THE True Crime DICTIONARY

From Alibi to Zodiac

THE True Crime DICTIONARY

From Alibi to Zodiac

THE ULTIMATE COLLECTION OF COLD CASES, SERIAL KILLERS, AND MORE

Amanda Lees

Published in the United States by:
ULYSSES PRESS
PO Box 3440
Berkeley, CA 94703
www.ulyssespress.com

First published as *From Aconite to the Zodiac Killer:
A Dictionary of Crime* in Great Britain in 2020 by
Robinson, an imprint of Little, Brown Book Group

ISBN: 978-1-64604-200-5
Library of Congress Control Number: 2021931495

Printed in the United States by Kingery Printing Company
1 3 5 7 9 10 8 6 4 2

US writer: Paula Lee
US project manager: Kierra Sondereker
US editor: Renee Rutledge
US proofreader: Kate St.Clair
US production: Yesenia Garcia-Lopez
Front cover design: Ashley Prine

For Delilah

INTRODUCTION

The crime bug bit me the day my father died although I didn't realize it until much later. I was only three at the time, so my memories are blurred, but the hints my mother dropped over the years sharpened a different kind of focus. She would refer to the secretive work he had done and to the infamous spies he knew, usually after a sherry or three. Then there were the oblique mentions of his sudden, untimely death, his glamorous first wife, and a mysterious fire that had burned down their London house. Mix in his Oxford education, murmurs of British intelligence and colonial missions lost in the mists of time, and the ramifications were obvious.

My dad was a spy, and he had probably been murdered. Or he could still be alive somewhere, a prisoner or even a defector. Almost every kid who has lost a parent thinks they might secretly be alive. Not every kid has a writer's nose for a story or the tantalizing details that could not be explained away. I used to scan faces at airports and wonder if one of them was my dad. I knew in my heart that he was dead, but I still picked at that murder theory. Yes, he probably did die of peritonitis, as I was told. But then again, you never know. You never know because people are far more complex than we think and, as I have learned, capable of anything.

It is that refusal to take anything at face value that has fueled my fascination with crime and led me down many dark alleyways. Some existed only in my mind. Others were more physical. I spent my days at a Devonian convent boarding school devouring Agatha Christie, who was coincidentally born in Torquay, where my school was located. Christie loved a coincidence and I identified strongly with this woman who had developed her expertise in poisons after volunteering as a nurse during the war and assisting a hospital pharmacist.

I grew up in the Hong Kong hospital where my mother was matron, with birth, death, and everything in between providing the backdrop to my childhood. It was the same hospital where my father was apparently misdiagnosed and died. The hospital that I suspected, in my youthful imagination, of a cover-up. Like Christie, I was intrigued by the power of substances to kill or cure. The Chinese have used potent herbs for thousands of years to do just that, as have monks and nuns since the Middle Ages. It was inevitable that I would want to tap into their horticultural legacy to spice up the stories I was already writing, the shadow of Christie falling over the pages I scrawled.

Later, I soaked up John le Carré, P. D. James, and every hard-boiled hack I could find before moving on to true crime, psychological thrillers and the cool, spare prose of Scandi noir. Spurning an English degree for drama, I learned to create characters and, more importantly, to dig for what motivated them. The play I wrote and directed for my finals centered on the abduction and murder of a child from a fairground and stunned the audience into silence. I received high honors for that play, laying the foundations of my future as a writer. But first I was determined to act—or, rather, act out—what I thought was my father's life of adventure. I plunged into it headlong with often terrifying results.

On the Baltic cruise ship where I wrote and performed murder mysteries to entertain some of the world's richest and most ruthless people, I gazed at the palm of the ex-head of the KGB and imagined those same hands brutally torturing dissidents. Later, I knocked back *rakia* with Bulgarian Mafiosi and fended off a British financial fraudster who went on the run to escape prison for the millions he had embezzled.

A lowlight of my acting career was playing Catherine Eddowes, Jack the Ripper's fourth victim, for a Japanese TV film directed by a man who screamed constantly for more violence. One of my closest friends was a Metropolitan Police officer; a relative was a criminal barrister. I sat in the gallery of the Old Bailey as a bunch of career criminals went down for one last botched holdup to shouts of "shame" from their families. I watched police tapes that no one should ever have to see.

All that time I was doing what so many of us do when we read or watch true crime and crime fiction. I was trying to make sense of it and the way it touched my world. We crime lovers are voyeurs, but we are also hackers, driven to crack the code. We want to know how and why, but we also want to know what we can do to protect ourselves. We want to help solve cold cases partly because we know it could happen to anyone. Yes, even to us. Especially to us.

That meeting with the ex-head of the KGB led, years later, to my taking on Putin's regime as part of a mission to save a dying man from prison. The man was chained to his bed in a Moscow cell, accused of crimes he did not commit. I used my skills as a writer to bolster the efforts of the lawyers who eventually won his release. The experience changed the direction of my writing, as did the simultaneous death of my mother. I returned to the darkness to which I had always been drawn, to write of the unspeakable things we can do to one another.

I had experienced evil firsthand. Now I wanted to make sense of it. I drew on my acting training to find the motives that drove my characters. Motive is one of the first things an investigator looks for when tackling a crime. Sometimes that motive seems irrational to everyone but the perpetrator. Those are the random crimes that hit the headlines and send ripples of fear through us. But hearing those stories does at least alert us to the possibility that anything can happen, that to stay safe we must consider the unthinkable. And that, I believe, is both the pull and the purpose of true crime and crime fiction.

We shudder at the gory details and sigh when a body is discovered. We stare at photos of the culprit and see the flat, blank sheen of evil in their eyes. Sometimes when we look in the mirror, we think we catch a glimpse of that same sheen and we turn away. Other times, we lie awake at night and listen to the creaks and sighs, wondering if it's our turn. All the while, one question throbs underneath our everyday thoughts. What if? What if someone snatched our child from the streets or a fairground? What if he really killed her? What if a dead father was alive, somewhere out there? What if it happens to me?

To control those thoughts, we seek answers in the pages of books, on our screens big and small, by listening to endless podcasts. Millions gather on forums and social media to solve cases the professionals have long consigned to a closed file. Mistakes are picked up and details pored over in a collective act of attempted closure. The unsolved is unsettling. The lazy cop or biased media create more bad apples to chew over. Crime is so compelling because it brings out the best and worst in us. It frightens us to the core while setting us free.

Every time I brush hands with danger, I feel more alive. Stupid, maybe, but true of so many people. But I don't get my thrills bungee jumping or performing hardcore parkour. The danger is not so much physical as psychological. I knew the ex-head of the KGB had long before given up espionage for more profitable pastimes. The Bulgarian Mafiosi were too busy parading their arrogance along with their bellies to worry about a lowly writer. Those police tapes I watched were just that. Tapes. Someone else's story played out for me to watch.

Their stories, however, stay lodged in my memory. The unsavory characters I have met leave their own taint. I am drawn to the rot and repelled by it, like some carrion beetle.

I want to burrow deep in the filth so that I can extract from it redemption, but happy endings are rare when it comes to true crime and even the coziest fiction leaves victims in its wake.

A crime thriller or mystery is both interactive and intensely intimate. We try to get inside the mind of the writer or protagonist so that we can solve the clues even as we anticipate the ending. It's a rush when we get it right. A gut punch when we're wrong. This is a visceral experience like no other and we can do it from the comfort of our living rooms. Often the characters are people just like us, except that something sinister has happened to them. They give us the chance to live vicariously, to flirt with danger. They allow us to exercise our minds and emotions in a way we may never experience in real life. Except that there is always the chance that we might. Which is why we keep getting back on the roller coaster for another ride.

The high stakes counterbalance the humdrum chaos of our own lives, especially if that chaos is domestic. Female crime fans outnumber male by a significant percentage, partly because their own lives are so full and fragmented with multiple responsibilities. Crime fiction lends order, especially if it is a police procedural. More than that, it takes us out of the ordinary. Good and evil are clear cut. Underlying themes are biblical or mythical in proportion. Passion, revenge, mayhem, and murder stir the blood in the most domestically dulled of veins.

I understand that need for a crime fix. I am also driven to supply it. I feed that supply through words, my favorite weapon. But I began to realize that the one barrier to crime fans was the thing they craved most: knowledge. If a reader or viewer does not understand a phrase or term used, then it adds friction to their experience. They cannot fully immerse themselves in the mystery or the solving of it and are therefore robbed of their full rush.

Crime readers are a discerning bunch. They thrive on fact and thorough research underpinning fiction. The blue line between true crime and crime fiction grows ever thinner as writers serve up stories with a palatable coating that barely disguises their roots in real life. Readers crave authenticity, but they don't want it to get in the way of a good plot. In trying to solve that problem like so many others, I came up with the idea of a crime dictionary, one that would not simply give definitions but also enough context and background to oil the wheels of the roller coaster. With it in hand, crime fans can simply jump on and enjoy one hell of a ride. That, after all, is the reason we do it.

The True Crime Dictionary: From Alibi to Zodiac is the culmination of my own restless search for answers. I am as guilty as anyone of needing to impose order. In my case, it is through my love of story and words, two gifts my father bequeathed me. I no longer search for his face in crowds. But I will always wonder. What I did not want was for any fellow crime fan to be left wondering too. Which is why, with this dictionary, you can now stand at the shoulder of monsters unencumbered. This is your companion on the ride, the friend who holds your hand as you scream at the scary bits. Take it with you as you climb aboard. It is the best ride you will ever take.

A

AA
See Air America.

ABFO scale
See American Board of Forensic Odontology (ABFO) scale.

ABH
See actual bodily harm.

ABI
See activity-based intelligence.

absorbance
Absorbance is the measurement of how much light is absorbed by a substance. It is used within spectrophotometry on **trace evidence**. Also known as optical density.

Abu Ghraib prison
A notorious prison located in Iraq and begun by dictator Saddam Hussein, Abu Ghraib was appropriated by the US military following its invasion of Iraq. When various news outlets revealed the extent and degree of systematic torture of detainees, including child rape, the ensuing public outrage led to the eventual conviction of 11 US soldiers of the minor crime of dereliction of duty. Abu Ghraib has become synonymous with human rights abuses and state-sanctioned torture of political prisoners by the US military.

abuse

Psychological, physical, sexual, financial, or emotional mistreatment of a human being or other living creature by another person or persons. (*See also* **domestic assault**.) Also the illegal, improper, or harmful use of something such as **alcohol** or **drugs**.

access

In **intelligence** terms, a way to approach and identify a target or the ability to approach, or access, an individual, place, or some information that enables the target to carry out the intended mission.

accessioning

Accessioning is the name given to the process of receiving, sorting, naming, and labeling **forensic** samples. The specimen accessioner is the person who conducts this process and who is also responsible for allocating the samples to the correct departments for testing.

accessory after the fact

If a person commits a felony crime, and you help them escape, you are acting as an accessory after the fact. This is a crime. The charge is typically brought against friends and family of a suspect, with sentencing depending on the severity of the original felony crime.

accessory before the fact

Someone who solicits or knowingly assists another person in the commission of a crime; often the person is not actually present at the time of the criminal act.

accessory (legal)

A person is considered an accessory to a crime if they had knowledge of the crime but are not physically present during the crime itself. Accessories are criminally liable, with sentencing depending on the nature of the crime; in

2021, for example, a female prison guard was successfully **indicted** and charged as accessory to the state-sponsored **murder** of 10,000 Jewish prisoners in a Nazi concentration camp.

accessory to a crime

Someone who is involved in a crime, prior to or subsequent to its commission, but not present when it is actually carried out.

accomplice (legal)

A person who knowingly assists in the planning or committing of a crime is an accomplice. Typically, they are physically present and assisting at the time the crime is being committed. Unless their cooperation was coerced, they will face the same criminal charges as the person actually committing the crime. A person who has knowledge of a criminal act who fails to prevent that crime from occurring (by, say, alerting the police) may also be named as an accomplice.

accusation

Statement that blames a specific person or persons for a criminal, illicit, or illegal act.

accused

Someone **charged** with breaking the law. This is used interchangeably with the term "defendant."

acint

See **acoustic intelligence**.

aconite (*Aconitum*)

Highly **poisonous** herbaceous perennial plant also known as monkshood, wolf's bane, devil's helmet, and the queen of poisons. Aconite is fast-acting and, with large doses, death is almost instantaneous. Initial symptoms include nausea, vomiting, and diarrhea followed by burning, tingling, and numbness in the mouth and burning in the abdomen. The main causes of death are paralysis of the heart and respiratory centers. The only postmortem sign is that of asphyxia, leading to a common misdiagnosis of heart attack as the cause of death. Despite the prevailing myth that it is undetectable, toxicology tests have existed for aconite for over two hundred years. It has featured as a murder weapon in the TV series *Midsomer Murders*, *Dexter*, and *The Cadfael Chronicles,* as well as in *American Horror Story* and James Joyce's *Ulysses*.

acoustic intelligence (acint)

Collection and processing of **intelligence** gained from listening devices, recordings, and other acoustic phenomena.

acquittal

At jury trial, a finding of not guilty (beyond a reasonable doubt) is called an acquittal. However, acquittal does not mean that the **defendant** is innocent, but that the jury could not convict on the basis of evidence presented at trial. Following acquittal, **double jeopardy** applies.

acronym

An acronym is formed from the initial letters of other words and often pronounced as a word. **Law enforcement** agencies and police forces worldwide use a variety of acronyms. Some examples of acronyms include: Advanced Fingerprint Identification Technology (AFIT); Alcohol, Tobacco, and Firearms (ATF); Be on the Lookout (BOLO); Combined DNA Index System (CODIS); Gunshot Residue (GSR); International Criminal Police Organization (INTERPOL); and Rapid Response Enforcement and Counterterrorism (REACT).

action (firearm)

Working part of a **firearm** that **loads**, fires, and ejects a **cartridge**. Lever, **pump**, and **bolt actions** are found in weapons that fire a single shot. Firearms that can shoot multiple rounds, also known as repeaters, include all these types of actions but only the **semi-automatic** does not require manual operation between **rounds**. A **machine gun** has a truly automatic action.

action (slang)

Referring to illegal profits, or participation in potentially lucrative illegal activity; that is, "a piece of the action."

activity-based intelligence (ABI)

Analysis of structured data from multiple **sources** to discover objects, relationships, or behaviors by resolving significant activity.

actual bodily harm (ABH)

Assault causing actual bodily harm (ABH) is assault or battery that causes actual physical harm to the victim, which can include bruises, scratches, and bitemarks as well as more serious injuries. The perpetrator need not intend to cause actual bodily harm but only to apply unlawful force to the victim. ABH is a criminal offense in the UK. In the United States, ABH generally falls under the rubric of **assault** and can be a misdemeanor or felony.

addiction

State of physical and/or mental dependence on a **drug**, including **alcohol** and **nicotine**, to such an extent that stopping is immensely difficult and creates severe physical and mental trauma. Addiction is a recurring theme in crime fiction and true crime and not always confined to the perpetrators or victims. Addiction to drugs or alcohol is often used to supply a detective such as Sherlock Holmes or Jo Nesbø's Harry Hole with a humanizing flaw. Conan Doyle planted clues throughout the Holmes series that point to his probable addiction to morphine and cocaine. Irvine Welsh's DI Bruce Robertson in *Filth* is a drug and sex addict as well as an alcoholic. The fictional detectives Jane Tennison, Inspector Morse, and John Rebus are also alcoholics or borderline alcoholics while Kathy Reich's Temperance Brennan, as befits her name, is an ex-alcoholic. In Paula Hawkins' thriller, *The Girl on a Train*, much of the action is seen through the blurred prism of the lead character, Rachel Watson, who often drinks until she blacks out.

A *British Medical Journal* study in 2013 quantified James Bond's consumption of alcohol and concluded that his weekly intake of 92 units a week was four times the recommended amount. At that rate, they calculated he would have died at the age of 56. Some fictional detectives, such as Lawrence Block's Matt Scudder with his attendance at AA meetings, use their battle to maintain sobriety as a central pivot to their actions or to develop their character and story further, as Michael Brandman did when he took over the Jesse Stone series after the death of Robert B. Parker. Other characters are colored by the experience of the authors, notably Raymond Chandler and Dashiell Hammett, who wrote at a time when a hard-drinking macho persona was preferable to the modern metrosexual who is more in touch with their feelings. Sue Grafton, author of the bestselling alphabetical detective series featuring PI Kinsey Millhone, acknowledged the effect her parents' alcoholism had on her writing and on the shaping of her protagonist, to whom she referred as her alter ego. James Lee Burke invented his character Dave Robicheaux in his own image as a recovering alcoholic. The flawed detective or **spy** may be a cliché or trope but it is one that is driven by the audience's appetite for figures with whom they can identify and who reflect the real-life addiction struggles of contemporary **law enforcement** officers as well as the readers themselves. ►**addictive** Causing addiction.

adjournment
Break in court proceedings, which can be for lunch, over-night, or for a longer period.

Administrative Maximum Security Facility (ADX)
Designed for the containment of extremely dangerous, violent, or escape-prone inmates, the ADX offers the highest level of security in the US prison system. In the US, there is only one such **supermax prison**: ADX Florence near Florence, Colorado. It holds extremely dangerous male inmates, including those who pose a serious threat to national security. Currently, the population of ADX Florence includes the former leader of the Sinaloa drug cartel, "El Chapo"; Oklahoma City bomber and domestic terrorist, Terry L. Nichols; domestic terrorist Ted John Kaczynski (the "Unabomber"); Eric R. Rudolph (the "Olympic Park" bomber); and Richard Reid (the "Shoe Bomber"). There is no ADX for female prisoners.

admissibility
Whether **evidence** is admissible. For evidence to be admitted in proceedings, it must be reliable and relevant to a factual issue in the **case**. Admissibility is always decided by the trial judge.

A

Adult Use of Marijuana Act (AUMA) (Proposition 64) (California)

A 2016 California voter initiative to legalize marijuana in the state, the Adult Use of Marijuana Act (more commonly known in California as Prop 64), passed with 57 percent of the popular vote, paving the way for legal commercial sale of marijuana in that state. Per AUMA, sales are regulated via the state's Bureau of Marijuana Control, and the state collects taxes on sales. AUMA also legalized the cultivation of no more than six marijuana plants for personal use, and permitted each adult individual to be holding no more than 1 ounce of marijuana. Overall, these measures are contributing to the **decriminalization** of marijuana-related offenses not just in California, but the US in general. Various other US states have similar voter initiatives that have either passed or have been submitted, but the size of California's economy gives it outside influence on the national push to legalize pot.

Advanced Fingerprint Identification Technology (AFIT)

First used by the **Federal Bureau of Investigation** in 2011, AFIT implemented new matching algorithms to increase accuracy in electronic automated **fingerprint** identification.

ADX

See **Administrative Maximum Security Facility**.

affidavit

Written statement of **evidence** confirmed on oath or by affirmation to be true and taken before someone who has authority to administer it. This can sometimes be used in court as witness evidence without the witness having to come to court.

AFIS

See **Automated Fingerprint Identification System**.

AFIT

See **Advanced Fingerprint Identification Technology**.

agency

In **intelligence** terms, an individual or organization that collects and/or processes information. Also known as a collection agency. ▶ **agent** Someone working for an **intelligence** service or agency, although the secret services usually refer to them as "officers" rather than agents, with the **Federal Bureau of Investigation** being one exception. ▶ **agent of influence** Also known as a secret agent. A person in an influential position who uses that position to benefit the country or regime operating that agent. This can be through influencing public, cultural, scientific, intellectual, and political opinion or decision making.

aggravated assault

An aggravated **assault** is a physical attack on another person that is aggravated by the use of a **deadly weapon**. It can also be considered aggravated if the intent was to cause serious harm to the victim or if injuries inflicted were serious.

AI

See **artificial intelligence**.

air ambulances

Emergency medical helicopter services in the US. The service is not centralized and can be either private or state-run. They are used by hospitals, local government agencies, for-profit companies, and the military. In addition to flying critically ill or wounded patients to hospitals, air ambulances can also be utilized for search and rescue operations. They are generally equipped with a nurse and a paramedic, with specialized personnel added as needed.

Air America (AA)

The US government owned and ran Air America as a passenger and cargo airline from 1950 to 1976, using it as a **cover** for military operations in areas where it could not otherwise operate. It was a dummy corporation for the **Central Intelligence Agency** and was later featured in a movie of the same name.

air gun

Gun that uses compressed air or gas to propel a **projectile**.

airsoft gun

Kind of **air gun** intended to look like a **firearm** and expelling small **pellets** typically made of plastic or compressed resin. *See also* **BB gun**.

AK-47

Refers to Avtomat Kalashnikov (AK), finished in 1947 ("-47"). Also known as "Kalashnikov," or "Kalash." Originally developed in the Soviet Union by Mikhail Kalashnikov, and first used in active service in 1948. Both reliable and cost-effective, the AK-47 has been adopted by military and paramilitary groups in over 100 countries. Models with semi-automatic settings are legal for civilian purchase in the US. Grandfathering provisions apply to AK-47s registered before the 1986 US ban on fully automatic assault rifles.

Alcatraz Federal Penitentiary

Also known simply as "The Rock," Alcatraz Federal Penitentiary (1934–1963) was a maximum-security prison located on Alcatraz Island in the San Francisco Bay. Before being decommissioned and turned into a major tourist

attraction, it began as a US military outpost called Fort
Alcatraz. As the "prison of last resort," The Rock quickly
developed a reputation for inhumane conditions so brutal
that inmates were driven to insanity. It was thought to be
impossible to **escape from Alcatraz**, though many
inmates tried, and three possibly succeeded. Notorious
inmates included gangsters Al Capone and Machine Gun
Kelly (George Kelly Barnes), and murderer Robert Stroud
("Birdman of Alcatraz"). The subject of many dozens of
books, films, and video games, the Rock also inspired
Azkaban wizarding island in the Harry Potter franchise
and played a major role in the plot of the film, *X-Men: Last
Stand*.

alcohol

Colorless, flammable liquid, produced by the fermenta-
tion of sugars, that forms the intoxicating element in
wine, beer, cider, spirits, and other drinks. It can also be
used as a solvent in fuel and in medicines. Used as a crutch
or character flaw by detectives, to facilitate crimes and
imbibed in legendary quantities by certain crime authors,
including Raymond Chandler, Dashiell Hammett, and
Patricia Highsmith. Broads and booze are hallmarks of
hard-boiled crime fiction while contemporary **thriller**
writers such as Paula Hawkins create protagonists broken
by the demon drink.

alias

Alternative or false name used to conceal a true identity.

alibi

Explanation, person, or people that may prove a suspect
was not at the scene of a crime when it happened.

all day

Serving a life **sentence** in prison—"I'm doing all day" (US contemporary slang). ▶ **all day and a night** Serving a life sentence without **parole** (US contemporary slang).

allegation

Claim or **accusation** of a crime that has been made but not yet proved.

All Points Bulletin (APB)

Typically issued by an American or Canadian law enforcement agency, an APB alerts other law enforcement entities about a person of interest or a fleeing suspect for whom they should be on the alert. It is identical to **BOLO**, or Be on the Lookout.

alternate light source

Also known as **forensic** light source. Powerful lamps used in **crime scene investigations** that contain ultraviolet (UV), visible, and infrared components of light. The light is filtered into individual color bands or wavelengths that help identify **evidence** through light interaction. UV light is used primarily to identify **latent fingerprints** as well as **biological fluids** such as blood, semen, and saliva because these have natural fluorescent properties. Fibers, shoeprints, human bone fragments, bitemarks, and **gunshot residue** are among the other applications.

Amber/AMBER alert

Alert sent out by police and **law enforcement** to ask for the public's help when a child goes missing and is suspected of having been abducted. Also known as a Child Abduction Emergency alert (CAE). The term originated in the US after ten-year-old Amber Hagerman was abducted and killed in Texas in 1996, and is now used worldwide.

American Board of Forensic Odontology (ABFO) scale

The ABFO scale is the US standard for measuring and photographing bitemarks. The scale is L-shaped and marked with circles and bars, to help compensate for camera-angle distortion and to determine exposure. The scale also includes millimeters to aid measurement.

ammunition or ammo (slang)

Collective term for the material such as **bullets** or shells that can be fired, dropped, or **discharged** from a weapon. Amounts of ammunition are measured in rounds. Ammo for firearms comes in hundreds of sizes and variations, and must match the caliber of the firearm.

amphetamine

Sold as a street **drug** as powder, pills, or a paste, often wrapped in small pieces of paper referred to as wraps. Amphetamine (alpha-methylphenethylamine) is a **synthetic stimulant** that increases energy levels, confidence and alertness. **Methamphetamine**, the stronger form of the drug commonly known as crystal meth because it usually comes in crystal form, is the second most popular illegal drug globally after **cannabis.** According to the US Drug Enforcement Administration (DEA), amphetamines (including methamphetamines) are **Schedule II** drugs; as controlled substances, they are only legal when prescribed for accepted medical conditions. The street and alternative names for amphetamine include: *acelerador*; Amy; amps; bam; b-bombs; beans; bennies; Benz; black and whites; black beauties; black birds; black bombers; black Mollies; blacks; blue boys; *bombita*; brain ticklers; brownies; bumblebees; cartwheels; chalk; chicken powder; chochos; chocolates; Christina; chunk; co-pilot; coast-to-coasts; crisscross; cross roads; cross tops; crosses; debs; dexies; diablos; diamonds; diet pills; dolls; dominoes; double cross; drivers; dulces; fives; flour; footballs; French blues; geeked up; goofballs; greenies; head drugs; hearts; horse heads; in-betweens; jelly babies; jelly beans; jolly beans; jugs; LA turnaround; leapers; lid poppers; lightning; little bombs; marathons; mini beans; mini bennies; morning shot; nuggets; oranges; pastas; pastillas; peaches; pep pills; pepper; pingas; pink hearts; pixies; pollutants; purple hearts; rhythm; rippers; road dope; roses; *rueda*; snaps; snow pallets; sparkle plenty; sparklers; speed; splash; sweeties; sweets; tens; thrusters; TR-6s; truck drivers; turnabouts; uppers; wake ups; West Coast turnarounds; wheels; whiffle dust; white crosses; whites; zoomers.

amphibious vehicle

Wheeled or tracked vehicle capable of operating on both land and water.

amyl nitrite

Often confused with amyl nitrate but in fact a completely different substance. Amyl nitrite is a pale-yellow liquid used to open or widen blood vessels to allow more blood flow. Amyl nitrite was originally sold in small vials or capsules that had to be cracked or popped open, so the **drugs** became known as "poppers." Poppers are also known as liquid gold, butyl nitrite, heart medicine (from the original use of amyl nitrite in treating heart patients) and room deodorizer. It is often sold in small bottles and inhaled. Swallowing amyl nitrite is highly dangerous and can be fatal. It first became popular among the gay community as a recreational drug and to enhance the effects of sexual encounters as it results in an increased sex drive and heightened skin sensitivity as well as relaxing the walls of the anus and vagina. It is now used as a psychoactive drug by a wide range of people and clubbers in particular. People also take it for the rapid sense of

euphoria it produces along with a temporary head **rush**.
In the US, it is illegal to sell poppers expressly intended for
use as a recreational drug.

analysis and production

In **intelligence** terms, converting processed information
into intelligence through the integration, evaluation, analysis and interpretation of all **source** data and the
preparation of finished intelligence products such as
intelligence reports to meet known or anticipated user
requirements. ▶**analyst** An **intelligence analyst** acquires,
evaluates, analyzes, and assesses information on behalf of
the secret intelligence services, the military, and the
police.

angel of death/mercy

An angel of death or mercy is a caregiver or medical
professional, usually a nurse, who deliberately harms or
kills their patients, often justifying their actions to themselves by claiming to act out of mercy in the face of
suffering. Others kill as a means of exerting sadistic
power and control over their patients or to obtain money
fraudulently from them. Another variant, known as malig-
nant heroes, deliberately harm patients so they can then
be lionized by the victim's family for "saving them." Often
serial killers, the typical medical professional who kills
patients will murder about two a month, usually by **lethal**
injection. Notorious examples include **Harold Shipman**
and nurse Beverley Allitt, whose **case** was dramatized in
the BBC's *Angel of Death* (2005).

ANPR

See **Automatic Number Plate Recognition**.

A

antemortem data

Medical records, samples and photographs taken prior to
death. These include, but are not limited to, **fingerprints**,
dental **X-rays**, body-tissue samples, and photographs of
tattoos and other identifying marks. These records are
compared to records completed after death to help establish a positive identification of human remains.

antimony

Antimony is a highly **toxic** metal that is found in many
everyday items. It has been described as the perfect
poison due to the fact it is odorless, colorless, and near
tasteless when dissolved, which means it is also easy to
ingest without noticing. When inhaled, antimony can
cause symptoms that include headaches, dizziness, antimony spots on the skin, gastrointestinal upset, psychosis,
convulsions, and coma. Antimony also acts as a natural
preservative, which means it may not be the perfect
murder weapon unless the perpetrator also ensures
the complete disposal of the corpse.

antique firearm

Muskets and flintlocks spring to mind when one thinks of
antique firearms, but what qualifies as "antique" is generally a combination of the gun's age and design.

According to the ATF (18 USC § 921), an antique firearm
is "any firearm not intended or redesigned for using rim
fire or conventional center fire ignition with fixed ammunition and manufactured in or before 1898 (including any
matchlock, flintlock, percussion cap, or similar type of
ignition system or replica thereof, whether actually manufactured before or after the year 1898) and also any
firearm using fixed ammunition manufactured in or
before 1898." This definition of "antique" stresses the
configuration of its ignition system over its age or
aesthetics. Under US law, an "antique firearm" does not fall

under the legal definition of a "**firearm**," hence the US **Gun**
Control Act does not restrict their import. For the same
reason, felons who are otherwise **prohibited persons** can
(sometimes) legally own them...if the laws of the state
where they reside also permit it. There are many repro-
ductions of muskets and flintlocks in the market that are
designed to look antique but are in fact new; typically,
their reason for existing is not nefarious but because they
are more affordable than authentic antiques.

antisocial personality disorder (APD)

Antisocial personality disorders include **narcissistic
personality disorder**, **sociopathy**, and **psychopathy**.
Though such people are destructive, however, they are
not necessarily criminal. Nonetheless, individuals with
APD are more likely to engage in risk-taking behaviors,
dangerous activities, and criminal acts. It is estimated that
as many as 70 percent of people in prison have APD, as
compared to 0.2 to 3.3 percent of the general population.

antiterrorism

Defensive measures including physical items such as
barriers and procedures used to reduce the vulnerability
of individuals and property to terrorist acts.

APB

See All Points Bulletin.

APD

See **antisocial personality disorder**.

appeal

Inside the legal system, an appeal is a request for a higher
authority to review the decision of the jury or other
deciding body. They are intended to correct errors or bias

in the system itself. Correspondingly, the US Supreme Court typically hears high-level cases on appeal.

APW
See **all points warning**.

area damage control
Measures taken before, during, and/or after an attack, natural, or manmade disaster to reduce the likelihood of damage and minimize its effects.

Armalite Rifle-15 (AR-15)-style rifle
The AR-15-style **semi-automatic** lightweight **rifle** is used by **law enforcement** in the US and UK as well as other countries around the globe but has also been used in a number of mass shootings, including five of the ten deadliest mass shootings in American history. A Colt AR-15-style rifle was also used in the 1996 Port Arthur massacre in Australia, which led to restrictions on private ownership of semiautomatic weapons capable of firing more than five **rounds**, even as the 2019 Christchurch mosque shootings in New Zealand resulted in a ban on semiautomatic weapons.

arming
When applied to explosives, weapons, and **ammunition**, the change from a safe state to a state of readiness for use.

armored rescue vehicle (ARV)
An armored rescue vehicle (ARV) is a wheeled personnel carrier designed for tactical response teams (military or police) facing high-risk situations. ARVs can have features such as a battering ram; tear gas deployment nozzle; powered turrets; blast shields; gun ports; electric winches; protection against **chemical, biological, radiological, nuclear, and high-yield explosives** (CBRNEs); Common

Remotely Operated Weapons Station (CROWS), and spotlights.

Some armored resource vehicles originally designed for overseas military use, such as **Mine-Resistant Ambush Protected vehicles (MRAPs)**, were transferred to domestic police forces via the **1033 program.** Other ARVs are purpose-built for the police and other law enforcement agencies, such as the FBI. The most widely recognized of such ARVs is the Lenco BearCat personnel carrier, which serves as the basic **SWAT team** transport vehicle.

arrest

Take a person into **custody** by restraint with the authority of law, for the purpose of charging them with a criminal offense terminating in the recording of a specific offense.

arrival zone

In anti**drug** operations, the area in or adjacent to the country affected, where the act of smuggling finishes and domestic distribution begins. This can be an airstrip (in cases of smuggling by air), or an offload or landing point (if by sea).

arsenic

Beloved of crime writers from Agatha Christie to Dorothy L. Sayers, arsenic **poisoning** was a common murder method in Victorian Britain. The 1939 play and subsequent 1941 film of *Arsenic and Old Lace* were successful dark comedies that may have been inspired by the real-life serial killer and nursing-home owner, Amy Archer-Gilligan.

A notorious **case** in Scotland in 1857 centered on a young woman, Madeleine Smith, **charged** with murdering her lover, Pierre Émile L'Angelier, after he tried to blackmail her with their love letters when she ended the relationship. Although high quantities of arsenic were found in L'Angelier's stomach, Smith had been recorded buying arsenic from her local apothecary—and L'Angelier's diary noted that he felt ill after drinking coffee and cocoa she served him—the case against Smith was found "not proven." It has been called the "Crime of the Century" and causes debate among **forensic** scientists and criminologists to this day.

The Victorian fascination with the case reflected the fact this was the golden age of poisons, with arsenic a poison of choice because it was so readily available and, being tasteless and odorless, easy to conceal. Its effects could be explained away as food poisoning, as in the Smith case. Arsenic was such a popular poison and so easy to obtain that the Arsenic Act of 1851 was passed, requiring it to be dyed indigo.

Arsenic eating was fashionable in the nineteenth century as people believed it resulted in a clear complexion and healthy hair, and also that they could build up a tolerance to it by ingesting small quantities over a period of time. This theory was the plot premise in Dorothy L. Sayers' *Strong Poison* (1930), in which two people sit down to a dinner laced with arsenic and only one dies. In fact, science has since proved that humans generally only have a low tolerance to arsenic but that a genetic mutation can result in a much higher tolerance. This mutation is mainly found in populations where the drinking water has higher than normal levels of arsenic, such as in some remote regions of Chile, where scientists from the University of Santiago conducted their research, publishing their results in 2017. No doubt some enterprising author will incorporate this into a plot as poisoning is once more a fashionable murder method.

arson

The crime of arson occurs when a person deliberately and maliciously sets fire to property, including buildings, vehicles, boats, and forests or land. A person who commits arson is known as an arsonist. Arsonists commonly use accelerants such as gasoline to start their fires, and the detection of such accelerants or the residue they leave is crucial in **forensic** fire **investigations**. One common reason to commit arson is to carry out an insurance **fraud**, although this is increasingly difficult as forensic detection methods become more advanced.

artificial intelligence (AI)

Artificial intelligence (i.e., machine learning), including machines capable of emulating skills such as speech and facial recognition, is used by police and **intelligence** both in the UK and the US as well as other countries to aid **investigations** and operations, although its use is controversial with some officers expressing concerns over possible data bias. In California, Bay Area departments use software that relies on data collected from crime-victim reports, **arrests**, suspect histories, and other pertinent data to predict when and where crime will occur. Tacoma, Washington, has seen a 22 percent drop in residential burglaries as a result of using AI. Shot detection systems based on AI alert authorities in real time and provide specific information about the type of gunfire and where it originated. The systems have multiple sensors that pick up the sound of a gunshot and then use a software algorithm to convert data into actionable intelligence.

While the use of AI is rapidly increasing in **law enforcement** and crime detection, doubts about ethical considerations and its efficacy remain. The use of facial recognition technology has been especially controversial, with ethical concerns over a Pentagon project (Project

Maven) prompting Google to drop it, but only for a different firm, Palantir, to take its place. Known as "the most secretive company in law enforcement," the Los Angeles Police Department (LAPD) utilizes Palantir's Gotham database. In spite of those doubts, data-driven policing is here to stay.

ARV

See **Armored Rescue Vehicle**.

Aryan Brotherhood

The Aryan Brotherhood aka the AB, the Brand, Alice Baker, and One-Two, is a white supremacist US prison gang and **organized crime** syndicate with a fearsome reputation. The gang operates with a "blood-in, blood-out" policy. You have to kill to get in, and only get out when you're dead. Entry is by invitation only.

assault

According to US common law, assault refers to "an attempt with force or violence to do a corporal injury to another; may consist of any act tending to such corporal injury, accompanied with such circumstances as denotes at the time an intention, coupled with present ability, of using actual violence against the person." Per 18 USC § 351(e), the criminal act of assault divides into two groups: 1) those that result in personal injury; and 2) all others. "Aggravated assault" refers to assaults involving deadly or dangerous weapons but without inflicting personal injury. The "**attempted homicide**" provision may apply when bodily or other harms are involved.

assault rifle

Selective fire **rifle** with a detachable **magazine**. It is capable of firing in different modes (both fully **automatic** and **semi-automatic** fire) and is typically the standard

infantry weapon in the armed forces. The **AK-47** is an
assault rifle. Civilian ownership of assault rifles capable of
full auto has been tightly regulated in the US since the
Firearm Owners Protection Act of 1986.

asset

Source of information within a country or organization
for an officer or **spy** who is spying on that country or organization. They are also sometimes referred to as **agents** or
informants. Can also be an object or item that aids an
intelligence operation. ▶ **asset validation** In **intelligence**
terms, the process used to determine an **asset**'s authenticity, reliability, utility, and suitability as well as the
degree of control the **case officer** or others has over them.

associate

Someone who works with the **Mafia** but is not an official
member of the organization.

Atascadero State Hospital

Officially known as California Department of State
Hospitals–Atascadero (DSHA), this all-male, maximum-
security institution holds mentally-ill felons deemed too
dangerous for other facilities. It has its own full-service
law enforcement agency, as well as a 24-hour clinical and
administrative staff. For security reasons, Atascadero is
not open to the public and only takes patients referred by
the California Superior Court, the Board of Prison Terms,
or the state Department of Corrections. Some notable
patients have included Arthur Leigh Allen (suspected of
being the **Zodiac Killer**) and serial killer **William Bonin**
(the Freeway Killer).

ATF

See **Bureau of Alcohol, Tobacco, and Firearms (ATF)**.

A   atropine

Atropine is extracted from the deadly nightshade plant, which is otherwise known as *Atropa belladonna*. Bitter tasting, atropine works by disrupting the nervous system. Symptoms of **poisoning** include a dry mouth, blurred vision, hallucinations, increased heart rate, coma, and death. Atropine is not only a poison but an antidote against **nerve agents** such as **sarin** and pesticides. It is also used in the treatment of bradycardia (slow heart rate). It has been used in a number of documented murders (on one occasion administered as eye drops) and **attempted** murders, as well as in crime fiction, notably by Agatha Christie.

attempt

An act that is more than the planning of a crime and, due to its nature, is a substantial element of finally committing the crime. An attempt is a separate and distinct offense in and of itself (e.g., attempted murder or attempted **robbery**).

attempted homicide

Homicide refers to the killing of a person by another person. Attempted homicide means that the victim survived.

Unlawful means that the homicide was not in legitimate self-defense, for example, or committed as a result of following military orders in combat.

Intentional means you cannot accidentally commit attempted homicide. The intent can be premeditated (first degree attempted murder charge, resulting in life sentence with possibility of **parole**) or spontaneous (second degree, resulting in 5–15 years). For the charge of attempted homicide to stick, prosecutors must prove that the accused demonstrated both the intent to act, and the intent to kill.

authentication

This can be a security measure designed to protect a communications system from a fraudulent transmission by establishing the validity of a transmission or message or its originator. It can also be a means of identifying individuals and verifying their eligibility to receive specific categories of information as well as **evidence** by proper signature or seal that a document is genuine and official. In personnel recovery missions, authentication is the process whereby the identity of the person to be recovered is confirmed so that the rescuers can be sure they have the right individual.

Automated Fingerprint Identification System (AFIS)

Biometric computer system that allows **forensic examiners** to encode, digitize, and search recovered **fingerprint** impressions against fingerprint record databases for identification purposes. **Advanced Fingerprint Identification Technology (AFIT)** replaced the **Federal Bureau of Investigation**'s AFIS segment of the **Integrated Automated Fingerprint Identification System** (IAFIS) in 2011 as part of the **Next Generation Identification** system.

automatic firearm

Any **firearm** that, once the first **round** has been fired, **loads** automatically and can, with each single pull of the **trigger**, fire a burst of many shots until the trigger is released (also known as a fully automatic firearm).

Automatic Number Plate Recognition (ANPR)

System that uses optical character recognition to read vehicle number plates and create vehicle location data. It does this through existing **CCTV** or road-rule enforcement cameras as well as cameras dedicated to this task. It is used globally for **law enforcement** purposes and to check if a vehicle is licensed and/or insured.

autopsy

An autopsy is the medical examination of a corpse to determine the cause(s) of death or the extent of a disease

away

In prison; that is, "he's been put away" (US/UK contemporary slang).

B

babysitter

Another name for a bodyguard, especially when used by the **security services**.

back door

A back door is a hole deliberately left in a software program to allow for updates. Back doors are also created by system developers as shortcuts to speed access through security during the development stage and are then forgotten and never properly removed during final implementation. Sometimes **hackers** and **crackers** will create their own back door to a system by using a **virus** or a **Trojan** to set it up, thereby allowing them future access at their leisure. Hackers, crackers, and bots exploit back doors for malicious purposes and to carry out **cyberattacks**.

back-door parole

To die in prison (US contemporary slang).

background check

A background check allows businesses and law enforcement to access various general and specialized databases (such as the sex offender registry and credit reports, or to conduct searches under the auspices of the **Patriot Act**). In the case of firearms, the **Brady Bill** requires sellers to run the personal information of prospective buyers through the **National Instant Criminal Background Check System (NICS)** to make sure they are not prohibited from buying/owning firearms.

backspatter pattern

Blood spatter pattern resulting from blood drops that travel in the opposite direction to the external force applied. Associated with an entrance wound created by a **projectile**.

backstop

Arrangements put in place to support the **cover** story and activities of an **agent** or officer so that their story will stand up if any inquiries are made. These can include setting up documentary, technical, legal, monetary, and other arrangements to make the cover story appear true.

bagman

Agent, person, or officer who collects and distributes often illicit funds in the form of bribes, and also to pay **assets** and **spies**.

bail

Release of a defendant from **custody** until their next court appearance, contingent upon payment of a specific sum determined by the court (i.e., "setting bail"). Individuals out on bail must also comply with specific conditions.

ballistics

Forensic ballistics is the examination of **evidence** relating to guns and **firearms** as well as the effect and behavior of **projectiles** or exploding devices at a **crime scene**. A forensic ballistics expert examines and matches fragments, **bullets,** and other evidence to a suspect's weapon as well as examining probable trajectories to ascertain the location from where the weapon was fired. Examination of weapons and bullets can reveal characteristic marks including **rifling** or marks from a specific gun on a bullet. Examination of **propellants** can reveal chemical components. Ballistics studies can be used to examine any type of thrown or fired projectile. Ballistics is usually divided into three parts:

- Interior ballistics, or the study of the projectile's movement inside the gun.
- Exterior ballistics, or the study of the projectile's movement between the **muzzle** and the target.
- Terminal ballistics, or the study of the projectile's movement and behavior in the target.

bang up

Lock in a **cell** or in prison (UK contemporary prison slang).

bar

Legal profession as a whole. Derives historically from the layout of an English courtroom and its attendant legal system, where a bar would separate spectators from barristers ("lawyers") and others officially involved with the trial. In the US, being "admitted to the bar" refers to a specific court system granting a particular individual permission to practice law in a specific jurisdiction. In other words, a person is admitted to the Massachusetts bar, or to the Florida bar, not to the bar of the United States of America. Failure to observe professional standards or committing crimes, among other things, can result in **disbarment**.

bar association

Professional association of lawyers. Each state has its own bar association. The American Bar Association is the largest voluntary body of lawyers in the world, and works to advance the professionalism of the US law profession as a whole.

Barney

Slang for police. Thought to derive from the beloved character of Barney Fife, deputy sheriff for the fictional town of Mayberry, North Carolina, as depicted on the television comedy, *The Andy Griffith Show* (1960–1968).

barrel

Cylindrical tube designed to contain the pressure of a **propellant** and direct the **projectile**. For many weapons it consists of a **chamber** ending in a rifled or **smooth bore**. In a **revolver**, the barrel does not have a chamber.

basic intelligence

Fundamental material and facts about a location or situation that could be used to plan an **intelligence** or military operation and to evaluate subsequent information gathered.

batrachotoxin

A neurotoxin extracted from certain birds, beetles, and the skin of several Central and South American frogs, including the golden dart frog, batrachotoxin is applied to the tips of the blow darts used by Colombian and other indigenous South American tribes. It acts on the heart muscles, causing arrhythmia and cardiac arrest. One frog contains enough **poison** to kill ten men and there is no known antidote.

BAU

See **Behavioral Analysis Unit**.

BB gun

BB guns are a type of compressed gas **air gun** that use metallic steel **projectiles** called **BBs** (.177in /4.5mm). Models exist as hand pistols as well as rifles.

BBs

Small spherical projectiles typically made of steel or lead, BBs serve as ammo for air weapons and typically measure .177 in (4.5 mm) in diameter. "BB" is sometimes used to refer to plastic pellets used in airsoft guns, but they are not interchangeable. (Among other things, they have a greater density than **airsoft pellets**.) However, BBs closely resemble birdshot, specifically the size measuring .180 in (4.6 mm). A tiny specialty gun exists that uses a single BB as ammo.

BDU

See **bomb disposal unit**.

beamer

Crack smoker (US/Jamaican contemporary gang slang).

beast

Police (US/Jamaican contemporary gang slang).

beef

Criminal **charge**—"I caught a **burglary** beef" (US contemporary slang); to have a problem with someone else—"I had a beef with him so I shot him" (US and UK contemporary slang).

behavioral analysis

In criminal **investigations**, the analysis of offenders and the way in which they behave in committing a crime. Specialist units include the **Behavioral Analysis Unit** (BAU) of the **Federal Bureau of Investigation** National Center for the Analysis of Violent Crime (NCAVC).

Behavioral Analysis Unit

A department of the National Center for the Analysis of Violent Crimes (NCAVC) of the **Federal Bureau of**

Investigations that uses **behavioral analysis** to assist in criminal investigations.

being inside
To be in prison. Ex: "Brutus has been inside so long he thinks K-Cups refer to bra size."

bench trial
A trial by judge, as opposed to a trial by jury.

bench warrant
In the event that a defendant fails to appear in court and/or pay fines and fees, a judge can issue a bench warrant (i.e., warrant from "the bench," which is to say, the judge) for their arrest. This written authorization directs law enforcement to jail them in order to bring them to court.

best evidence policy
Forensic laboratory policy that some items will not be examined based on the results of other testing, or due to other factors such as the manner of collection, **degradation,** or limitations of the science.

bifurcation
Point in a **fingerprint** where a friction ridge divides or splits to form two ridges.

bilateral operation (bilat)
Operation jointly run between two **intelligence** agencies from either the same or different countries.

bilk
Swindle or cheat.

bindle paper

Clean sheet of paper that is folded in a specific manner
and used to collect **evidence**, typically **trace evidence**
such as hair, dust, paint chips, or other tiny particles that
are light and therefore easily lost. It often forms part of a
trace evidence kit.

bind over for sentence

Order that requires the defendant to return to court on an
unspecified date for sentencing.

bing

Solitary confinement. Originally slang for solitary on
Riker's Island, but eventually seeped into general prison
lingo. (Ex: "Sue attacked a guard, now she's in the bing.")

binky

Homemade syringe, usually created from an eyedropper,
pen shaft and guitar string, for shooting up **drugs** (US
contemporary prison slang).

biohazard bag

Plastic or paper bag specifically used to safely transport
evidence samples from a crime or accident scene to
another site, typically a laboratory. Biohazard bags
prevent **contamination** of the evidence and also protect
the handler from any harm presented by the samples.

biological agent

Microorganism, or a toxin derived from it, that can be
used as a weapon in biological warfare, causing disease in
people, plants, or animals, or causing the degradation or
destruction of material. ▶ **biological weapon** Biological
agents used to cause disease to threaten or destroy human
life. These can include bacteria, toxins, fungi, and viruses.
The use of biological weapons in modern warfare is a war

crime. Biological weapons are a staple of fiction, TV, and film.

biological fluid

Fluid that originates from a human or animal. The most typical biological fluids found at a **crime scene** are blood, saliva, semen, vaginal fluid, urine, and perspiration.

biological hazard

Organism, or substance derived from an organism, that can damage human or animal health.

biological material

Material that has a human or animal origin, most commonly encountered at **crime scenes** (e.g., blood, saliva, semen, skin cells).

biometrics

Measurement and analysis of unique human biological and behavioral characteristics. Often used to secure entry access or data with biological information such as **fingerprint** or iris recognition. ▶**biometric characteristic** Also known as a biometric attribute or simply as a biometric. The biological and behavioral characteristic of an individual from which distinguishing, repeatable biometric features can be extracted for the purpose of recognition.

biscuit

It is one of the more unusual slang words for a gun, yet also one of the most familiar because of its ubiquity in **gangsta** rap. There is no agreed-upon explanation for its origins. Another common slang word for gun is "side-piece" (carried on one side of your body), and a biscuit also goes "on the side" (of your main meal); therefore, gun = biscuit. For similar reasons, however, "biscuit" is also slang in gangsta rap for an attractive woman.

bitemark identification

Forensic odontologists use specific marks and patterns to identify a suspect from a bitemark on a victim. The practice first became accepted in 1974 in the US after a bitemark on the nose of an elderly murder victim was used to identify her killer, but it has recently been the subject of controversy and scientific scrutiny. There have to date been 31 exonerations in the US after **cases** based on bitemark **evidence** were reexamined. This has led to questions being raised over the validity of such evidence, which may result in it being banned.

blab

To inform or reveal secrets or the details of a criminal operation or plot (historical and contemporary slang).

black

When used by **intelligence** or military services, black means being free of any hostile **surveillance**. Going black in **tradecraft** jargon means ensuring freedom from such surveillance before engaging in an operation or act connected to an operation. Can also mean **clandestine** or **covert**, especially when used by the **Central Intelligence Agency**, or being in an undetected or unknown location.
▶**black operations (ops)** Covert or clandestine operations carried out by governments, military, and private organizations that are not officially authorized and are deniable by the agencies that have instigated them.

black-bag job

Federal Bureau of Investigation version of breaking and entering. Gaining **covert** entry into residences or other buildings for the purposes of **intelligence** gathering. Often used to obtain files and other documents relating to **foreign intelligence agents** operating on US soil. Can also entail installing wiretaps and planting microphones without a warrant.

Black Codes

During Reconstruction, in the wake of the American Civil War, white landowners sought to control formerly enslaved people by enacting laws that drastically restricted their rights. Known as the Black Codes, these laws were a form of racialized state terror: they placed severe limits on the rights of the formerly enslaved to buy and own property; to marry; to make contracts and testify in court; and to hold any profession except "farmer" without paying prohibitively expensive annual "dues" to the state. Labor contracts were written in such a way that failure to have annual formal employment agreements was tantamount to a crime, and being arrested for vagrancy could result in beating, extrajudicial murder by the police, or being forced into "unpaid labor" (slavery by another name) on plantations. Being denied the right to vote meant that Black people did not have the power to change legislation that would ban these unfair laws. All-white police and state militia forces, often made up of former Confederate soldiers, enforced the Black Codes. The enduring legacy of the Black Codes directly informs the **prison abolition movement** today.

black hat

Cracker who exploits vulnerabilities in computer systems for illicit purposes. Black hats often share information with other black-hat crackers so they can exploit the same vulnerabilities before the victim becomes aware and takes appropriate measures. Can also refer to all kinds of illicit or illegal computer or internet activity.

Black List

When used by the **intelligence** or military services, this is a list of individuals and their locations who are known or suspected to be hostile and whose capture and detention is a priority. (*See also* **Gray List** and **White List**.)

blackmail

A form of **coercion**, blackmail occurs when a criminal threatens to reveal damaging or incriminating information about their victim unless their demands are met. For example, the then-married, now former CEO of Amazon, Jeff Bezos, was threatened with extortion and blackmail after photographs of his mistress were stolen off his phone. Blackmail is a **felony**.

black market

A black market is a marketplace (physically concrete or virtual) where economic transactions take place outside of legal channels. Sometimes known as an "underground market," they are not necessarily malign, as they can spring up in oppressive regimes that might force people to seek goods outside legal channels just to meet basic needs. Whether out of laziness or to avoid paying taxes, for example, parents who pay their babysitter in cash are also technically engaging in a black-market transaction. However, the idea of the black market typically conjures up goods that are illegal (as opposed to the market itself being illegal, in the manner of paying the nanny under the table or international arms dealing). Examples of common black-market goods include designer fakes and banned narcotics. Examples of common black-market transactions include ticket scalping and illegal firearms sales, as well as human trafficking (babies, prostitution, slavery). The **dark web** facilitates black market transactions.

black powder

Earliest known form of **gunpowder**, which was invented over a thousand years ago and consists of nitrate, charcoal, and sulfur.

black propaganda

Untraceable disinformation that is deniable by its source.

black site

Highly controversial, definitely unethical, and probably illegal, a black site is a place where unacknowledged military operations (**black operations** or black ops) are being carried out. In the US, black sites include secret prisons being run by the CIA. In 2006, President George W. Bush acknowledged that the US government was running black sites related to the **War on Terror**; in the same speech, he also informed the public that many of these **ghost detainees** were being shifted to **Guantánamo Bay**.

black swan event

Occurrence so rare and with such an extreme impact that it could only have been predicted in retrospect. *See also* **grey rhino** event.

Blackwater

American private military company founded by ex-Navy SEAL Erik Prince. It was renamed Xe Services in 2009 and Academi in 2011.

black widow

Derived from the name of the spider who kills her mate after mating, a black widow killer is a woman who kills her husbands or lovers for money or some other material gain in the course of her criminal career. Females make up fewer than 20 percent of all serial killers and, unlike male serial killers, are unlikely to have a sexual **motive.** Many also kill other family members or those close to them, again to profit, and some are also caregivers who kill or harm the people in their care. Infamous examples include Velma Barfield, who killed her fiancé, mother, and two elderly people in her care; and Linda Calvey, who killed her lover, Ronnie Cook, and whose other lovers all ended up either dead or in prison.

blank cartridge
Gun **cartridge** that is **loaded** without a **projectile**, so it only causes a sound and/or flash effect.

blank-firing weapon
Object or device that may or may not have the appearance of a **firearm**, originally designed and intended to produce only a sound or flash effect and whose characteristics exclude the firing of any **projectile** (e.g., alarm firearm, starter **pistol/revolver**).

blister agent
Chemical agent that injures the eyes and lungs, burning or blistering the skin. Also known as a vesicant agent.

blood agent
Chemical compound that includes the **cyanide** group and affects bodily functions by preventing the normal utilization of oxygen by body tissues.

blood-borne pathogen
Pathogenic organisms that can cause disease and are present in human blood. These include the human immunodeficiency virus (HIV), hepatitis B (HBV) and hepatitis C (HBC).

bloodstain

Deposit of blood on a surface. ▶**bloodstain pattern** A grouping or distribution of bloodstains that indicates, through a regular or repetitive form, order, or arrangement, the way in which the pattern was deposited or created. ▶**bloodstain pattern analysis** Bloodstains at a **crime scene** can help **forensic** investigators deduce what happened and when from the shapes and patterns formed. As blood has to follow the laws of physics, these shapes and patterns are reliable although their analysis is inevitably subjective. A skilled and experienced investigator can yield vital information from bloodstain patterns, including the precise nature of events and in what order they occurred, as well as whether the crime scene has suffered any disturbance. The analysis can also help pinpoint the positions of victim(s) and perpetrator(s) as well as any witnesses. Bloodstain patterns depend on the speed and distance at which the blood traveled, its volume, the surface it hit, and the angle at which it landed, among other factors. Bloodstain pattern analysis can help to corroborate or refute other **evidence**. Bloodstains are either impact stains, passive stains, or transfer stains. Blood spatter falls into different categories: **impact spatter** occurs when a force acts upon the blood and causes it to travel through the air before landing on a surface; **projection bloodstains** occur from arterial projection; a spatter of **cast-off bloodstains** occurs when a centrifugal force causes blood to fall or be cast off from a moving, bloodied object; and **expirated bloodstains** are formed from blood exhaled from the mouth.

blood typing

A serologist takes blood samples if relevant at a **crime scene** and then tests them to identify blood type using the

ABO system. This system measures antigens and antibodies in the blood.

blow
Slang for **cocaine**.

blow cover
To expose a **covert agent**, officer, activity, or operation, often unintentionally. To have your **cover** blown means to suffer such exposure. Also to inform or reveal information regarding a criminal or crime.

Bobbitt, Lorena and John
In 1993, Lorena Bobbitt made world headlines when she was accused of cutting off her husband John's penis with a carving knife, then driving away and throwing the appendage out the window. At the trial, both prosecution and defense accepted that she had been abused by her husband for years. In light of that history, and following her claim of violent spousal rape, her lawyers used the risky **mental disorder defense** to explain her sudden attack on John. The defense succeeded. On the grounds of temporary insanity, she was acquitted of all charges. Her husband, John Wayne Bobbitt, was also acquitted of the charge of marital rape. After his penis was successfully reattached, he went on to star in porno films in an attempt to profit from his newfound notoriety. Their dynamic illustrates the toxic emotional undercurrents that can fuel **crimes of passion**. The Bobbitt's story has become the stuff of popular legend and countless jokes, but also raised awareness of spousal rape and the psychological toll of **intimate partner violence**.

body
A corpse or dead human being.

body farm

A body farm, or human taphonomy facility (HTF), is a **forensic** research facility that studies the decomposition of the human body. It does so by placing donated human bodies in a variety of situations to decompose naturally, including underwater, buried in various types of soil and hung from trees. Bodies are also placed in situations that replicate **crime scenes** including being left partially clothed, wrapped in plastic, and placed in a car trunk or in a garbage bin.

There are seven body farms in the US, with the first established in 1981 at the University of Tennessee, Knoxville, by the anthropologist Dr. William M. Bass. The **Federal Bureau of Investigation** Laboratory's Recovery of Human Remains course is held at the Knoxville facility every year. Body farms are useful to forensic science, especially **forensic anthropology**, and the solving of crimes because they provide information and **evidence** that can help pinpoint the time and nature of a crime. Research at one body farm in the US helped to identify some of the victims of the serial killer **John Wayne Gacy**.

Body farms obtain bodies through donation, either from the family of someone who has died or the person themselves if they have stipulated they want their remains to be used in this manner. A **medical examiner** may also decide to donate an unclaimed and unidentified body to a body farm in the interests of science. All the body farms in the US are part of a university and, as they are located around the country, offer different ecological, climatic, and geographical environments for the study of decomposition in varying conditions.

There is also a body farm in the Netherlands and one in Australia, the Australian Facility for Taphonomic Experimental Research (AFTER), which was established because US research on decomposition is often not relevant to the results produced by the Australian environment. Plans to open a body farm in the UK are currently being explored although, at present, body farms or HFTs are illegal.

body snatcher

In the eighteenth and nineteenth centuries, a thief who stole bodies from morgues and cemeteries to sell to medical schools and students.

body-worn video (BWV)

Body-worn videos (BWV), sometimes referred to as body-worn cameras, are small, visible devices that are attached to a police officer's uniform, usually on the chest. They are used to capture both video and audio **evidence** when officers are attending incidents. The position of the camera records what happens from the police officer's perspective, acting as an independent witness. Footage is recorded onto an internal, secure storage device and is uploaded to external, secure storage at the end of the officer's shift for use as evidence at court or other legal proceedings. If it is not required for police purposes, it is automatically deleted. BWVs are popular with police forces both in the UK and US as they help build trust in areas where police and community relations are strained, providing evidence in the event of any **allegation** of police brutality or use of unreasonable force, and enforcing transparency and accountability.

BOLO

BOLO is a familiar police acronym for Be On the Lookout. It is broadcast by law enforcement to other members of law enforcement regarding a suspect or person of interest who is believed to be in the area.

bolt action

Action of a gun that includes a movable part that ensures the closing and the locking of a manual repeating **firearm**.

bomb disposal unit (BDU)

Special unit of the New York State Police (NYSP) tasked with disposing explosive devices and hazards in the state of New York except for New York City, which is covered by the **bomb squad** of the New York City Police Department (NYPD).

bomb squad

An informal name for an Explosive Ordnance Disposal Unit, "bomb squad" refers to a special unit of the police force (municipal or state) tasked with dispensing with explosive devices or hazardous devices. The Los Angeles Police Department (LAPD) and New York Police Department (NYPD) each have a bomb squad. By contrast, the bomb squad of North Carolina responds to threats throughout the state, including its major cities.

bona fide

Document or other resource used by the **intelligence** services that backs up or proves an **agent** or officer's claimed identity, often supporting a **cover** story.

Bonin, William

Bonin (1947–1996), aka the Freeway Killer, was an American **serial killer**, rapist, **hebephile**, and ephebo-phile. The product of a neglected, abusive childhood where he was often left in the care of his convicted child molester grandfather and placed in an orphanage, Bonin started to molest children, including his younger brother, as a teenager. He went on to serve in the Vietnam War where he earned a medal for bravery but also assaulted two soldiers at gunpoint, although this went unreported.

After returning to the US, he began to abduct and **rape** teenage boys, some of whom were hitchhikers, at times acting alone and on other occasions with an **accomplice** named Vernon Butts. His victims were often sodomized, brutally beaten, tortured, and then strangled. Bonin also acted with three other accomplices, including William Ray Pugh, a boy he attempted to abduct and rape but who then aided and abetted Bonin in another killing for which he (Pugh) was convicted of **manslaughter**. Those accomplices testified against Bonin at his trial and he was given the death penalty. In total, Bonin killed at least 21 boys and young men, and is suspected of killing 15 others.

He was married once, largely to please his mother who hoped it would cure his evident homosexuality, and dated at least one other young woman. He spent 14 years on death row where he got to know another "Freeway Killer," Randy Kraft. There is a third, unrelated "Freeway Killer" named Patrick Kearney. Bonin was executed by **lethal** injection at San Quentin Prison on February 23, 1996, the first person to be executed in this way in the state of California after the gas chamber was declared to be a "cruel and unusual method" by the state.

book
Gambling racket based on sporting events. A bookmaker runs "the book," taking illegal bets.

booking
Police process by which a suspect is officially **arrested** and **charged** with a crime.

books

Membership records of **Mafia** families in the US.

BOP

See **Federal Bureau of Prisons**.

borgata

Italian term meaning neighborhood or village adopted by the US **Mafia** to mean *famiglia,* or family, the established structure and hierarchy of the organization.

boss

Gang or **Mafia** leader (contemporary slang).

Boston Strangler

The Boston Strangler is the name given to the person or persons who brutally **assaulted** and murdered at least 11 and possibly 13 women in and around Boston, Massachusetts, between 1962 and 1964, strangling them with items of their clothing. A local criminal, Albert DeSalvo, confessed to the murders and two more while under **arrest** for the "Green Man" **rapes** but later recanted his confession. There was no physical **evidence** to link him to the murders, and he was stabbed to death in prison in 1973. In 2013, **DNA** from the scene of one of the Boston Strangler's victims, Mary Sullivan, was matched to DNA secretly obtained by police from a water bottle used by DeSalvo's nephew, Timothy. Albert DeSalvo's body was exhumed and the DNA match confirmed, but it is still unclear which crimes he committed as some people believe there was more than one Boston Strangler. There have been several movies based on the Boston Strangler murders.

bot

A bot or robot is an automated program that performs designated tasks. Some bots run automatically while others only respond to inputted commands. Some bots are used for malicious purposes and in the perpetration of **cybercrime**. These include denial-of-service (DoS) bots, that bombard websites and applications with multiple access requests in an attempt to override the site or application's security gateway, and spambots, which capture email addresses and add them to **spam** email lists.

▶ **botnet** A botnet is a group of linked computers that have been infected with malicious software and then act together to carry out DoS attacks to try to gain access to other computers and systems.

boundary, barrier

Designated perimeter or area that surrounds a **crime scene** or items of physical **evidence** found at a crime scene. Also known as the perimeter or barrier. Ideally a crime scene has three boundaries or barriers consisting of an outer or public barrier, an inner one for personnel working on the crime scene, and a core barrier for the crime scene itself. The first step to securing an outdoor crime scene is to set up the public or outer barrier to prevent **contamination** by the public. This is sometimes called the perimeter containment barrier and is typically when a street, park, or open area is cordoned off with **police tape,** or vehicles positioned to stop the public from entering.

box

Solitary confinement; that is, being "put in the box." Can also refer to a **cell** within a cell, also known as a cage.

box   47

Brady Bill loophole

Signed into law in 1983, the **Brady Bill** was one of the last significant pieces of twentieth-century legislation related to US gun regulation. It imposed a then-new requirement of **background checks** on prospective purchasers of firearms, but criminals quickly exploited several loopholes that continue to make it possible for **prohibited persons** to purchase a firearm.

1) The default sale loophole. Under the Brady Bill, prospective buyers' personal information is run through the **National Instant Criminal Background Check System (NICS)**, and the check is usually completed on the spot. If a background check takes longer (that is, several days), this is generally an indication that there are red flags in this person's background, such as an unresolved criminal charge. Despite this, if a background check is not completed within three business days, the sale can proceed by default. The 2017 **mass murder** of nine worshippers at Emanuel A.M.E. Church in Charleston, South Carolina, took place because of this loophole.

2) The private sale loophole. Also known as the **gun show loophole**, it stems from the fact that private transactions between individuals are not required to run a background check because they have no means to do so. Private sellers of firearms can be found in bartering communities, survivalist forums, online exchange sites for firearms enthusiasts, classified ads, and various resale websites. These kinds of private sales are not **black** market because the gun is legally held by the seller, and resale market transactions (peer-to-peer sales that cut out the middleman) are also legal. *See also* **Brady Handgun Violence Prevention Act**.

Brady Handgun Violence Prevention Act (Brady Bill; 1993–)

Named after James Brady, who in 1981 was shot and wounded during the attempted assassination of Ronald Reagan, the Brady Bill was signed into law by Bill Clinton in 1993. Its key feature was mandating firearm-purchase **background checks**. Initially, the Brady Bill imposed a five-day waiting period on purchases as well, but it was no longer required after 1998 with the implementation of the **National Instant Criminal Background Check System (NICS)**. *See also* **Gun Control Act (GCA)** and **Brady Bill loophole**.

brain fingerprinting

Also known as Farwell brain fingerprinting, this is a controversial technique that uses electroencephalography (EEG) to record the electrical activity of the brain and find out whether specific information is stored within it. A subject is asked specific questions about a crime with the aim of obtaining a P300 response, a particular kind of brain wave, during a **Concealed Information Test** in which a number of questions are asked about the crime but only one relates to what really happened. It is used as a lie-detection method, but it has raised concerns in the wider scientific community.

breakdown

Shotgun (US contemporary gang slang).

brevity code

Code used to shorten a message but not conceal its content.

brew

Any hot beverage, not just coffee; also **alcohol.**

brick

A brick of **cocaine** or a packet of drugs.

brick agent

A nonpejorative term referring to competent, nonmanagement **FBI agents**.

brief

A legal argument written by a licensed lawyer to be presented to the court that will be hearing the case. Inside an adversarial legal system such as exists in the US, the brief argues the merits of your side: either defense, or prosecution. The word *brief* derives from the Latin word *brevis*, meaning "short (of length)." In American courts, however, the legal brief can be quite lengthy, including but not limited to: statutes and regulations being cited; presentation of issues under review; statement of relevant facts; summary arguments of legal standard of review; and discussion of the legal and/or policy arguments in favor of the defendant.

Browder, Kalief (1993–2015)

In 2010, a Black 16-year-old New Yorker named Kalief Browder was accused of stealing a backpack. Though he denied the crime, and neither the backpack nor any of its contents were found on his person, he was arrested, charged with robbery, grand larceny, and assault, and sent to the men's jail on **Riker's Island**. Eventually, due to fighting back against repeated attacks on him by gang members and correctional officers, Browder ended up spending two years in solitary confinement, where he was kept locked up for 22 hours a day.

At Riker's, he made two serious attempts at suicide; he later stated that he'd been goaded by correctional officers. As a result of his attempts to kill himself in order to escape these horrors, his file recorded that he was mentally ill (most likely a reference to clinical depression).

At trial, he pled not guilty, and the case against him was dismissed due to lack of evidence. He'd spent three years at Riker's waiting for trial, of which two-thirds of the time was spent in solitary. Unable to overcome the trauma of his unjust incarceration, in 2015, he succeeded in killing himself. Before his death, he had sued the New York City Police Department, the District Attorney of the Bronx, and the Department of Corrections for his wrongful imprisonment; his family eventually won a substantial civil settlement. More importantly, his tragedy cast a spotlight on systematic abuse inside the prison system, prompting Barack Obama to sign an executive order banning **solitary confinement** of juveniles in federal prison.

brush contact

Covert brief encounter between **intelligence** operatives, often prearranged, during which information or material is passed either physically or orally. Also known as a brush pass or a brief encounter.

brute-force attack

A brute-force attack is an attempt to gain access to a computer or system by using multiple successive login attempts with different password and username combinations. The attack can be carried out manually or by using an automated script. **Hackers** often run several systems at the same time similar to a DoS attack (see **bot**) to try to gain access as they may eventually hit upon the right combination, especially if the username or password is short or common. Brute-force attacks are the most common way of compromising online accounts.

BTK

See Rader, Dennis.

bubird

Pronounced boo-bird. An official **Federal Bureau of Investigation** airplane or helicopter.

bucar

Pronounced *boo-car*. An official **Federal Bureau of Investigation** car.

buccal swab

Buccal means "relating to the cheek or mouth." A buccal swab, also known as buccal smear, is a way to collect **DNA** from the cells on the inside of a person's cheek. Buccal swabs are a relatively noninvasive way to collect DNA samples for testing. Their use is very common in police **investigations** where they can include or exclude individuals as suspects.

buck

To shoot someone in the head (US/Jamaican contemporary gang slang).

buckshot

Shot with a diameter of greater than 6.1 mm (.24 inches) in the English system. In the international metric system, buckshot starts at 5 mm (.197 inches).

bug

Concealed listening device, microphone or other equipment used in audio **surveillance**. ▶ **bugged** Room or item that contains a concealed listening device.

bullet

Unique **projectile**, most often fired from a gun, which can be spherical or nonspherical and made from a variety of materials. Bullets are shaped or composed differently for a variety of purposes:

- Round-nose–the most commonly found multipurpose **lead bullet**. The end of the bullet is blunted.
- **Hollow-point**–used for controlled penetration. There is a hole in the bullet that expands when it hits its target, creating more damage.
- Jacketed–the soft lead is surrounded by another metal, usually copper, that allows the bullet to penetrate a target more easily (see **full metal jacket**, **total metal jacket**).
- Wadcutter–a bullet specially designed for firing at paper targets. The front of the bullet is flattened.
- Semi-wadcutter–intermediate between round nose and wadcutter.

▶**bullet diameter** The maximum dimension measured across the largest cylindrical section of a bullet. ▶**bullet jacket** The metallic, polymer or plastic envelope surrounding the core of a compound bullet.

▶**bullet trajectory** The curved path of a projectile or bullet from the **muzzle** of a **firearm** to the target. This is more or less straight over short distances close to the muzzle. ▶**bullet wipe** The discolored area on the immediate periphery of a bullet hole, caused by the transfer of residues from the bearing surface of the bullet. These are dark gray to black residues that typically contain carbon, lead, bullet material, and possibly other constituents such as bullet lubricant and **primer** residues. Bullet wipe may occur at any range of fire. Also known as burnishing or leaded edge.

bum beef

False **accusation** or **charge**, or wrongful conviction (US contemporary slang).

bum steer

False information or misdirection (US historical slang).

Bundy, Ted

Ted Bundy (1946–1989) was one of America's most notorious serial killers who **kidnapped, raped,** and murdered young women and girls during the 1970s. The exact number of his victims remains unknown; although, before he was executed, he confessed to 30 homicides he had committed between 1974 and 1978. A former law student, Bundy was good looking and charismatic, using both attributes to help him win the trust of his victims.

He would often pretend to be injured or to have a disability and would approach his victims in a public place, asking them to help him put something in his car, the notorious brown Volkswagen Beetle he drove. He would then bludgeon them unconscious before driving them to a secluded spot where he would rape and kill them. He would sometimes revisit the corpses of his victims to groom and perform sexual acts on them until decomposition and destruction by wild animals made this impossible.

He also decapitated at least 12 of his victims and kept some of the severed heads in his apartment, where he slept beside them. Bundy escaped from **custody** on several occasions but, after his final recapture in 1978 in Florida, he received three death **sentences** in two separate trials. Bundy was executed in the electric chair at Florida State prison in 1989. Those who encountered and worked with him described him as a sadistic sociopath and the definition of evil. Bundy described himself as "the most cold-hearted son of a bitch you'll ever meet." In 2011 Bundy's complete **DNA** profile was added to the **Federal Bureau of Investigation**'s DNA database in the hope that it might aid the **investigation** of unsolved murder **cases**.

Bureau

Federal Bureau of Investigation agents generally refer to the organization as "The Bureau," especially when speaking to other agents.

Bureau of Alcohol, Tobacco, and Firearms (ATF)

Currently operating as part of the **US Department of Justice (DOJ)**, ATF is a law enforcement agency that focuses on four areas of criminal concern: 1) the illegal use and trafficking of firearms, 2) the illegal use and storage of explosives, 3) acts of arson and bombings, acts of terrorism, and 4) the illegal diversion of alcohol and tobacco products. Originally part of the US Treasury Department, ATF was responsible for enforcing the National Prohibition Law of 1919. In 1930, AFT was still part of the US Treasury when special agent Elliot Ness and his team of "Untouchables" (thus called because they were believed to be impervious to bribery) finally brought down bootlegger gangster Al Capone for tax evasion. Today, ATF special agents are trained to handle criminal activity relating to arson, alcohol, explosives, firearms, and tobacco.

burglary

Burglary is the **theft**, or **attempted** theft, of money or objects from premises where access has not been or is not authorized. Damage to premises that appears to have been caused by a person attempting to enter to commit a burglary is also counted as burglary. Residential and commercial burglaries are distinguished by the function of the building.

burned

When an **intelligence agent** or officer is **compromised**, they are said to be burned. This can also be used to describe when the target of a **surveillance** operation realizes that they are being watched or followed. The popular television series Burn Notice (2007–2013) followed the life of a "burned" agent.

burner

A temporary, disposable mobile phone bought with prepaid minutes and paid for in cash so it cannot be easily traced (UK/US contemporary slang).

burst-fire weapon

Type of **automatic firearm** that fires a predetermined number of shots with each pull of the **trigger**.

butt

In **handguns** it is the bottom part of the **grip**. In longer guns such as **rifles**, it is the rear or shoulder end of the **stock**.

BWV

See **body-worn video**.

C

C

cache

Hidden stock of supplies that typically contains items such as food, water, medical items, and/or communications equipment, which is packaged to prevent damage from exposure. A cache can be buried, submerged, or concealed in some other way and is usually designed to support an **agent**, officer, or operative who is isolated and operating alone.

CAD

See **Computer-Aided Dispatch**.

caliber

A measurement of **barrel** diameter, but commonly used to identify, in association with other elements such as the length of the **cartridge case** or brand, the type of cartridge a gun is designed to fire.

call sign

Any combination of characters or pronounceable words that is used to establish and maintain communications, and which identifies a communication facility, a command, an authority, an activity or a unit.

Camargo Barbosa, Daniel

Camargo Barbosa (1930–1994) was a Colombian serial killer who **raped** and murdered up to 150 young girls in the 1970s and 1980s, making him one of the most prolific serial killers of all time. He chose poor, vulnerable young girls because he was obsessed with virgins and the pain he inflicted upon them gave him greater satisfaction. Camargo Barbosa was stabbed to death in prison at the age of 64 by a fellow prisoner who turned out to be the nephew of one of his victims.

Camp Peary

Camp Peary is a 9,000-acre training facility in Virginia, which hosts a **covert Central Intelligence Agency** training facility known as "The Farm." It is also known as Camp Swampy. Although it is well known that this facility exists, it has never been formally acknowledged by the US government.

cannabis, marijuana

The most used illegal recreational **drug** in the world, cannabis or marijuana is a psychoactive drug from the cannabis plant that is also used for medical purposes. It is usually smoked or eaten. Various names given to cannabis refer to the different methods of preparation. Weed refers to the dried buds and leaves of the plant, whereas hashish or hash is prepared from cannabis resin. Weed and hashish are commonly smoked in hand-rolled cigarettes known as joints but can also be smoked in pipes or bongs. Cannabis is also cooked into food, especially cookies and brownies, before being eaten. Cannabis is an important part of the illegal global **drug-trafficking** trade and is the drug seized in the greatest quantities worldwide. Also known as: 420; A-bomb (cannabis mixed with **heroin**); Acapulco gold; Acapulco red; ace; African black; African bush; airplane; alfalfa; *alfombra*; Alice B. Toklas; all-star; *almohada*; Angola; animal cookie (hydroponic); Arizona; ash; Aunt Mary; AZ; baby; bale; *bambalachacha*; Barbara Jean; *bareta*; bash; bazooka (cannabis mixed with **cocaine** paste); B. C. Budd; Bernie; bhang; big pillow; biggy; bionic (cannabis mixed with **PCP**); black bart; black gold; black Maria; blondie; blue cheese; blue crush; blue dream; blue jeans; blue sage; blueberry; bobo bush; boo; boom; branches; broccoli; bud; budda; *burrito verde*; bush; cabbage; café; *cajita*; cali; camara; Canadian black; catnip; *cheeba*; Chernobyl; cheese; Chicago black; Chicago green; chippie; *chistosa*; Christmas tree; chronic; churro; cigar; citrol; cola; Colorado cocktail; cookie (hydroponic); *cotorrito*; crazy weed; creeper bud; crippy; crying weed; *culican*; dank; devil's lettuce; dew; diesel; dimba; dinkie dow; *diosa verde*; dirt grass; ditch weed; dizz; *djamba*; dody; dojo; domestic; *Donna Juana*; doobie; downtown brown; drag weed; dro (hydroponic); *droski* (hydroponic); dry high; *elefante pata*; endo; *escoba*; fattie; fine stuff; fire; flower; flower tops; fluffy; fuzzy lady; *gallina*; *gallito*; garden; *garifa*; gauge; gangster; ganja; gash; gato; Ghana; gigi (hydroponic); giggle smoke; giggle weed; girl scout cookie (hydroponic); Gloria; gold; gold leaf; gold star; gong; good giggles; gorilla; gorilla glue; granddaddy purp; grass; grasshopper; green; green crack; green-eyed girl; green eye; green goblin; green goddess; green Mercedes Benz; green paint; green skunk; greenhouse; *grenuda*; *greta*; *guardada*; gummy bears; *gunga*; hairy one; hash; Hawaiian; hay; hemp; herb; *hierba*; holy grail; homegrown; hooch; *hoja*; *humo*; hydro; Indian boy; Indian hay; Jamaican gold; Jamaican red; jane; jive; jolly green; jon-jem; joy smoke; *Juan Valdez*; *juanita*; jungle juice; kaff; kali; kaya; KB; Kentucky blue; KGB; khalifa; kiff; killa; kilter; King Louie; kona gold; kumba; kush; laughing grass; laughing weed; leaf; *lechuga*; lemon-lime; *leña*; *liamba*; lime pillows; little green friends; little smoke; *llesca*; loaf; lobo; loco weed; loud; love nuggets; love weed; Lucas; MJ; machinery; *macoña*; *mafafa*; magic smoke; Manhattan silver; *manteca*; *maracachafa*; Maria; marimba; *mariquit*a; Mary Ann; Mary Jane; Mary Jones; Mary Warner; Mary Weaver; matchbox; *matraca*; Maui wowie; Meg; method; mersh; Mexican brown; Mexicali haze; Mexican green; Mexican red; MMJ; mochie (hydroponic); *moña*; monte;

moocah; mootie; mora; *morisqueta*; *mostaza*; mota; mother; mowing the lawn; muggie; my brother; narizona; northern lights; nug; O-boy; OG; OJ; owl; paja; palm; Paloma; *Palomita*; Panama cut; Panama gold; Panama red; *pakalolo*; parsley; *pasto*; pasture; *peliroja*; *pelosa*; phoenix; pine; Pink Panther; pintura; plant; platinum cookie (hydroponic); platinum Jack; pocket rocket; popcorn; *porro*; pot; pretendo; Prop 215; puff; purple haze; purple OG; Queen Ann's lace; red hair; ragweed; railroad weed; rainy day woman; Rasta weed; red cross; red dirt; reefer; reggie; *repollo*; righteous bush; root; rope; Rosa Maria; salt and pepper; Santa Marta; sassafras; sativa; shoe; sinsemilla; shmagma; shora; shrimp; shwag; skunk; Skywalker (hydroponic); smoke; smoochy woochy poochy; smoke Canada; sour OG; spliff; stems; sticky; stink weed; sugar weed; sweet Lucy; Tahoe (hydroponic); tangy OG; terp; terpene; Tex-Mex; Texas tea; tigitty; *tila*; tims; top shelf; Tosca; train wreck; tree; trinity OG; tweed; *valle*; wake and bake; weed; weed tea; wet (cannabis dipped in **PCP**); wheat; white-haired lady; wooz; Yellow Submarine; yen pop; yerba; *yesca*; young girls; *zacate*; *zacatecas*; *zambi*; zip; zoom (cannabis mixed with PCP).

cant, thieves' cant

Cant is a jargon belonging to and used by a particular group or subgroup. From the sixteenth to nineteenth centuries in England, thieves and other marginal members of society had their own cant, known as thieves' cant, which they used to communicate without being discovered or found out by the authorities. The Artful Dodger in Dickens's *Oliver Twist* speaks almost entirely in cant, and Dickens helpfully included a thieves' cant glossary at the back of the book. Thieves' cant was also known as "flash" or "peddler's French" and existed across Europe in different forms.

It began to flourish in sixteenth-century England when there was less work available and, as a result, crime started to rise. The new burgeoning underclass of thieves and rogues met in public gathering places or "flash houses" in order to share tips and information. Much as people have an interest in true crime today to arm themselves with knowledge, so the general population became fascinated with this underclass and several thieves' cant dictionaries were published as a result.

These dictionaries contained not just definitions of the words or jargon used by thieves and vagabonds but also descriptions of their various scams so the public could be forewarned. An early example was John Awdeley's *The Fraternity of Vagabonds*, where Awdeley explains that he gathered the information for his book by interviewing "ruffling and beggarly" people who insisted on remaining anonymous for fear of being killed in retribution by their brethren.

Thieves' cant dictionaries were so popular they were published in other countries, including the US where, in 1859, a New York police chief named George W. Matsell published *The Rogue's Lexicon*. There was also a French–English cant dictionary. The origins of thieves' cant remain a mystery, but it is generally believed to be a mixture of English, Romani, French, Yiddish, Latin, and Italian influences with some words from other European languages including German and Portuguese. Thieves' cant fell out of use after the nineteenth century but remnants of it may be found in children's songs, cockney rhyming slang and Polari, a form of nineteenth-century cant used by the gay subculture, actors, showmen, the British Merchant Navy, and wrestlers as well as thieves and prostitutes.

The game Dungeons and Dragons keeps the tradition
alive with its own fictional criminal cant.

C

capital murder

A capital murder is a crime so terrible that the perpetrator
is eligible for the death penalty; that is, **capital punishment**. The term is considered antiquated and is only in
use in eight states.

capital punishment

Otherwise known as the "death penalty," capital punishment is the highest form of retributive punishment by the
state, and is handed down for crimes such as treason or
heinous murder. It is imposed on a state-by-state basis. In
1971, for example, cult leader **Charles Manson** was
sentenced to death for murdering two people and orches-
trating the killings of seven others. But, in 1972, California
suspended the death penalty as unconstitutional. As a
result, Manson was resentenced to life in prison without
possibility of parole. The Supreme Court of the United
States has ruled that capital punishment should not be
used on those under 18 at the time of the offense, or those
judged mentally defective.

capo

Used to mean the **boss** in **Mafia** terms but now refers to a
captain or lieutenant within a Mafia family. ▶*capo dei capi*
The ultimate leader or crime boss in a Sicilian or
American Mafia family.

car

Group of prisoners who stick, or "ride," together in the
prison yard and back each other up if necessary. Cars are
organized by race, religion, gang, or other affiliation. ▶in

the car In on a deal or taking part in a plan involving other inmates while in prison (US contemporary prison slang).

carbine

Rifle of relatively short length and light weight originally designed for mounted troops.

carbon

Paper that is impregnated with chemicals that can reveal **secret writing**. This is often concealed within a writing pad to appear like a normal sheet of paper.

CARD team

See child abduction rapid deployment (CARD) team.

carfentanyl

A synthetic opioid not intended for human use, the veterinary purpose of carfentanyl is chiefly as a tranquilizer, for use on large animals such as elephants. It is 1,000 times more powerful than **fentanyl**, and 10,000 times stronger than morphine. Recently, carfentanyl (or carfentanil) has surfaced as a recreational drug used by humans, who consume it, sometimes unknowingly, after it is cut into powdered **cocaine** or sold as **heroin**. Classified as a **Schedule II** drug, even tiny amounts on the skin pose lethal safety risks. It is linked to a sharp rise in American drug deaths by overdose.

carry

"Carrying" refers to carrying a firearm on one's person, and can be **open** or **concealed**. All 50 states acknowledge the right to carry, but some require licenses or permits. There are many places where private citizens, including those who have gun permits, are not allowed to carry a firearm, including schools and school grounds, hospitals, airports, nuclear facilities, public transit, and private homes, without permission.

car toss

Type of **dead drop** in which the documents or information are concealed and thrown into a preselected location from a car traveling along a designated route. Concealment devices might, for example, be drink cans or bottles, and could include a tracking device so that the intended **agent** could find the item. (See **toss**.)

cartridge

Unit of **ammunition** made up of a cartridge case, **primer**, powder and **bullet**. Also called a **round** or **load**. A gun cartridge consists of a self-contained unit comprising the primer, **propellant** and one or more **projectiles**, unless it is a **blank cartridge**, all housed within a cartridge case. ▶cartridge case Component of a gun cartridge that contains the primer and propellant. ▶ **cartridge case mouth** Open end of a cartridge case or **shotgun** cartridge from which the projectile or **shot charge** is expelled in firing. ▶cartridge head End of the gun cartridge case in which the primer or priming is inserted and the surface upon which the headstamp identification is imprinted. The head impacts against the breech during firing. ▶ **cartridge headstamp** Numerals, letters, and symbols or a combination of these stamped into the head of a cartridge case or shotgun cartridge to identify the manufacturer, year of manufacture, **caliber** or **gauge**, and other additional information.

CARVER

Developed by US Army Special Forces during the Vietnam War, CARVER stands for Criticality, Accessibility, Recuperability, Vulnerability, Effect, and Recognizability.

It is used to identify, assess, and rank targets so that military resources can be used most efficiently.

carving

Forensic carving, also known as data carving, is the process of extracting a collection of data from a larger data set in **digital forensics**. Data carving frequently occurs during a digital **investigation** when the unallocated file system spaces are analyzed in order to extract files. The files are "carved" from the unallocated space.

case

The **investigation** of a crime from the time it is reported/discovered until it is resolved or closed. ▶**case file** Collection of documents relating to a particular case or investigation. These can be kept in files, folders, boxes, cabinets, and drawers, and can include photographs, video and audio recordings as well as laboratory reports, media clippings, and recordings, and documented **evidence**. ▶**case identifier** Unique combination of letters, numbers and sometimes symbols used to identify a particular case. ▶**caseload** Number of cases that an investigator is actively investigating. ▶**case officer** In the **intelligence** services, case officers manage **agent** networks, principal agents, agents, and **assets**. They also spot potential agents and recruit them as well as training them in **tradecraft**. ▶**case review** Comprehensive review of all case-related documents and evidence for the purpose of solving the case. ▶**case summary** Documentation summarizing the status of a **cold case** after review.

cast

Technique to preserve and replicate impression **evidence** in soft material such as soil, tissue or snow. Casts can be made of shoeprints, bitemarks, tire prints and tool marks. When done properly, casting produces excellent positive replicas of the impression, but casts are not exact duplicates.

Castle doctrine

If a man's home is his castle, he has a right to defend it from trespassers, up to and including deadly force if necessary. Inside one's home, the reasoning goes, one does not have a duty to retreat. Its application has not been without controversy; in the US, the Castle doctrine is bound up with an ideological argument called **stand your ground**. Legally, it is argued under the presentation of justifiable homicide. The Castle doctrine applies on a state-by-state basis.

cast-off bloodstain

Cast-off **bloodstains**, as their name suggests, occur when centrifugal force causes blood to fall or be cast off from a moving, bloodied object such as a weapon that has been flung through the air. Cessation cast-off patterns occur when that object suddenly stops moving (e.g., when the weapon lands on the floor after it has been flung). These bloodstains are particularly difficult to interpret as there are so many possible variations of movement, speed, angle, and whether or not the blood has been repeatedly thrown. There are, however, characteristic patterns that occur and that can offer some clue as to what took place at the **crime scene**.

catfish

Fake or stolen online identity used, especially on social media, to deceive, abuse, or troll people. Catfishing is frequently used for romance or relationship scams on dating sites and/or to defraud unsuspecting victims. Sexual predators including **pedophiles**, **cyberbullies**, and trolls are all known to catfish, and it is also used in **espionage** to blackmail or discredit the target. Catfishing can result in serious **sexual assaults** including **rape**, the loss of money and reputation, and even suicide as a result of the impact on the victim. Although catfishing in itself is not, in most instances, a **cybercrime**, it is often used to facilitate it.

CC
"Cop on the corner" or in the area (US contemporary gang slang).

CCTV
See **closed-circuit television**.

CCW
See **concealed carry**.

CEHTTFs
See **Child Exploitation and Human Trafficking Task Forces**.

cell
Usually small room in a prison, police station, or other institution to which someone is confined. Also, a subordinate organization formed around a specific process, capability, or activity within a designated larger organization, and which is often used in relation to terrorists.

cement shoes
Popular murder method, to get rid of someone who has fallen out of favor with an **organized crime** gang or the **Mafia**, where someone is weighted down, dead or alive, before being thrown in water in the hope that they will sink and never be found.

Central Intelligence Agency (CIA)

The Central Intelligence Agency is a US government **agency** responsible for collecting, evaluating, analyzing, and disseminating national and foreign security **intelligence** to assist the President and senior officials in making decisions affecting national security. It officially consists of the Directorate of Intelligence, the Directorate of Science and Technology, the Directorate of Support, and the NCS (National Clandestine Service). The Special Activities Division (SAD) is the NCS's **covert** and **clandestine** operations unit.

CEOP Command

See **Child Exploitation and Online Protection Command**.

chaff

Reflector that consists of thin, narrow metallic strips of various lengths and frequency responses. It is used to reflect radar echoes to create confusion.

chain gang

In the US, the chain gain is perhaps the most visible form of convict leasing, which provided **prison labor** to plantations and corporations requiring menial or hard physical work such as timber cutting, coal mining, and road work. Though convict leasing was abolished in 1941, the chain gang–which refers to the practice of shackling these leased inmates together to deter escape–has resurged in the contemporary American South. They have been featured in films such as *I am a Fugitive from a Chain Gang* (1932), *Cool Hand Luke* (1967), and *The Shawshank Redemption* (1994).

chain of custody

Also known as the chain of **evidence**. The chronological paper trail that documents who collected, handled, analyzed, or otherwise controlled a piece of evidence during an **investigation**. It is vital that a proper chain of custody is established and adhered to without gaps or discrepancies to rule out the possibility of mishandling or tampering with the evidence. Evidence can be ruled inadmissible and therefore suppressed where the chain of custody has not been properly secured—and there is therefore no way of being able to trust the accuracy of, for example, **fingerprint** analysis or blood tests.

chamber

Essential part of a **firearm** into which the **cartridge** is inserted prior to being fired. In a **revolver**, the chamber is not part of the **barrel** but is instead made by holes in the **cylinder** that have been formed to accept a cartridge.

change detection

Image-enhancement technique that compares two images of the same area from different time periods, eliminating identical picture elements in order to leave the parts that have changed.

charge

In relation to a gun **cartridge**, the amount, by weight, of a component of that cartridge (i.e., priming weight, **propellant** weight, **shot** weight).

charge (legal)

See **criminal charge**.

cheap thief

Someone who steals from places of worship (US historical slang).

chemical agent

Chemical substance used with the intention to kill, seriously injure, or incapacitate through its physiological effects.

chemical, biological, radiological, nuclear, and high-yield explosives (CBRN or CBRNE)

A CBRNE defense protocol consists of three parts:
1) passive protection, 2) contamination avoidance; and
3) mitigation. These protocols were developed in anticipation of CBRNE warfare or terrorism, including mass casualty events. In some countries, jurisdiction for CBRNE events falls to the police. In the US, it is military. Training in CBRNE is required for all members of the US Navy and is a specialty focus inside other branches of the military.

chemical enhancement

Use of chemicals that react with particular types of **evidence** such as blood, **latent fingerprints,** and semen that might otherwise be difficult to detect. These chemicals include fluorescein and **luminol** for blood, and iodine, silver nitrate, ninhydrin, and cyanoacrylate (or superglue) for fingerprints.

chemical hazard

Any **toxic** chemical manufactured, used, transported, or stored that can cause death or other harm. This includes toxic industrial chemicals as well as **chemical agents** and **chemical weapons** prohibited under the Chemical Weapons Convention.

chemical weapon

Under the Chemical Weapons Convention, the definition of a chemical weapon includes all **toxic** chemicals and their precursors, except when used for purposes permitted by the Convention. Any munitions or devices specifically designed to inflict harm or cause death through the release of toxic chemicals are chemical weapons, including but not limited to mortars, artillery shells, missiles, bombs, mines, or spray tanks. This includes any equipment specifically designed for use "directly in connection" with the employment of the munitions and devices identified as chemical weapons.

Chikatilo, Andrei

Andrei Romanovich Chikatilo (1936–1994) was a Soviet citizen who was one of the most prolific serial killers of all time, operating between 1978 and 1990. Chikatilo sexually **assaulted** and mutilated his victims, all of whom were women and children, including boys. He was known as the Butcher of Rostov, the Red Ripper, and the Rostov Ripper, Rostov being the region of Russia where most of the murders took place. He enjoyed tasting his victims' blood as well as consuming body parts that included tongues and nipples. When he was caught in 1990, he confessed to 56 murders, was **charged** with 53, and **sentenced** to death for 52 of them. Chikatilo's **case** is noteworthy not just because of the number and brutality of his crimes but also because he belonged to a rare group of people known as nonsecretors whose blood type can only be inferred from a blood sample as it did not match that of his other bodily fluids. Chikatilo's blood was Type A and his semen Type AB. Police only had a sample of semen from the victims when they first caught and **arrested** him in 1984 for a series of minor offenses so he escaped a murder charge. He was finally caught thanks in part to psychological **profiling** carried out by a psychiatrist, Alexander Bukhanovsky, who refined an earlier profile. When Bukhanovsky's profile was read out to him, Chikatilo was so flattered, he confessed to the murders and even led police to the remains of bodies that had hitherto been undiscovered. Chikatilo was executed with a single shot to the back of his head in 1994 in Moscow Prison. Bukhanovsky went on to become a sought-after expert on sexual crimes and serial killers.

child abduction rapid deployment (CARD) team
The FBI will deploy a CARD team as soon as possible after a child abduction has been reported to an FBI field office or related branch of law enforcement.

Child Exploitation and Human Trafficking Task Forces (CEHTTFs)
Combines the resources of the FBI with state and local law enforcement at the state level to investigate cases involving crimes against children.

Child Protective Services (CPS)
Umbrella term referring to US state agencies in charge of child welfare. Such agencies respond to accusations of child abuse or endangerment. CPS falls under the administrative aegis of state-run social services (such as Departments of Health and Human Services, or HHS) and often works with, but not for, state and local law enforcement. On the federal level, CPS is governed by a variety of laws, including the Child Abuse Prevention and Treatment Act (CAPTA) of 1998.

child sexual abuse material (CSAM)
Any material involving the sexual abuse of a child. CSAM is an investigative priority of the **Crimes Against Children Program** of the FBI.

CHIS
See **covert human intelligence source**.

chloroform

Chloroform is well known for its use in anesthesia but it is also a deadly **poison**, requiring only 1.5 ounces or around a shot-glass measure to kill. In 2018, three-year-old Mariah Woods from North Carolina died from chloroform **toxicity** and her mother's boyfriend, Earl Kimrey, was **charged** with first-degree murder. In the UK in 2015, two brothers were jailed for the murder of Sameena Imam with chloroform after she had demanded one of them leave his partner for her. Craig McCreight was jailed for life in Scotland in 2002 for the murder of his partner with chloroform but had his conviction quashed in 2009 due to flawed scientific **evidence**. Even when chloroform was used as an anesthetic, numerous accidental deaths occurred due to its high levels of toxicity, which is why its use is now tightly regulated, although it can be made from combining easily available household substances including bleach and acetone.

CI

See confidential informant.

CIA

See Central Intelligence Agency.

CID

See Criminal Investigation Department.

cipher

A cipher is a way to conceal words or text using encryption. Cipher can also refer to the words or text that have been encrypted, the key used to encrypt, or the method of encryption. A cipher pad is a pad of paper sheets that have a nonrepetitive key printed on them. A sheet is used once to **encipher** text and another sheet is used once to decipher it.

circumstantial evidence
See **evidence**.

CIT
See **Concealed Information Test**.

clandestine
In **intelligence**, military, and police terms, any activity or operation sponsored or conducted by governmental departments or agencies with the intent to assure secrecy and concealment. (*See also* **black**.)

clap
To have been shot by or to shoot someone with a firearm (US/Jamaican contemporary gang slang).

classified
Official designation given to a document or information that is deemed of sufficient importance or interest to require protection against **unauthorized disclosure** in the interests of national security.

clean
Free of any kind of **surveillance** or unknown to hostile **intelligence**. Can refer to an object such as a phone or an environment as well as a person.

clearance rate
Percentage of crimes known to the police or **law enforcement** that were "cleared," or solved, by **arrest** or other special circumstances. The clearance rate is calculated by dividing the number of known crimes by the number of cleared or solved ones.

clickjack

Exploit that occurs when a cybercriminal tricks someone into clicking on a hyperlink, thinking they are being taken to a particular site or URL when they are, in fact, taken elsewhere, usually for malicious purposes including downloading **malware** or harvesting their personal information.

clip

Cartridge container used to rapidly **reload** the **magazine** of a **firearm**. Also known as a stripper clip.

closed case

Case where all suspects have been identified and, if possible, successfully prosecuted.

closed-circuit television (CCTV)

Closed-circuit television (CCTV) is used for monitoring and **surveillance**. CCTV consists of unmanned, remotely mounted video cameras that transmit live pictures back to a closed monitoring system. It is used in town centers and on roads, as well as in airports, hospitals, government buildings, and on public transport. CCTV footage can help identify suspects in a crime but can also serve criminal purposes; for example, via tiny cameras attached to ATMs recording PINs as they are entered.

In the United States, as of 2021, no federal laws regulate or prohibit the use of CCTV by employers monitoring their workplace. General privacy laws still apply, such as the Privacy Act of 1974, which, per the **US Department of Justice (DOJ)**, "establishes a code of fair information practices that governs the collection, maintenance, use, and dissemination of information about individuals that is maintained in systems of records by federal agencies." Critics of public monitoring (via CCTV and other means) point to sweeping federal laws such as the **Patriot Act,** which gave various law enforcement agencies the power to conduct warrantless domestic surveillance of civilians, as a sure indication that civil liberties and freedoms being eroded in the name of national security and public order.

In urban centers abroad, mass surveillance has already become the norm; this is especially true in China but is not confined to that country: in 2020, there are 691,000 CCTV cameras in London (chiefly operated by private businesses and not police entities). Its ratio of 1 camera per 14 people can be compared to Beijing's ratio of 1 camera per 8 people.

close-up photograph

Close-up photographs are taken to capture specific items of **evidence**. They should provide enough detail for positive identification of the evidence and for **forensic** analysis when appropriate. A ruler is used to show scale when taking close-up photographs, placed on the same plane as the evidence.

cocaine

Cocaine is a highly **addictive** stimulant drug. It is commonly snorted in the form of a powder. Alternately, it can be inhaled (as **crack cocaine**), freebased (smoked), or, most dangerously, injected. It triggers a flood of dopamine, which causes a state of euphoria. Over time, the **drug** alters the way the brain releases dopamine so that frequent users need more and more of it to attain the same state or even to feel normal. It increases the risk of stroke and heart attacks. Prolonged use, if snorted, causes damage to the nose cartilage that separates the nostrils. Cocaine is a **Schedule II** drug in the US and illegal in most other countries except, in some instances, for personal or medical use. Globally, it is the second most popular illegal recreational drug after **cannabis**. Also known as: Adidas; all-American drug; *ancla*; angel powder; Angie; animals;

A-1; Apache; *apodo*; *arriba*; Audi; Aunt Nora; *azucar*; baby powder; *barrato*; *basuco*; bazooka (cocaine paste mixed with **cannabis**); beach; Belushi (cocaine mixed with heroin); Bernice; Bernie's flakes; Bernie's gold dust; big bird; big bloke; big C; big flake; big rush; Billie Hoke; bird; birdie powder; *blanca nieves*; *blanco*; blast; blizzard; blonde; blocks; blow; BMW; board; bobo; *bolitas*; Bolivian marching powder; *bombita* (cocaine mixed with heroin); booger sugar; bose; bouncing powder; *brisa*; bump; C-dust; *caballo*; *caca*; Cadillac; California pancakes; calves; *canelon*; candy; car; carney; carrie nation; cars; case; *cebolla*; Cecil; cement; charlie; chevy; Cheyenne; *chica*; *chicanitas*; *chinos*; *chiva*; *cielo*; clear kind; clear tires; coca; Coca-Cola; *cocazo*; coconut; coke; cola; Colorado; *comida*; *comida dulce*; Connie; cookie; *cosa*; *coso*; *cosos*; crow; crusty treats; *cuadro*; Death Valley; designer jeans; devil's dandruff; diamonds; diente; dienton; diesel; diosa blanca; dona blanca; double bubble; double letters; dove; dream; *dulces*; Duracell; *durazno*; *duro*; dust; *escama*; *escorpino*; *falopa*; Fef1; *fichas*; fiesta; fire (cocaine base); fish (liquid cocaine); fish scale; flake; flea-market jeans; Florida snow; flour; food; foolish powder; fox; freeze; friskie powder; frula; funtime; *gabacho*; galaxy; *gallos*; *gato*; gift of the sun; gin; girl; girlfriend; glad stuff; gold dust; green gold; *gringa*; *gringito*; grout; *guerillo*; *gueros*; guitar; H1; hai hit; hamburger; happy dust; happy powder; happy trails; heaven; heaven dust; heavy one; hen; Henry VIII; HH; HHJ; high heat; HMH; hooter; *hundai*; hunter; ice cream; icing; Inca message; Izzy; jam; *Jaime blanco*; *jaula*; jeep; jelly; John Deere; joy flakes; joy powder; *juguetes*; jump rope; junk; K13; king's habit; *kordell*; *la familia*; lady; lady snow; late night; *lavada*; leaf; *libreta*; line; loaf; love affair; LV; maca flour; *madera*; Mama Coca; *mandango*; *manita*; Maradona; *marbol*; material; mayback (62 grams); mayo; *melcocha*; *media lata*; Mercedes; milk; *milonga*; mojo; Mona Lisa; *monte*; *morro*; mosquitos; movie-star drug; *muchacha*;

muebles; *mujer*; napkin; *nieve*; *niña*; nine-two-one; normal; nose candy; nose powder; old lady; oyster stew; paint; Paloma; *paleta*; *palomos*; *pantalones*; papas; paradise; paradise white; parrot; pearl; *pedrito*; *perico*; personal; Peruvian; Peruvian flake; Peruvian lady; *pescado*; *peta*; *pez*; *pichicata*; pillow; pimp; *pingas*; pingos; *pintura blanca*; *poli*; *pollo*; *polvo*; powder; powder diamonds; puma; *puritain*; *quadros*; *queso blanco*; racehorse charlie; Rambo; *refresco*; *refrescas*; regular kind; regular work; reindeer dust; Richie; rims; rocky mountain; Rolex; Rolex HH; rooster; scale; *schmeck*; schoolboy; scorpion; scottie; seed; Serpico; seven; seven-seven; seven-seven-seven; sierra; six-two; shirt; ski equipment; sleigh ride; sneeze; sniff; snow; snow bird; snow cone; snow white; snowball; snowflake; society high; soda; *soditas*; soft; space (cocaine mixed with **PCP**); special; speedball (cocaine mixed with heroin); stardust; star-spangled powder; studio fuel; suave; sugar; Superman; sweet stuff; *tabique*; *tablas*; *talco*; *talquito*; *tamales*; taxi; *tecate*; teenager; teeth; tequila; thunder; tire; tonto; toot; *tortes*; *tortuga*; Toyota; T-shirts; tubo; *tucibi* (pink variety); turkey; tutti-frutti; *vaquita*; wash; wet; whack (cocaine mixed with PCP); white; white bitch; white cross; white dove; white girl; white goat; white horse; white lady; white Mercedes Benz; white mosquito; white paint; white powder; white rock; white root; white shirt; white T; white wall tires; whitey; whiz bang; wings; woolly; work; *yayo*; *yeyo*; *yoda*; *zapato*; zip.

cock

To place the **hammer, firing pin,** or striker of a **firearm** in position for firing.

code

System in which arbitrary letters or symbols are substituted for words or text to conceal them. ▶ **code book** Book containing **codes** and the plain text equivalents used by the **intelligence** services and military.

CODIS

See **Combined DNA Index System**.

coerced confession

When police obtain a **confession** using unlawful means, such as torture or trickery, it is understood to have been coerced. Depending on the level of duress, coerced confessions can be inadmissible as evidence in a court of law. Detainees will often confess to crimes they did not commit in order to make the torture stop.

coercion

Coercion occurs when someone is forced to behave in a particular way; for example, by threats of violence. The person concerned does not act freely.

cognitive bias

Tendency to evaluate or perceive information based on the experience and unconscious preferences held rather than on the facts alone. A confirmation bias is a type of cognitive bias and is the tendency to look for or interpret information that confirms a preexisting belief or hypothesis. Cognitive biases can result in overt subjectivity and distorted thinking, leading to flawed decision making or interpretation during **investigations** or **forensic** examinations.

cokehead

Cocaine addict (contemporary slang).

cold case

Criminal **investigation** that has not been solved and is not being actively investigated due to lack of **evidence** or

leads. There is always the possibility that new information could be received or emerge, which may reopen the active investigation. Famous cold **cases** include the Black Dahlia, **Jack the Ripper,** and the **Zodiac Killer.** *Cold Case* (2003 to 2010) was also a US TV series based in a fictional Philadelphia police department specializing in cold cases.

▶ **cold-case unit** Dedicated police or **law enforcement** unit that consists of two or more investigators whose specific job it is to investigate cold cases.

cold hit

Connection identified between two criminal **cases** that were not previously known to be related. A **DNA** cold hit is a connection made between a crime-scene DNA profile and a DNA profile found in a DNA database in the absence of any prior investigative **leads**.

cold pitch

An attempt to recruit an **asset**, contact or **agent** without prior development, interaction, or contact.

Combined DNA Index System (CODIS)

This is the **Federal Bureau of Investigation** system that can link **DNA** found at **crime scenes** and so identify serial offenders. There are three levels of CODIS: the Local DNA Index System (LDIS), used by individual laboratories; the State DNA Index System (SDIS), which serves as a state's DNA database containing DNA profiles from LDIS laboratories; and the National DNA Index System (NDIS), managed by the FBI as the nation's DNA database containing all DNA profiles uploaded by participating states.

comedown

Occurs when the effects of a **drug** begin to wear off, and the user experiences symptoms similar to a hangover from **alcohol**. In both instances, the body is trying to process the **toxic** effects of what are essentially **poisons** to the system with the resulting headache or heavy head and need to sleep or lie down.

command and control

Command and control (C & C) is the authority and capability of an organization to direct the actions of its personnel and the use of its equipment. The principles of command and control can be scaled and used to resolve incidents and operations ranging in size and scope, from the policing of a local community event to a major criminal **investigation** such as a major terrorist attack that involves mobilizing several police forces.

communications intelligence (comint)

Information or **intelligence** that has been found, intercepted or otherwise obtained by agencies or governments other than the intended recipients.

communications network (comnet)

Organization of stations capable of intercommunication, but not necessarily on the same channel.

communications security (comsec)

Security measures designed to deny unauthorized access to valuable information that might be gained from telecommunications or to mislead unauthorized people in their interpretation of those telecommunications.

Company

Those on the inside of the **Central Intelligence Agency** refer to it as "The Company."

comparison sample

Generic term used to describe physical material or **evidence** discovered at **crime scenes** that may be compared with samples from people, tools, and physical locations. Comparison samples may be from either an unknown or a known source.

Comparison Question Test (CQT)
Also known as the Probable Lie Test, this is a directly accusatory method of questioning, used alongside a **polygraph test**, which detects deceit in the subject's physiological responses to questions such as "Did you kill her?"

complaint
Formal written **accusation** made by someone, often a prosecutor, and filed in court or to an official body, alleging that a specific person, or persons, has committed a specific offense.

compromised
When an operation, **agent,** or **asset** has been uncovered and is no longer secret, or when a piece of **classified** information has been passed to hostile **intelligence** or governments.

Computer-Aided Dispatch (CAD)
Computer-Aided Dispatch is the allocation and dispatch of police and other emergency services, with the aid of computer software, in response to emergency calls. When a crime is reported, a CAD number is allocated to it. Computer-Aided Dispatch is also used in the private sector by, for example, taxi firms.

computer forensics
See **digital forensics**.

con
Convict or a confidence trick (police and general slang).

concealed carry

In the US, the practice of carrying a concealed weapon, usually a **handgun**, is referred to as concealed carry or CCW (carrying a concealed weapon). Some states limit the carrying of a concealed weapon to handguns while others include knives, batons, and electronic weapons such as tasers. Per federal law, felony offenders forfeit their right to own a firearm, thus convicted felons can never legally carry concealed weapons, even if their state offers unrestricted carry (no permit required, also called "constitutional carry"). Permits are issued by the states, the majority of which do not allow unrestricted carry.

Concealed Information Test (CIT)

Also known as the Guilty Knowledge Test, this is a method of questioning popular with Japanese **law enforcement** and the **Federal Bureau of Investigation** where a subject is asked a series of questions about a crime, only one of which actually relates to what happened. Its aim is to prove that the subject possesses information only a guilty person would know. The test is normally used alongside a **polygraph test** or **brain fingerprinting**.

concurrent sentence

Sentence of imprisonment that runs at the same time as another sentence, as directed by a court.

confession

Generically, to confess means to admit to wrongdoing of some kind. Confession has been an important element in criminal justice for as long as civilization has existed, but modern law is particularly attentive to its legal dimensions. A suspect can't simply be caught on tape confessing to an undercover officer, "Yeah, I did it," and go straight to prison as a result. Though this kind of ruse is often used as a plot device in cop shows, a confession may and can be simply recanted; ruled inadmissible if the suspect was not read their **Miranda rights**; thrown out if the confession was obtained via coercion (police torture), and so on. In other words, confessions are not convictions in and of themselves, and even properly obtained confessions must be supported by other forms of corroborating evidence.

confidential informant (CI)

According to the FBI, a confidential informant (CI) is an individual who provides useful and credible information regarding criminal activity to a law enforcement agency on an ongoing basis. CIs are frequently criminals themselves, and agree to act as CI in exchange for reduction in a potential sentence or vacating of prior convictions. Unlike **cooperating witnesses**, CIs usually do not testify at trial, as preserving their anonymity is of paramount importance.

connected

Someone who is connected is associated with the **Mafia** or **organized crime** in some way.

consigliere

Advisor to a **Mafia** family who is always consulted before a decision is made.

consumer

In **intelligence** terms, a person or **agency** that uses information or intelligence produced by either its own staff or other agencies.

contamination

In **forensic** terms, the undesirable introduction of substances or trace materials to items that will be subject to forensic examination.

contempt of court

Intentionally obstructing a court in the administration of justice, or acting in a way calculated to lessen its authority or dignity, or failing to obey its lawful **orders**.

contract killer

Also known as hitmen, contract killers are murderers-for-hire. Insofar as it is not a credentialed occupation, "professional" contract killers rely on reputation to find work and may have military backgrounds as well as connections to organized crime. In hiring a hitman, you are committing at least two crimes: 1) conspiracy to commit murder (a **felony**); and first-degree murder (also a felony). The most prolific contract killer is believed to have been Julio Santana, who stopped counting his kills after he reached 492 victims. Because their primary incentive for killing is financial gain, contract killers are generally considered to be a category of killer separate from **serial killers, spree killers,** and **mass killers.**

contract prison

A contract prison is a private, for-profit prison contracted by the **Bureau of Prisons**. Their use has long been controversial, as it incentivizes the legal system to find people to jail. In January 2021, Biden ordered the **Department of Justice** to terminate all private prison contracts.

controlled substance

A controlled substance is any behavior-altering or **addictive drug**, such as **heroin** or **cocaine**, of which the manufacture and sale are regulated by federal law. Enforcement of drug laws falls under the purview of the **Drug Enforcement Agency (DEA)**. When certain states passed laws legalizing marijuana (such as, for example, the **Adult Use of Marijuana Act (AUMA; Proposition 64)** in California), the Obama administration suspended federal enforcement of marijuana in those states. *See also* **decriminalization**.

Controlled Substances Act (CSA) of 1971

This statute placed all federally regulated substances into one of five **schedules** based upon the substance's medical use, potential for abuse, and safety or dependence liability. The schedules also rank the drugs according to these criteria. Scheduling also applies to certain chemical precursors.

control zone

A controlled airspace extending upward from the surface of the Earth to a specified upper limit.

conventional force (CF)

This is a force capable of conducting operations using nonnuclear weapons. It can also mean a force other than designated **special operations** forces.

converted firearm

Firearm that has been modified in one or more of its essentials characteristics (e.g., to fire live **bullets** if it was designed to fire blanks). Often used in gun crime to avoid or subvert gun import restrictions.

cooking the books

An accounting scam.

cooperating witness (CW)

Cooperating witnesses are individuals who have negotiated special terms of consideration with the **Department of Justice (DOJ)** in exchange for testifying publicly at trial.

copycat crime

Crime that has been inspired by prior exposure to a previous crime or media content concerning a crime, including fictional or game content. ▶ **copycat effect** The copycat effect occurs when publicity or media attention around a crime or suicide inspires similar incidents. This is most marked when that media content is sensationalist in nature. The term was first coined *c.* 1916 when reporting of the **Jack the Ripper** murders inspired copycat killings.

corner men

Members of a drug gang positioned at street corners, where they serve as lookouts for police.

coroner

An elected or appointed official who conducts or oversees **investigations** and inquests into the cause and manner of death as well as investigating and confirming the identity of an unknown deceased person. Coroners do not have to be medical professionals and might therefore not be authorized to conduct autopsies or other invasive procedures themselves. These are the responsibility of a **forensic pathologist**.

Cosa Nostra

Meaning "our thing," the **Mob** term for a family or the **Mafia**.

count

In the US, each separate offense, attributed to one or more persons, as listed in a **complaint**, information, or indictment.

counterdrug activity

Measure or activity undertaken to detect, disrupt or stop any activity that is reasonably related to illicit **drug trafficking**.

counterespionage (CE)

Counterespionage is the offensive, proactive form of **counterintelligence** and consists of activities designed to gather information about a hostile **intelligence** service using, or attempting to use, that service's own operations.

counterfire

Fire from a ballistic weapon intended to destroy or **neutralize** enemy weapons.

counterguerrilla operation

Activity or operation conducted by security forces against an armed paramilitary wing of an insurgency (guerrillas).

counterintelligence (CI)

Term for activities carried out or information gathered to identify, deceive, thwart, disrupt, or otherwise protect against other **intelligence** activities carried out by hostile agencies or governments.

countersurveillance

Actions taken to counteract hostile **surveillance**. Can include systems and techniques designed to detect that surveillance.

counterterrorism

Activities and operations undertaken to **neutralize** terrorists, their organizations and networks, in order to stop them from using violence to instill fear and to coerce governments or societies so they can achieve their goals.

court hierarchy (American)

The US court system is highly complex. At its most basic, the system architecture divides into federal court and state court.

The federal court system typically hears cases related to: the constitutionality of a law; the laws and treaties of the US; disputes between two or more states; and admiralty law and similar high-level issues.

The Supreme Court, or "court of last resort," is the highest court in the US system. Beneath the Supreme Court, inside the federal court system, there are two main types of courts: 1) District Courts and 2) Courts of Appeals.

There are 94 District Courts or district-level trial courts. There is at least one per state and all US territories (Guam, Mariana Islands, Puerto Rico, US Virgin Islands) except American Samoa, plus the District of Colombia (DC). They consist of one judge and a jury of up to 12 individuals.

There are 13 Courts of Appeals or appellate courts, consisting of three judges but no jury. Specialized Courts of Appeals hear cases related to specific legal issues such as bankruptcy (Bankruptcy Courts); and Article I Courts of Appeals hear cases related to taxes, veterans affairs, and the armed forces.

State courts typically hear cases related to crimes; wills and estates; contract cases; personal injury; and family law (divorce, child custody, adoption).
Confusingly, state and federal laws can conflict. For example, in 2021, marijuana is legal in some states but remains illegal at the federal level.

The Constitution and laws of each state establish the state courts. Each state has its own supreme court, which is not to be confused with the Supreme Court of the United States (federal). States also have courts to handle specific legal issues such as probate court (wills and estates); juvenile court; and family court.

courtroom drama

The courtroom or legal drama or **thriller** focuses on the legal process, featuring lawyers, jurors, witnesses, defendants, and plaintiffs, or complainants. At least half the plot or action will take place in the courtroom and may be based on real-life events or be partly or completely fictional. At the heart of the story are the moral dilemmas that are an inevitable part of the legal system and that reflect real life.

cover

A cover is a protective measure or series of measures designed to conceal an **agent**, plan, place, or operative's true identity and purpose. The term can be applied to anything that masks the true nature of an activity. ▶**cover legend** A cover legend is a story or scenario designed to provide an agent or operative with an explanation for past and present activities in a way that backs up the cover that has been created for them. ▶ **cover within a cover** If an agent or operative is caught and questioned by hostile forces or **intelligence**, a cover within a cover may be used in which they confess to something lesser than **espionage** in the hope of explaining their suspicious activities.

covert

Way of operating that conceals the identity of the organization, government, or entity that sponsored the operation as well as the relationship of the participants. Covert differs from **clandestine** in that clandestine conceals the nature of the operation itself. ▶**covert human intelligence source (CHIS)** A CHIS is a police **informant** or, more informally, a snitch or **grass** (UK police acronym).

cozy mystery

The term "cozy" for a mystery or crime book or series was coined in the late twentieth century and refers to a genre in which an amateur detective solves a crime in what is usually a small town or village setting where an unsuspecting victim has suffered foul play. The amateur detective is often female and middle-aged or elderly, highly educated, and with a useful contact in the local police force or **forensic** services. Supporting these main characters is an array of often eccentric minor characters and there are plenty of clues and red herrings to follow. The reader follows these clues along with the amateur detective but is often surprised by the identity of the real perpetrator. Sex and violence are deliberately downplayed in a cozy mystery and profanity rarely used. The villain is almost always a member of the same small community within which the victim lives, or lived, and the murder method does not involve graphic violence but is unusual or relatively blood free, such as **poisoning**, and takes place "offstage." The emphasis in the cozy mystery is on problem and puzzle solving as well as development of the main characters. They are often written as part of a series and are hugely popular.

CPS

See **Child Protective Services**.

CQT

See **Comparison Question Test**.

crack cocaine

Crack cocaine is the crystallized form of **cocaine** that is heated and smoked. It comes in solid rocks or blocks and is usually white, pale yellow, or rose in color. The name "crack" comes from the popping or cracking sound it makes when heated. Crack cocaine is much stronger than regular cocaine, ranging from 75 to 100 percent pure, and gives users an immediate and powerful high. This effect only lasts for around 15 minutes and so users will smoke more and more crack to replicate its initial potency. It is one of the most addictive **illegal drugs** currently available with some users developing an **addiction** after just one use. It is also relatively cheap, which means it is readily available but that cost skyrockets as the addict needs to buy ever-increasing quantities to feed their addiction. Crack cocaine has many physical and mental ill-effects and is the root cause of many crimes, including **burglary**, street **theft,** and of course, the manufacture and supply of the drug itself. Also known as apple jacks, badrock, ball, base, beat, candy, chemical, cloud, cookies, crack, crumbs, crunch & munch, devil drug, dice, electric Kool-Aid, fat bags, French fries, glo, gravel, grit, hail, hard ball, hard rock, hotcakes, ice cube, jelly beans, Kryptonite, nuggets, paste, piece, prime time, product, raw, rock(s), rock star, Rox/Roxanne, scrabble, sleet, snow coke, sugar block, tornado, troop, 24-7.

crackhead

Crack cocaine addict (contemporary slang).

cracking

Cracking is **hacking** a computer system with malicious intent to destroy files, steal personal information such as credit card numbers or data, infect the system with a **virus**, or do many other things that cause harm. ▶**cracker** A cracker is someone who breaks into a computer system or network without authorization and with the intention of doing damage. Hackers see themselves as elite programmers who build systems while crackers break them, and are therefore above such activity. Although looked down on by hackers who consider themselves programmers, the two have become synonymous. Cracker derives from "safe-cracker" as a way to differentiate it from the various uses of "hacker" in the cyber world. A cracker may destroy files, steal personal information such as credit card numbers or data, infect the system with a virus, or do many other things that cause harm.

crapped out

To die suddenly without warning (contemporary slang).

crash

To raid or invade (contemporary slang).

crew

Group of "soldiers" under a **Mafia** officer's command. Also a gang (contemporary slang).

crime

Criminologists group crimes into several major categories, including: 1) violent crime; 2) property crime; 3) white-collar crime; 4) organized crime; 5) **hate crime**; and 6) consensual or victimless crime. But what is crime? Its definition is circular: a crime is that which is illegal, and that which is illegal is a crime. Or, as novelist Ursula Le Guin famously said: "To make a thief, make an owner; to create crime, create laws."

Theft is wrong, but it can also be understood primarily as an ethical lapse or cognitive failing, which is why children are not criminally liable for unlawful behaviors, up to and including murder, until the age of **criminal responsibility**. At all times, what one thinks of as "crime" must be understood as an artifact of culture and history. For example, "killing" (an act) only becomes "murder" (a crime) when it breaks the law, and a surprising number of killings are perfectly legal. Some US-specific examples of legal killing of humans by human actors include: **Castle doctrine**; self-defense; death penalty/execution by the state; military combat; some police actions; and suicide.

crime of passion

In the US, crimes of passion generally fall under the rubric of temporary insanity or the **mental disorder defense.** The "crime" is not necessarily homicide but involves any act that is driven by heat-of-the-moment violence as opposed to careful premeditation. In this context, "passion" should not be misunderstood as love. Rather, it refers to the overly strong emotional state of the perpetrator at the time the criminal act was committed. In the case of homicide, claiming "crime of passion" is useful for reducing charges from first degree homicide to the lesser charge of manslaughter, and can result, if rarely, in acquittal. In the US, one of the most famous crimes of passion emerged from the violent marriage of John and Lorena **Bobbitt.**

Crimes Against Children Program

A special division of the FBI investigating criminal offenses against children, including cybercrimes. As part of the Crimes Against Children Program, the international Violent Crimes Against Children International Task Force (VCACITF) combines 68 online child sexual exploitation investigators from almost 46 countries. It is the largest task force of its kind in the world.

crime scene

A crime scene is any physical place, including a person, building, vehicle, or open-air location, that may provide an investigator with **evidence** in the **investigation** of a crime. ▶**crime scene reconstruction** The process of determining what actually occurred at a crime scene from an evaluation of physical evidence and other relevant information.

crime scene investigator (CSI)

Thanks to *CSI: Crime Scene Investigation* (2000–2015) and its many spinoffs, American viewers are familiar with the general parameters of CSI work. Falling under the purview of the **forensic** sciences, CSIs include evidence technicians, crime scene analysts, and forensic investigators. Their job is to conduct crime scene processing, fingerprint identification, and forensic imaging, in order to assist police department entities and other law enforcement agencies with their investigations. Using strict methods, they collect, preserve, package, transport, and document physical evidence found at a crime scene. They are not law enforcement officers but support services.

criminal charge

A formal complaint brought by an entity of the state (such as a **district attorney** or **grand jury**) that an individual has committed a criminal act. Charges fall into the category of **felony**, **misdemeanor**, or **summary offense**.

criminal damage

Criminal damage occurs when property is intentionally destroyed or damaged, not necessarily to gain entry to premises or a vehicle.

Criminal Investigation Division (CID)

The largest branch of the FBI, the Criminal Investigation Division (CID) investigates globalized criminal organizations deemed to pose a threat to US national security, including international drug cartels and syndicates, and money-laundering entities. It also pursues cybercrimes, public corruption, and civil rights issues. To these ends, it has partnered with agencies in Mexico, Europe, Asia, South America, and Southeast Europe.

C criminalistics

Branch of **forensic** science that involves the examination and interpretation of physical **evidence** in order to aid forensic **investigations**. It includes **crime scene reconstruction**, **drug** analysis, **firearms**, and tool marks, fire-debris analysis, molecular biology, photography, and trace-evidence analysis.

criminalization

Criminalization is the sociocultural process of turning an act, activity, or state of being into a crime. Examples include the criminalization of abortion, breast feeding in public, childhood, homosexuality, homelessness, poverty, mental illness, assisted suicide, and euthanasia; currently, some US lawmakers are trying to criminalize miscarriage and public protest, while also attempting to **decriminalize** the act of running over political protesters.

Nonetheless, criminalization is not necessarily negative. Pedophilia, date rape, spousal rape, polygamy, and domestic abuse are examples of behaviors that activists fought to have criminalized in order to save their own lives as well as that of other girls, women, and children in general. That work is ongoing.

criminal responsibility, age of

Refers to the age at which a child can be legally held responsible for a crime. This age varies considerably from state to state. In South Carolina, which has the lowest age of criminal responsibility, a six-year-old can be charged with a crime. In 35 other states, the age is seven. At the federal level, the age is 11. *See also* **juvenile justice system**.

critical intelligence

Intelligence that is crucial and requires the immediate attention of the commander or other senior officer.

cruel and unusual punishment

The Eighth Amendment of the Constitution prohibits the federal government from imposing "cruel and unusual punishment." However, this wording is extremely vague, leading to a great deal of legal argument and social debate over what is acceptable. For example, **solitary confinement** may be cruel, but it is not unusual, and it may even be requested by inmates whose circumstances make them targets while **inside**. Ultimately, it is a reflection of social norms; in the US, there is a general trend toward less physically gruesome forms of punishment than in previous centuries.

CSA

See **Controlled Substances Act (CSA) of 1971.**

CSAM

See **child sexual abuse material.**

CSI

See **crime scene investigator.**

cult

A cult is any social group defined by unique or unusual set of beliefs that causes them to isolate from the rest of society; they are often led by a charismatic individual to whom the group is excessively devoted. There can be doomsday cults, religious cults, terrorist cults, and racist cults (Ku Klux Klan), and the line between religion and cults can be very thin. Famous American cults include the People's Temple led by Rev. Jim Jones, whose 918 followers were so devoted to him that they drank poisoned Kool-Aid and committed mass suicide; and the Manson Family, a cult devoted to **Charles Manson**, whose members committed heinous murders for him.

current standards

Principles of behavior that exist for the **investigation** of a **case** and can include suspect and witness interviews, documentation of **evidence** and other procedures. In terms of a **cold case**, this means reviewing the case and updating the file and documentation to comply with current standards.

custody

Temporary restraint or detention of a person by lawful authority or process. Also the responsibility for the control, transfer, and movement of weapons and components as well as access to them.

cut

Place in prison not covered by **CCTV** cameras so a prisoner "in the cut" can carry out illicit activity such as **drug** deals (US contemporary prison slang).

CW

See **cooperating witness**.

cyanide

One of the **poisons** of choice in the Victorian era, particularly as it acted fast, often within minutes. Unfortunately for potential poisoners, its signature effects, which include nausea, vomiting, cardiac arrest, unconsciousness, and death, are unmistakable and not easily explained as anything other than murder. From the Second World War onward, **agents** and operatives in fact and fiction were often supplied with cyanide or "suicide pills" in case of capture. Serial killer Leonard Lake committed suicide in 1985 using a cyanide pill after his **arrest** for possessing an illegal silencer (**sound moderator**) and **handgun**.

cyberbullying

Like physical bullying, cyberbullying is often aimed at children and young people and involves harassing, embarrassing, threatening, or humiliating them through their smartphone, computer, or tablet; through their social media accounts and in chat rooms; as well as sending harmful, distressing, or threatening messages or images via messaging services, email, and text. Repeatedly calling a victim's mobile or cell phone is also considered cyberbullying. ▶**cyberstalking/cyberharassment** Cyberstalking or cyber-harassment is the term used instead of cyberbullying when adults are involved.

cybercrime

Use of a computer and a network to carry out illegal acts. These can include using **malware**, ransomware and **botnets**, **hacking** and **cracking**, distributing child pornography, inciting child and **human trafficking**, and for terrorist purposes. Pure cybercrime is that which involves attacks on computer and information systems where the aim is to gain access or to deny legitimate users access. Cyber-enabled crimes include theft, fraud, and the distribution of illegal pornography as well as the commissioning of crimes through networks such as the **dark web**. Cybercrime is global, has no borders, and is a major source of revenue for **organized crime** as well as terrorist groups. New trends and methods constantly emerge, which makes the policing of it extremely difficult. ▶**cyberattack** Disruptive or destructive action that targets computer infrastructures, information systems, networks, or personal devices. ▶**cyberweapon** Any software program, **malware**, **Trojan**, **worm**, or exploit that is used to attack another system, often one belonging to an enemy nation state or **intelligence agency,** or a major tech, utility, or financial institution.

cylinder
Part of a **revolver** holding **rounds** in separate **chambers**. The chambers are sequentially rotated in line with the **barrel** prior to each round being **discharged**.

D

DA
See **district attorney.**

Dahmer, Jeffrey

Jeffrey Dahmer (1960–1994) was an American **serial killer** who murdered 17 mostly African American men between 1978 and 1991, committing sex acts with their corpses before dismembering and disposing of them, although he would often keep their skulls and genitals as souvenirs. Dahmer was careful to select victims who were homeless or on the fringes of society and would therefore be less likely to be missed. He would meet them at bus stops and in malls and bars, luring them to his home with promises of money or sex, and giving them **alcohol** laced with **drugs** before strangling or bludgeoning them to death. He liked to take photographs of the stages of his murders and subsequent dismemberments so he could relive his crimes. In 1989, Dahmer was convicted of child molestation for engaging in sexual acts with a 13-year-old Laotian boy and managed to get away with a one-year prison **sentence** on day release. In 1991, that same boy's 14-year-old brother was seen running naked down Dahmer's street and the incident was reported to the police by a concerned neighbor. The police believed Dahmer when he told them that the boy was his 19-year-old lover and, after a cursory look at Dahmer's home, left, whereupon he killed the boy. He went on to kill four more times before police picked up a 32-year-old African American named Tracy Edwards who was found wandering the streets with handcuffs dangling from his wrist claiming that a "weird dude" had drugged him. This time, the police decided to investigate and went to Dahmer's home where they found his photographs of his previous killings, along with skulls in the fridge and freezer and jars containing genitalia. Dahmer was **arrested** and subsequently sentenced to 16 life sentences. He was killed by a fellow prison inmate in 1994. Dahmer inspired an eponymous movie as well as several books.

damages

The court will award damages, or monetary compensation, to a complainant suing an entity (person or institution) for financial or property losses, breach of contract, emotional or physical injuries, loss of earnings, costs of care, and other kinds of losses. Damages can range from nominal (very small sums, where the lawsuit is to demonstrate technical wrongdoing as a matter of principle) to punitive (very large sums, awarded above and beyond basic compensation as a form of deterrence). For example, in Liebeck v. McDonald's Restaurants (1994), a jury awarded Stella Liebeck $2.7 million in punitive damages (later reduced to $480,000) on top of $160,000 in compensatory damages for the severe burns she received from a dangerously hot cup of McDonald's coffee.

dark web, deep web

The dark web is the unindexed part of the World Wide Web that can only be accessed by using an anonymized browser such as Tor. While the pages are public, the IP addresses are hidden and the web sits on darknets, or overlays, on the internet. The dark or deep web is a hive of criminal and illicit activity including trading in stolen information, **drugs**, arms and pornography, but is also used for communication purposes by journalists and people living under oppressive regimes as well as legitimate companies wanting a presence in an arena seen as edgy. Bitcoin initially flourished thanks to the dark web, and vice versa, and is still the major currency used to trade there, along with other cryptocurrencies.

D

database hit
Link between two or more crimes that results when computer databases connect information or **evidence** from separate crimes or connect physical evidence with a potential suspect.

date rape
Also known as acquaintance **rape**. Date rape specifically refers to a **sexual assault** that occurs during a voluntary social engagement or "date" where the assailant is known to the victim, who specifically has not consented to and resists the advances. To date rape means to carry out the act as described in the previous definition. ▶ **date-rape drug** A substance used to facilitate a sexual assault, often by incapacitating the victim. Although it is popularly believed that **drugs** such as **GHB** are the most widely used date-rape drugs, **alcohol** and **cannabis** are more commonly detected. Widely available prescription drugs such as Valium, Xanax, and Ambien (zolpidem) are increasingly being used.

Datura stramonium
Also known as jimsonweed, devil's apple, devil's trumpet, thorn apple, and locoweed, *Datura stramonium* is a **poisonous** flowering plant from the nightshade family containing hyoscyamine and scopolamine. *Datura* is a deliriant rather than a **hallucinogen**, producing an inability to differentiate reality from fantasy as well as bizarre and sometimes violent behavior. All parts of the plant are poisonous but especially the seeds and flowers. In some parts of Europe and especially India, where it has

been long used in Ayurvedic medicine, *Datura* has also been a popular poison.

DB

An acronym for Dead Body.

DCFS

See **Department of Child and Family Services.**

DEA

See Drug Enforcement Administration.

deactivated weapon

A deactivated weapon is a **firearm** that has been modified in such a way that it can no longer **discharge** any **shot, bullet,** or other missile. Deactivation is intended to be permanent and these weapons should be incapable of being reactivated without specialist tools and skills, although criminals often find a way to do so. The **reactivation** of deactivated weapons and conversion of **blank-firing weapons** are among the main sources of illegal firearms trafficked in Europe, often coming from Eastern Europe and ending up in the UK.

dead drop

A form of **tradecraft** used to pass items, including USB sticks and micro discs, and information between two individuals that does not require them directly to meet or contact one another. The dead drop, also known as a dead-letter box, is a secret location where one party, possibly a **case officer**, leaves the item or information and the other, possibly an **agent** or other officer, collects it and may leave something in return. Once the item has been dropped, a **signal** such as a chalk mark on a lamppost is left to indicate to the other party that it is ready for collection. Dead-drop locations have included particular stones in parks, wall cavities, bushes, and even within the body cavities of dead animals. To prevent the latter from being eaten by predators, both the **Central Intelligence Agency** and KGB came up with the ruse of pouring hot sauce over the carcass.

Dead Man Walking

The phrase originally refers to condemned prisoners on **death row**, making the final journey from their cell to their place of execution. It now refers to anyone who knows they are going to die or faces a terrible, unavoidable circumstance.

deadly physical force

In the US this means physical force that can be reasonably expected to cause death or serious physical injury.

deadly weapon

A deadly weapon in the US is one that can cause mortal or great physical harm and usually includes a **firearm** from which a shot can be **discharged**, various knives including switchblades, and metal knuckles.

death penalty

See **capital punishment**.

death row

Death row refers to a special holding place inside certain prisons, such as **San Quentin**, where inmates who have been sentenced to death await their execution. The condemned are heavily guarded and must be shackled any time they are outside of their cells. Because the **appeals** process can be time consuming, some inmates will stay on death row for decades. For example, a prisoner named Gary Alvord arrived on death row in 1974 and died 39 years later of a brain tumor. Most states still honor the tradition of the "last meal," for which the condemned gets to order what they wish except alcoholic beverages. The social, legal, and ethical flaws of death row were explored in the drama, *Dead Man Walking* (1995), as well as *The Green Mile* (1999).

deblurring

Type of image restoration used in **forensics** to reverse image degradation, such as motion blur or out-of-focus blur. It is accomplished by applying algorithms based on knowledge or an estimate of the cause of the original degradation.

decriminalization

Where there is **criminalization**, there is also decriminalization, which typically seeks to undo or soften laws in the context of revised social views. In the US, much of this conversation revolves around the decriminalization of marijuana, a process accelerated by the actual **legalization** of pot in various states. Across the country, marijuana is still illegal according to federal law, but even in states that have not legalized, the system will tend to impose civil fines or penalties over criminal charges.

The underlying philosophy of decriminalization is thought to reflect liberal or progressive views, as it seeks to avoid snarling people in the **prison industrial complex** via **overcriminalization**, which results from relying on the criminal justice system to respond to conflicts better addressed through social services and policies. With this in mind, in 2021, New York State introduced a bill to decriminalize sex workers (who are often exploited women and girls) while still holding pimps and sex traffickers criminally accountable.

defendant (legal)
In a court of law, the defendant is the person who is charged with committing a crime.

defense (legal)
The strategy mounted by the legal team for the **defendant**.

degradation
Fragmenting, or breakdown, of **forensic evidence** by chemical, physical, or biological means.

Department of Child and Family Services (DCFS)
A state-administered, family-oriented variant of Child Protective Services (CPS).

Department of Justice (DOJ)
Founded in 1870 by an act of Congress to handle the legal affairs of the country, the US Department of Justice (DOJ) is helmed by the Attorney General, the top lawyer position in the United States (not to be confused with the Justices of the Supreme Court of the United States, who are the top judges). Overseeing the **Federal Bureau of Investigations (FBI)** and the **Federal Prison System (FPS)**, the DOJ controls high-level criminal prosecutions and civil suits in which the United States has an interest. For example, in 2020, Attorney General William Barr authorized the DOJ to investigate Donald Trump's claims of national election fraud.

deployment
Movement of forces, **agents** or officers into and out of an operational area.

deposition

In law, a deposition is the sworn testimony of a witness or person with knowledge pertinent to a civil or criminal case. Depositions are not taken inside the trial itself, as they are part of the pretrial **discovery** process.

designer drug

Legally restricted or prohibited **drug** that has been chemically altered to enhance its properties or to circumvent drug laws.

desired point of impact (DPI)

Precise point associated with a target and assigned as the optimal impact point for a single weapon to create a desired effect.

detective fiction

A subgenre of crime fiction, classic detective fiction involves an intellectually superior detective or investigator solving an often seemingly perfect crime through a series of deductions, leading to a denouement that often surprises the reader. If the police are involved, they are usually inept. The details of the mystery to be solved and the clues are presented to the reader from the outset so that they may attempt to deduce the identity of the perpetrator alongside the detective.

diamorphine

Diamorphine, otherwise known as **heroin**, is an opioid and strong painkiller that can only be obtained by prescription in the UK. It is not used for medical purposes in the US. Dr. **Harold Shipman** (1946–2004), the UK's most prolific serial killer, used 30 mg doses of diamorphine, which is six times greater than the usual amount, to kill his elderly victims who are believed to have numbered at least 218 over 23 years.

digital forensics

Digital or **computer forensics** is the application of scientific investigatory techniques to digital and **cybercrimes** and attacks. It involves the collection, preservation, examination, and analysis of digital **evidence** using scientifically accepted and validated processes. Digital forensics may be used in the private and public sector, in business and in law, and to solve **cyberattacks** as well as crime.

DILLIGAF

"Do I Look Like I Give a Fuck?" Vulgar term allegedly used by the police and military personnel.

dimed

Informed to the police (US/Hispanic contemporary gang slang).

ding wing

Prison psychiatric unit (US contemporary slang).

DIN

Departmental Identification number with the New York state correctional system. A DIN number is assigned to every inmate entering the system. *See also* **New number.**

direct evidence

Direct **evidence** is that which directly links a perpetrator to a crime such as an eyewitness account or video footage of the actual crime occurring. If believed, it proves a fact without any need for presumption or inference.

direct fire

Fire delivered on a target using the target itself as the point of aim for either the weapon or the person controlling the weapon.

Directorate of Operations (DO)

The Directorate of Operations, formerly the National Clandestine Service, operates as the **clandestine** arm of the **Central Intelligence Agency**, serving as the "national authority for the coordination, deconfliction, and evaluation of clandestine **human intelligence** operations across the **Intelligence Community**." The DO conducts clandestine activities to collect information that cannot be obtained by other means. The DO also conducts **counterintelligence** and special activities as authorized by the US president.

dirty

Drugs (US contemporary gang slang).

disbarment

The most severe professional punishment for a lawyer, disbarment refers to the formal decision to revoke a lawyer's license to practice law. Disbarment can be incurred for malpractice, incompetence, breach of professional ethics, or criminal activity on the part of the lawyer. It is typically imposed by the lawyer's bar association at the state level. A disbarred lawyer cannot legally practice law but may work as a paralegal or similar law-adjacent professions. At least five years must pass from the date of disbarment before a disbarred lawyer can petition for readmission to the bar.

discharge

To cause a **firearm** or other weapon to fire.

discovery (legal)

In US law, the process of discovery refers to a pretrial exchange of information between opposing sides. Hence, should you choose to sue another person in civil court, you simultaneously open yourself up to discovery. There are three basic forms of discovery: written, document production, and **deposition**.

disguised firearm

Firearm constructed in such a manner that it doesn't look like a firearm. Examples have included guns disguised as pens, mobile phones, and torches, all capable of **lethal discharge**.

dispatcher

Police stations will have a communication center to coordinate law enforcement response to crime and accident scenes. The role of the dispatcher is to respond to and field phone calls and alarm notices, and alert the appropriate units (law, fire, ambulance) to respond. Dispatchers are civilian support and are not themselves police officers. They can be, though are not necessarily, synonymous with **9-1-1** calls.

dissemination

In **intelligence** terms, the delivery of intelligence to users in a suitable form.

district attorney (DA)

Also known as a state's attorney, the district attorney is an elected official who serves as the chief lawyer for the state in a district or county of that state. As law enforcement officers, DAs can issue subpoenas, investigate individuals, file formal charges, and offer sentencing deals; they generally determine if a case is headed for a plea bargain or will go to trial.

DNA

In police slang, this is an acronym for Do Not Approach.

DNA (deoxyribonucleic acid)

Molecule that contains the genetic code of human beings and almost all other organisms and that contains the instructions for cell formation. Nearly every cell in a person's body has the same DNA. There are different kinds of DNA that are especially useful to **forensics**.

- Familial DNA: when a routine search of a DNA database has failed to come up with an exact match, a search for familial DNA may be carried out. This is based on the concept that first-order relatives such as a parent, child, or sibling will share more DNA than unrelated individuals and so a perpetrator might be tracked down through one of these family members. Jason Ward, the killer of 87-year-old Gladys Godfrey, was the first murderer to be traced and later convicted through familial DNA in 2003 in Nottinghamshire. It was later used to track down the Golden State Killer in the US, Joseph James DeAngelo (who pleaded guilty on June 29, 2020, and was sentenced to life imprisonment without the possibility of parole), as well as solve several **cold cases**.

- mtDNA: mitochondrial DNA exists outside the nucleus of a cell and is inherited from the mother. It does not degrade as much as nuclear DNA and is therefore helpful in identifying **biological material**, such as human remains, that may have degraded. This is therefore particularly helpful in identifying remains that cannot be identified by other means.

- Y-STR DNA: short tandem repeat markers located only on the male Y-chromosome. Useful in cases of **sexual assault** when bodily fluids may need to be identified and separated as belonging to males and females.

DNA (deoxyribonucleic acid) profiling

Also known as DNA fingerprinting, DNA profiling reflects the fact that technology has advanced to the point that it is now possible to use DNA trace evidence to identify an individual based on genetic markers. When combined with **forensic** genetic genealogy, DNA profiling has been shown to be effective in resolving cold cases, such as the 2018 arrest and 2020 conviction of Joseph James DeAngelo, thus revealed as the "Golden Gate Killer."

DO

See **Directorate of Operations**.

DOJ

See **Department of Justice**.

domestic assault, domestic violence

Sometimes referred to as DA for domestic abuse. Domestic **assault** or violence is defined in the US and the UK as any incident or pattern of incidents of controlling, coercive, or threatening behavior, violence or abuse between those aged 16 or over who are or have been intimate partners or family members regardless of gender or sexuality. This can encompass but is not limited to psychological, physical, sexual, financial, and emotional abuse. Controlling behavior is defined as a range of acts designed to make a person subordinate and/or dependent by isolating them from sources of support, exploiting their resources and capacities for personal gain, depriving them of the means needed for independence, resistance, and escape, and regulating their everyday behavior. Coercive behavior is defined as an act or a pattern of acts of assault, threats, humiliation, and intimidation or other abuse that is used to harm, punish, or frighten the victim.

don

Boss of a gang. The title was originally used by the Sicilian **Mafia** and has now been adopted by many criminals including Jamaican and Eastern European gangs.

dossier

Official file consisting of information concerning an individual.

double action

Method of firing a gun where a single movement of the **trigger** cocks and releases the **hammer** or **firing pin**.

double agent

Agent in contact with two opposing **intelligence** services, only one of which is aware of the double contact.

double barrel

Two **barrels** in a **firearm** mounted to one frame. The barrels can be aligned vertically, known as **over-and-under**, or horizontally, known as **side-by-side**.

double jeopardy (legal)

If a defendant is acquitted of a crime but then faces a new trial for the same crime, this is known as double jeopardy. It is legally prohibited by the Fifth Amendment, even if new evidence emerges after acquittal that shows they are guilty. The subject was explored in a hit thriller, *Double Jeopardy* (1999).

double OG

Second generation of gang members (US contemporary gang slang).

double tap

Refers to two shots in quick succession at the same spot on the target. The opposite of **spray and pray**, the double-tap technique places emphasis on speed and precision. Police tactical teams, military personnel, and special forces train in the technique due to its effectiveness at disabling opponents in real-life situations (as opposed to simulations or competition settings).

down

To "go down" is to be sent to prison (US contemporary slang).

down and dirty

Police **informant** or selling **drugs** on the side (US contemporary gang slang).

down with the 5-0

Police **informant** (US contemporary gang slang).

DPI

See **desired point of impact**.

drama

Fight or **assault** (US contemporary prison slang).

drip pattern

Bloodstain pattern resulting from a liquid that dripped into another liquid, at least one of which was blood. ▶ **drip stain** A **bloodstain** resulting from a falling drop that formed due to gravity.

drone

After a gunman massacred 58 people at a Las Vegas music festival in 2017, US police have been looking for new ways to heighten event security and they have found an effective method with the use of Unmanned Aerial Systems (UAS), more commonly known as drones. Drones provide a cost-effective way to patrol events, monitor traffic, and improve responses to incidents. Police departments also use drones to map fatal car crashes in minutes, when this process used to take hours. In the UK, drones are also used at soccer matches and events as well as to aid real-time **surveillance**, thanks to visual and thermal imagery, of a suspect police are pursuing. They are also used at protests, **crime scenes,** and in disaster zones to aid police operations.

dropping a dime, drop-a-dime
The meaning is identical to "dropping a nickel," which is US street slang for informing on someone to the police. It is thought to originate from public pay phones, which originally required a dime per call. It now generically refers to any form of betrayal.

dropping a tab
A prisoner's improvised method of signaling administration. The phrase derives from tab-pull-style lids of, say, a can of peaches. After being pulled off, the sharp-edged lid can be used as a weapon. To frame a rival, an inmate might hide a lid in that rival's cell, then "drop a tab" to alert a guard to its presence. Example: "Veronica dropped a tab on Betty, and now Betty's in the **bing**."

drug
Any substance other than food that, when ingested or otherwise taken into the body, changes the way the body works or the way the person thinks or feels. **Illegal drugs** are those that are proscribed or forbidden under law. The supply of those illegal drugs is big business and often involves **organized crime**, for which it is the most profitable business model. **Drug trafficking** crosses

international borders and jurisdictions, involving national, international, and global operations. ▶**drug abuse** Substance abuse involving the use of illegal drugs or misuse of medicines, which usually follows a pattern in which the user ingests harmful quantities of the substance(s) in question. ▶**drug culture** Lifestyles of people who abuse drugs, their way of dressing, and the behavior common to abusers of different types of drugs. Also the degree to which drugs pervade so many aspects of society and fundamentally influence culture. ▶**drug dealer** Person who sells illegal drugs. ▶**drug trafficking** Drug trafficking, or the illegal transportation and distribution of illicit substances, is big business on a global scale and infamous as an important source of revenue for **organized crime**. It is also used to finance terrorism. Corruption and ineffective **law enforcement** along the supply chains ensures that drug trafficking continues to flourish. ▶**druggler** Drug dealer (US/Jamaican contemporary gang slang).

Drug Enforcement Administration (DEA)

The Drug Enforcement Administration is sworn to uphold the **rule of law** and the Constitution of the United States. Founded by Richard Nixon in 1973 to combat the global "drug menace," its mission is to enforce the controlled substances laws and to investigate individuals suspected of violating those laws. At Quantico, it operates its own dedicated training center for its special agents and law enforcement counterparts. In 2008, it opened a new Clandestine Laboratory at Quantico, which includes a lab and a raid house. Other branches of the DEA include a **forensic** lab and an **Intelligence** arm.

drug slang code words

Drug Enforcement Agency (DEA) agents must familiarize themselves with slang for various drugs—what the agency calls "code words"—in order to recognize when individuals are discussing the sale or distribution of illicit substances. There arc so many "live" (rapidly changing) words for various **controlled substances**, designer drugs, and synthetic substances, that the DEA issued an unclassified, seven-page report listing thousands of them from A (amphetamines) to X (Xanax). The shortest entries are for Ritalin (just one entry, "Kibbles and Bits") and Klonopin (K, K-Pin, Pin, Super Valium), whereas **heroin**, **marijuana**, and **cocaine** have hundreds of entries.

dry clean

Any technique used to detect and elude **surveillance**. A precaution commonly used by **intelligence officers** and **agents** when actively engaged in an operation.

due process

Due process refers to the legal understanding that the state will respect a defendant's legal rights according to the **rule of law**, and as set out in the Due Process Clauses of the **Fifth** and **Fourteenth Amendment**.

DUI manslaughter or murder

DUI, or Driving Under the Influence, can elevate a charge from accident to **manslaughter** to **murder**, should you happen to get into an accident that causes others to die as a result. The maximum penalty for DUI manslaughter or murder is 14 years.

dummy cartridge

Inert gun **cartridge** designed for **firearms**-handling purposes only, which contains neither **primer** nor **propel-lant** and cannot be fired under any circumstances. Also known as a dummy **round** or drill round.

dumpster diving

Act of rummaging through the rubbish or trash of an individual or business to gather information that could be useful for identity **theft** or for a cybercriminal to gain access to a system.

duty to retreat

In some US jurisdictions, if a person is threatened with violence by another, they have a legal duty to retreat, which is to say, to run away and avoid direct confrontation if at all possible. In states where duty-to-retreat applies, the use of deadly force is only legally justifiable if retreat is either impossible or poses another set of dangers. This contrasts with **stand your ground**, which argues the opposite position.

E

ECAP
See **Endangered Child Alert Program.**

economic espionage
Misappropriation of trade secrets for the benefit of a foreign government, foreign **agent,** or instrument that is an entity controlled by the government of a foreign country. Misappropriation includes, but is not limited to, stealing, copying, altering, destroying, transmitting, sending, receiving, buying, possessing, or conspiring to obtain trade secrets without authorization.

ECRIS
See **European Criminal Records Information System.**

edge characteristic
Physical feature of the periphery of a **bloodstain.**

eGuardian
The **Federal Bureau of Investigation**'s sensitive but unclassified (SBU) terrorism-related threat reporting system that aids **law enforcement** by allowing them to rapidly circulate and compare or combine Special Activity Reports (SARs) that contain information regarding a potential threat or suspicious activity.

electronic masking
Controlled radiation of electromagnetic energy to protect the emissions of communications and electronic systems

without significantly degrading the operation of those systems.

electronic monitoring (EM)

Electronic tagging or electronic monitoring (EM) allows prisoners to be released from prison before the end of their **sentence** to serve the rest of that sentence with an electronic monitoring device or tag. Prisoners serving a sentence of between three months and four years can be considered for such release. Early release is usually between two weeks and four and half months before the automatic release date, depending on the length of the sentence. An EM is considered a privilege and not an absolute right of a prisoner. Not all prisoners, such as those who have committed violent or sex crimes, are eligible. When a prisoner is released on an EM they are required to stay at a designated address and the electronic tag, which resembles a bulky watch, is fitted to them. The tag is waterproof so they can wear it to bathe. It communicates with a monitoring box fitted at their designated address so if they leave it during their curfew hours, normally 7 a.m. to 7 p.m., the control center will be notified, and the prisoner will be in breach of their EM. They will then normally be returned to prison to serve the rest of their sentence until their automatic release date.

electronic tracking device

Tracking device such as a vehicle-locator unit, radio-frequency beacon or transmitter as well as those devices that use a Global Positioning System (GPS) or other satellite system for monitoring noncommunication activity.

elicitation
In **intelligence** terms, the acquisition of information from a person or group in a way that does not disclose the intent or motive behind the interview or conversation.

elimination prints
Finger or handprints taken from people known to have had access to an item examined for **latent prints** so they can be eliminated.

embezzlement
Financial crime that involves the unlawful misappropriation of funds or assets entrusted to an offender.

Eme
La Eme (Spanish for "the *m*") is the Mexican **Mafia**, a highly organized Mexican American criminal gang network based in the US and operating throughout the Californian and federal prison systems among others.

encipher
To convert plain text into unintelligible or **coded** form through the use of a **cipher** system.

Endangered Child Alert Program (ECAP)
A program run by the FBI in collaboration with the **National Center for Missing and Exploited Children**, ECAP works to proactively identify unknown individuals engaged in producing **child sexual abuse material (CSAM)**.

escape from Alcatraz
In June 1962, four inmates at **Alcatraz Federal Penitentiary** attempted their escape. At various points in time, brothers John and Clarence Anglin, along with Allen West and Frank Morris, had been prisoners together in Atlanta

Penitentiary and had already developed a degree of mutual trust. Following their eventual transfer to Alcatraz, the quartet ended up in adjacent cells and began to formulate their plan.

Masterminded by Morris, the plan required patience, creativity, and daring. They got out of their cells by breaking into and then carefully widening each of their cells' ventilation shafts (that ultimately led to the roof), then used this secret route to set up a clandestine workshop. Hidden from view, they made a rubber raft out of donated raincoats, and realistic dummy heads out of an improvised version of papier-mâché. On the night of their escape, they placed these dummy heads on their pillows, then created the illusion of a sleeping body by mounding up towels and clothes under their blankets. The ruse successfully fooled the guards, who did not discover their absence until the next morning.

But Allen West had gotten stuck in his ventilation shaft; by the time he managed to get to the roof, it was already sunrise, and the others had left him behind. Turning **rat**, he gave law enforcement precise information regarding the direction where Morris and the Anglin brothers were headed—which, he said, was nearby Angel Island, only two miles away.

Did they make it? On December 31, 1979, after a 17-year investigation, the **FBI** publicly concluded that the remaining three men drowned in San Francisco Bay. However, no bodies have ever been found. To this day, the case remains open with the **US Marshals** Service. Officially, there have been no successful escapes from Alcatraz.

espionage

Commonly known as **spying**. **Intelligence** activity that involves the acquisition or **theft** of information through secret or **clandestine** means and which is usually prohibited by the laws of the country in which the espionage is carried out.

European Criminal Records Information System (ECRIS)

The European Criminal Records Information System (ECRIS) was established in April 2012 in order to improve the exchange of information on criminal records throughout the European Union (EU). All EU countries are currently connected to ECRIS. The ECRIS database exchanges information between EU countries on convictions, provides judges and prosecutors with easy access to comprehensive information on the criminal history of the people concerned, including in which EU countries that person has previously been convicted, and removes the opportunity for offenders to escape convictions by moving from one EU country to another.

evidence

In a court of law, evidence used to prove innocence or guilt can be *circumstantial* or *direct*. Direct evidence refers to proof of the so-called smoking gun type, such as a videotape showing the individual in the act of committing a crime, or the testimony of a credible eyewitness who witnessed a murder as it occurred. Circumstantial evidence requires inference or logical leaps to connect it to the crime in question, which renders the testimony open to multiple reasonable interpretations. An example of circumstantial evidence would be a credible eyewitness who sees a person running away from a murder scene but who does not actually witness that person committing a murder. The trial judge decides the **admissibility** of and weight to be given to a piece of evidence within proceedings. **Forensic** evidence is evidence obtained through scientific methods such as fingerprint analysis, **DNA**, and chemical testing. Evidence tampering is when someone

hides, falsifies, destroys, or alters evidence to interfere with a criminal investigation and is in itself a crime.
▶**evidence identifier** The tape, labels, containers, and string tags used to identify the evidence, the person collecting the evidence, the date the evidence was gathered, basic information about the criminal offense, and a brief description of the evidence are all evidence identifiers. ▶**evidence procedure** Standard put in place for receiving, processing, safeguarding, and disposing of physical evidence.

execution warrant
An execution warrant, also known as a death warrant or black warrant, is a writ in the US that authorizes someone's execution. An execution warrant is not to be confused with a "license to kill," that operates like an **arrest** warrant but with deadly force, or the death of subject, instead of arrest as the end goal.

exfiltration
Removal of individuals, operatives, or units from areas under enemy control by stealth, deception, surprise, or **clandestine** means. It can also mean a clandestine rescue operation intended to remove a defector, refugee, or operative and their family from harm or potential harm.

exhibit
Item or **forensic** sample recovered as part of an **investigation**, including but not limited to items found at a **crime scene** such as weapons, **fingerprint lifts**, **casts** of footprints, objects, and fibers.

expanding bullet
Bullet designed to extend and expand its surface upon impact with the target.

expert witness

In a trial setting, an expert witness is a credentialed professional hired to provide insight into a particular area relevant to a criminal or civil trial, such as DNA analysis, or analysis of fire debris. Expert witnesses do not necessarily testify for prosecution or defense, and may be called by the court itself to explicate points of particular complexity to the jury.

expirated bloodstain

This is the result of blood being exhaled, coughed out, or otherwise released from the mouth. This type of **bloodstain** is often diluted by the presence of saliva or mucous, and the bloodstain forms a characteristic pattern of small, round stains that resemble a fine mist.

explosive cargo

Material such as **ammunition**, bombs, depth charges, demolition material, rockets, and missiles in the process of being transported.

explosive hazard

Any material posing a potential threat that contains an explosive component such as unexploded explosives, booby traps, improvised explosive devices (IEDs), and bulk explosives.

extortion

Extortion is a theft crime involving physical threats or other coercive means to obtain payment or some form of cooperation from the victim. It is always a felony.

extractor mark

Also known as an ejector mark. This is a mark created on a gun **cartridge case** by the metal-to-metal contact between the cartridge case and the extractor and ejector mechanisms in the weapon. The extractor mechanism removes a cartridge from the **chamber**, while the ejector throws the cartridge away once it is extracted. **Revolvers** do not have ejectors, but **automatic** and **semi-automatic** weapons such as **pistols** and **rifles** do. As a result, the cartridge cases used in these weapons are designed differently from **ammunition** used in revolvers.

extradition

Extradition can occur between jurisdictions, states, or countries, and refers to a cooperative agreement where one sovereign jurisdiction (such as the US) agrees to physically transfer a criminal suspect to another sovereign jurisdiction (such as Mexico). The US does not have extradition agreements with numerous countries, including China, Russia, Namibia, the United Arab Emirates, North Korea, and Bahrain.

eyewash

False entries made in files by **clandestine agents** and officers to protect the security of a **source**.

F

facial recognition

A facial recognition system is one that can recognize someone from a digital source such as a photograph or video. Controversially used by the police and **law enforcement** at events and protests to identify known perpetrators or simply participants.

facial reconstruction

Facial reconstruction is a **forensic anthropology** technique used when a victim's remains are unidentifiable, usually because they are skeletal or near skeletal. The reconstruction may be two-dimensional, based on photographs of the skull, or three-dimensional either based on sculptures created with modeling clay and other materials or on high resolution 3D computer images. The FACES (Forensic Anthropology Computer Enhancement System) and CARES (Computer Assisted Recovery Enhancement System) computer programs assist in creating faster 2D facial reconstructions but both methods normally require an artist and a forensic anthropologist. Forensic facial reconstructions are controversial and are not a legally recognized technique for positive identification or **admissible** as expert testimony in the US, England, and Wales.

fall guy

Someone who takes the blame to protect other people, often other members of a gang (US historical slang).

false flag recruitment

This is when an **intelligence** service recruits someone who believes that they are cooperating with representatives of a specific country or entity, when actually they have been deceived and are cooperating with an intelligence service of another country or entity altogether. The action of the **agent** who recruits them is known as a "false flag approach."

family annihilator

A subtype of **mass murderer** and murder/suicide, the family annihilator is generally a man who kills his children and/or his wife, then himself. The motives can range from extreme narcissism (in the case of divorce, the father would rather kill his family rather than let his wife and children leave him) to misplaced saviorism (in a cruel world, it's morally wrong to let them keep living). Because she stood out from the pattern, one of America's most infamous family annihilators was Andrea Yates, who drowned all five of her young children in 2001. She was eventually found not guilty due to reasons of **insanity**.

Faraday bag

Special **forensic** collection bag for electronic parts with a lining that protects the contents from electromagnetic forces.

farmero

A member of the *Nuestra Familia*, a prison gang based in the US (US/Hispanic prison gang slang).

FBI

See **Federal Bureau of Investigation**.

FCIP

See **Foreign Counterintelligence Program**.

Federal Bureau of Investigation (FBI)

The Federal Bureau of Investigation, headquartered in Washington, DC, is the principal federal **law enforcement agency** of the United States and functions as its domestic **intelligence** and **security service**. It is comparable in some areas of its national operations to **MI5** in the UK and, as well as operating across the US, it also maintains offices in US embassies and consulates around the world. Despite its domestic focus, the FBI can and does carry out **clandestine** activities overseas, usually in conjunction with foreign security services and in joint operations with other agencies such as the **Central Intelligence Agency**, although there is famously rivalry between the two. The FBI has featured in numerous books, films and TV series since the 1930s including *The X-Files* (1993–2018).

Federal Bureau of Prisons (BOP)

Created in 1930 within the US **Department of Justice**, its original purpose was to oversee and regulate all federal prisons and correctional institutions. Currently, it is charged with coordination and administration of the United States' 122 federal "institutions" (i.e., prisons). Federal prisons are divided into 5 security ranks: 1) minimum, 2) low, 3) medium, 4) high, and 5) administrative. On the low end of the scale, Federal Prison Camps (FPCs) are minimum security prisons with dormitory housing and limited guards, and their inmates typically participate in some kind of work program. At the opposite end of the security spectrum are **Administrative Maximum Security Penitentiaries (ADX)**, designed to hold the most dangerous and escape-prone felons.

Federal Firearm Licensee (FFL)

Under current federal law, individuals intending to sell firearms as a business must first obtain a license from **ATF**. FFLs will require potential purchasers of a firearm to fill out **Federal Form 4473**, which is then submitted to the **National Instant Criminal Background Check System (NICS)** for a **background check**. It is illegal to sell a firearm to a **prohibited person**.

Federal Form 4473

This form must be filled out by every customer making a purchase from a **Federal Firearm Licensee (FFL)**. It is an essential document in the **background check**. Lying on this form is a **felony**.

Federal Prison Industries (FPI)

See **prison labor**; UNICOR.

Federal Prison System (FPS)

In 1891, Congress passed the Three Prisons Act, which established the Federal Prison System (FPS). The US **Department of Justice (DOJ)** had limited oversight over these first three federal prisons, which were 1) FPS Atlanta; 2) FPS Leavenworth; and 3) FPS McNeil Island.

felony

A felony is the most serious form of criminal offense, and includes arson, kidnapping, grand larceny, and **manslaughter**. Class A/Level One felonies are the most serious, and include **first-degree murder** or rape. The minimum punishment for a felony crime is a year; the maximum punishment is death. A person convicted of a felony is known as a felon.

fence

Receiver of stolen goods (historical slang still in contemporary use).

fentanyl

In 2020, fentanyl, a **synthetic** opioid, is the leading cause of **drug** overdoses in the US. Much more powerful than **heroin**, fentanyl is often added to it, which results in a **lethal** combination. A single tablespoon of fentanyl could kill up to five hundred people, which is why **Drug Enforcement Agents** take precautions not to touch or inhale the drug and often carry the antidote Narcan (naloxone) to reverse its effects. There are concerns that fentanyl could be used as a weapon of terror or mass destruction. Currently, more deaths result from its misuse than from car accidents in the US. Street names include: Apache; *birria* (fentanyl mixed with heroin); blonde; blue diamond; blue dolphin; blues; butter; China girl; China Town; China white; Chinese; Chinese buffet; Chinese food; crazy; crazy one; dance fever; dragon; dragon's breath; F; food; Freddy; fuf (furanyl fentanyl); Facebook (fentanyl mixed with heroin in pill form); fent; fenty; fire; friend; girl; goodfella; great bear; gray stuff; He-Man; Heineken; *huerfanito*; humid; jackpot; King Ivory; lollipop; Murder 8; nal; nil; nyl; opes; pharmacy; poison; shoes; snowflake; tango and cash; TNT; toe tag dope; white girl; white ladies.

FFL

See **Federal Firearm Licensee.**

FI

See **foreign intelligence.**

Fifth Amendment

The Fifth Amendment to the US Constitution addresses criminal protections accorded to citizens. Its influence is perhaps best recognized through the line, "pleading the Fifth," which refers to a clause regarding the right of witnesses to refuse to answer questions in a court of law on the grounds of self-incrimination. This clause ultimately yielded the requirement that police issue **Miranda** warnings to criminal suspects. The Fifth Amendment also includes the **double jeopardy** clause, which states that a defendant may only be tried once in federal court for the same offense.

filch
To steal (contemporary slang).

Financial Crimes Enforcement Network (FinCEN)
FinCEN safeguards the US financial system from financial crime, including terrorist financing, **money laundering** and other illicit activity. FinCEN aids **law enforcement, intelligence,** and regulatory agencies by sharing and analyzing financial intelligence, and works globally, cooperating with counterpart foreign **financial intelligence units**, networks, and people.

financial intelligence unit (FIU)
Each member of the EU must have a national financial intelligence unit, which receives, analyzes, and disseminates information gathered from **Suspicious Activity Reports**. The UKFIU is based within the **National Crime Agency**.

FinCEN
See **Financial Crimes Enforcement Network**.

fingerprint
Impression of the friction ridges of all or any part of the finger.

FIO
See **foreign intelligence officer**.

fire

Police approaching (US/Jamaican contemporary gang slang).

firearm

As defined by the 1968 Gun Control Act, a firearm is "any weapon (including a starter gun) which will or is designed to or may readily be converted to expel a projectile by the action of an explosive; B. the frame or receiver of any such weapon; C. any firearm muffler or firearm silencer; or D. any destructive device." This definition excludes **antique firearms, air guns,** and other devices that fire projectiles without combustion. It is illegal in the US to possess a firearm with obliterated serial numbers, and federally restricted to possess **sawed-off shotgun**s and machine guns manufactured after 1986. **Prohibited persons** may not own or handle firearms in the US.

firearm license

Some states (Massachusetts, for example) require all gun owners to be licensed. This license is not a permit to carry a concealed weapon. Upon the purchase of a firearm or ammo, this license card must first be shown to the vendor.

Firearm Owners Identification Card (FOID)

FOID is not a concealed carry permit but a simple firearm license. Most states do not require one, and those that do have been subjected to repeated legal attempts to remove it.

fired standard

Component of a collection and catalogue of test-fired **bullets, cartridge cases,** and **shot** shells from known **firearms** kept in a **forensics** laboratory. Also called known standards, **ammunition** standards, or reference ammunition.

firing pin

Part of a **firearm** that strikes the **ammunition primer** or the rim of the **cartridge**, igniting the **propellant** and discharging the **projectiles**.

first-degree murder

The most serious form of **homicide**-related offenses, felony murder, or first-degree murder, refers to the willful, premeditated, and intentional killing of another person with **malice aforethought**. By contrast, second-degree murder is intentional but not premeditated. When murder happens but there is neither intent nor premeditation, it is called **manslaughter**.

first offender programs

Associated with **juvenile justice** but open to all ages, first offender programs are a form of alternative sentencing that allow convicted individuals to stay out of the prison system.

first-person shooter (FPS) video games

Immensely popular, first-person shooter games such as *Call of Duty* and *Halo* let the gamer experience the onscreen action through the eyes of the protagonist. Increasingly realistic and well narrated, these games typically present the gamer with an arsenal from which to choose, often set within a wartime or survivalist narrative to justify the violence. The astonishing sophistication of FPS and VR (virtual reality) games increasingly blurs the boundaries between physical and virtual reality. Research is divided regarding the impact of violent video games on developing minds, but gun-rights organizations tend to blame the startling number of US mass school shootings on the influence of these games. *See also* **Grand Theft Auto**; **Sandy Hook**; and **SWATting**.

first responder

First police, ambulance, or other officer arriving at a **crime scene**, who is responsible for the immediate action taken at that scene including the preservation of human life and, in the case of **law enforcement**, crime-scene examination. Their responsibility ends when the officer with official responsibility for the crime scene takes over. Also known as the first intervener.

fish

New and usually naive prisoner who is educated in the ways of prison life by other inmates (US contemporary prison slang).

FIU

See **financial intelligence unit**.

flaps and seals

Intelligence term for the **clandestine** or secret opening, reading and resealing of envelopes or packages without the recipient's knowledge.

flat joint worker

Someone who assists in a gambling scam (US historical slang).

flat worker

Someone who steals from homes and apartments (US historical slang).

flick knife

A switchblade.

flow pattern

Bloodstain pattern resulting from the movement of a volume of blood on a surface due to gravity or the movement of the target.

fluorescence

Fluorescence is a form of luminescence that has been found to be helpful in the **forensic** examination of **crime scenes** and materials. Different wavebands cause different substances or materials to fluoresce. UV light is used to detect body fluids and **drug** residues while blue or violet light causes some human and animal hair as well as body fluids to glow. UV and blue light are also used for **fingerprints**. Blue/green light is used to detect **gunshot residue**, accelerants, and explosives. ▶**fluorescent powders** Powders that contain fluorescent chemicals, which reveal **latent prints** under an **alternate light source**.

FMJ

See **full metal jacket**.

FPI

See **Federal Prison Industries**.

FPS

See **Federal Prison System**.

FOID

See **Firearm Owners Identification Card**.

Folsom State Prison (FSP)

Folsom State Prison (1880–) is a maximum-security prison in Folsom, California, with a disturbing history of violence inside its walls. It firmly entered pop culture when Johnny Cash wrote a song about it and recorded an album there. In 2013, Folsom added a standalone facility to hold low-risk women prisoners. Notorious **cult** leader **Charles Manson** was once held at Folsom, which also once held singer Rick James; actor Danny Trejo; psychedelics advocate and clinical psychologist Timothy Leary; and music executive Suge Knight.

football numbers

A prison sentence in double digits, in the manner of football jerseys: 10, 15, 25 years (US prison slang).

Foreign Counterintelligence Program (FCIP)

The military division of the US National Intelligence Program (NIP) that conducts **counterintelligence** activities in support of the US Department of Defense.

foreign intelligence (FI)

Intelligence or information about the intentions, capabilities, and activities of foreign powers, organizations, or people. It does not include **counterintelligence** except for information on international terrorist activities. ▶ **foreign intelligence officer (FIO)** Member of a foreign intelligence service.

forensics

Forensics refers to scientific methods or techniques used in the detection or **investigation** of a crime. The term can also be used informally to refer to the laboratory or department where these tests are conducted. ▶ **forensically clean** When applied to **digital forensics**, digital media that are completely wiped of nonessential and residual data, scanned for **viruses** and verified before use. ▶ **forensic anthropology** Application of anthropological methods and theory, particularly those relating to the recovery and analysis of human remains, to help solve crime. ▶ **forensic crime fiction** Subgenre of crime fiction that centers on the work of **medical examiners** and pathologists. In this genre the forensic expert takes on the role of the investigator and solves the crime by scientifically examining the clues left on the body or at the **crime scene**. ▶ **forensic entomology** Study and analysis of insects and arthropods to aid investigations, especially where cadavers are concerned. The developmental stages of the insect or arthropod in a decomposing body can offer a wealth of information to investigators. ▶ **forensic examiner** Someone who conducts and/or directs the analysis of **evidence**, interprets the data, and reaches conclusions. ▶ **forensic genealogy** Combined use of family histories and partial **DNA** matches to identify the likely donor of a DNA sample. The GEDmatch database in Florida is an open data personal genomics and genealogy database that helped to identify the Golden State Killer. ▶ **forensic odontology** Dentistry dealing with the proper handling and examination of dental **evidence** and the proper evaluation, interpretation, and presentation of such evidence in the interest of the law. A forensic odontologist deals with the identification of unknown human remains through dental records; assists at scenes of mass disaster; estimates the age of living and dead people; analyzes bitemarks found on victims, other evidence and various materials; and presents that evidence in court. They can also analyze weapon marks using the principles of analysis for **bitemark identification**. ▶ **forensic pathology** Determination of the cause of death through the examination of a corpse. A forensic pathologist who has specialized medical and forensic training will carry out a postmortem or **autopsy** to determine the cause of death, acting as a medical expert for justice. ▶ **forensic toxicology** Gathering, identifying, and evaluating evidence relating to **drugs** and **poisons** to aid criminal investigations or legal proceedings. Forensic toxicologists are often senior and highly experienced toxicologists, or experts on the harmful effects of chemicals on humans, and use techniques such as analytical chemistry to isolate, identify, and quantify drugs and poisonous substances in forensic samples. They consider all kinds of factors such as chemical metabolism and how that can affect concentration or **toxic** effects as well as drug interactions, tolerance, postmortem redistribution, and the differences between people that have an effect such as age, height, weight, and medical history. Forensic toxicologists are often called upon as expert witnesses and to give an expert opinion as to whether a particular substance could have proved toxic or even fatal.

▶**forensic wipe** Verifiable procedure for sanitizing a defined area of digital media by overwriting each byte with a known value.

for helvede

Danish vulgar slang comparable to "for fuck's sake," a phrase that often appears in **Scandi noir**.

forward spatter pattern

Bloodstain pattern resulting from blood drops that traveled in the same direction as the impact force.

Fourteenth Amendment

In the legal context, the Fourteenth Amendment is responsible for the Due Process clause, which states that no person shall be "deprived of life, liberty, or property without due process of law." Due process remains instrumental in protecting the rights of citizens from **coercion** by police.

fraud

Fraud occurs when a person criminally or wrongfully deceives another for the purposes of personal or financial gain or to deprive them of a legal right. Fraud may be a civil or criminal offense depending on the circumstances.

fröken, frøken

Fröken is the Swedish and *frøken* the Danish and Norwegian for "Miss," a respectful title for a young, unmarried woman or teacher. The word often appears in **Scandi noir**.

front

Someone without a criminal record who acts as the public-facing person for a known criminal who is the real owner of a club or business. Also an apparently legitimate business operation that conceals the real, illegal business operating on its premises or under its aegis.

FSP

See **Folsom State Prison.**

fugitive

An individual on the run, for the purposes of evading law enforcement. Along with **US Marshals**, the figure of "the fugitive" became an archetypal antihero with the hit television show (1963–1967) and film (1993) of the same name.

fugu

Fugu, the name given to the Japanese pufferfish and the **poison** it contains (tetrodotoxin), is deadlier than **cyanide**, paralyzing and then suffocating the unfortunate victim who remains conscious to the end. When prepared properly, fugu poses little risk but every year in Japan around 50 poisonings occur, although they are rarely fatal thanks to extensive knowledge of the symptoms. James Melville used fugu poisoning as a murder weapon in his fifth Inspector Otani novel, *Sayonara Sweet Amaryllis*, while James Bond survived a near fatal dose of fugu in *Dr. No*.

full

Arrest (US historical slang).

full metal jacket (FMJ)

Projectile in which the **bullet jacket** encloses most of the
core, with the exception of the base (see **total metal
jacket**). Also known as full jacketed, full patch, and full
metal case.

G

G

A grand or a thousand dollars in **Mafia** and other gang slang.

Gacy, John Wayne

John Wayne Gacy was an American **serial killer** who was known as the Killer Clown because he would dress as Pogo or Patches the clown to entertain children at charitable events. Gacy **raped**, tortured, and murdered at least 33 young men and boys between 1972 and 1978. Born in 1942 in Illinois, Gacy committed his first known offense in 1967, sexually **assaulting** a 15-year-old boy for which he was **sentenced** to 10 years in prison. Released after 18 months on **parole**, Gacy sexually assaulted another teenage boy in 1971, but the boy failed to appear in court and the **case** was dropped. Gacy then bought a house in Cook County, Illinois, with help from his mother. It was at this house that all his subsequent murders were committed. He married his second wife in 1972, at which point his mother moved out of the house. In 1975, he told his wife he was bisexual and that they would not be having sex again. That year, after his wife saw him bringing teenage boys to their garage and found gay pornography in the house, she petitioned for divorce. After she also moved out in 1976, Gacy ramped up his activity during what he referred to as his "cruising years," and the majority of his murders were committed between then and 1978. After the disappearance of 15-year-old Robert Piest, who had last been seen speaking with Gacy about a possible job, police placed Gacy under surveillance, having also learned about his previous conviction. Gacy became so chummy with the detectives on the surveillance team that he invited them out for meals, remarking over breakfast with them, "You know . . . clowns can get away with murder." After he then invited these same detectives into his house, one noticed a smell that was similar to that of a rotting corpse. This, along with testimony from two of his victims who had survived, was enough to convince the police to apply for a second search warrant for Gacy's house. Gacy, in the interim, confessed all to his lawyer and then to police who confronted him with the fact they had found bodies in the crawl space in his house. Gacy stood trial in 1980 and was sentenced to death. He served 14 years on death row and, after his final appeal was rejected, was executed on May 9, 1994. His brain was removed after he was declared dead and remains in the possession of Helen Morris, who was a witness for the defense and conducts research into violent sociopaths. Several of Gacy's victims remain unidentified and his crimes helped inspire the Missing Children Act of 1984, which led directly to the AMBER alert system in use all over the world today. Many on the investigation team believe he did not act alone but had at least one accomplice, a fact borne out by witness testimony. Gacy himself claimed that there were others who aided him in his crimes and also committed them, but no accomplice has ever been found or brought to justice.

gang banger
Gang member or gang activity. ▶ gang banging Gang activity (US contemporary gang slang).

gangsta
An evolution of "gangster" in the Prohibition-era sense, "gangsta" can mean actual membership in a present-day gang. But, in pop culture, including gangsta rap, it more

often signals an attitude that evokes the kind of hard, violent life that is represented by gangs, as opposed to affiliation with gangs.

ganja baron
Major **drug** smuggler (US/Jamaican contemporary slang).

gap
In **spy** jargon, "in the gap" means being free of **surveillance** for a few seconds but not as long as a minute.

garbage business
Euphemism for **organized crime**, so-called because one universally popular gangster business is waste disposal. In New York City the **Cosa Nostra** dominated the trash collection industry from the 1950s until Mayor Rudy Giuliani seized control of it in the 1990s. The construction industry was also infamously dominated by the US **Mafia**. Worldwide, the practice still continues although larger organized crime operations focus on more profitable sectors such as **drug trafficking** and **human trafficking**.

garnish
Money demanded of, and paid by, prisoners to their fellow inmates on their admittance to prison (UK thieves' **cant**, historical slang).

gas firearm
Object or device that may or may not have the appearance of a **firearm**, originally designed and intended to produce only a gas expulsion and whose characteristics exclude the firing of any other **projectile**. Normally the **cartridges** are filled with a noxious substance such CS gas to temporarily disable an attacker. Gas firearms are often **converted** in the course of illicit gun trafficking so that they can be used as **lethal** weapons. ▶ **gas-operated**

firearm Fully **automatic** or **semi-automatic** **firearm** in which the **propellant** gases are used to unlock the breech bolt and then to complete the cycle of extraction and ejection. This is accomplished usually in conjunction with a spring, which returns the operating parts to battery. Gas-operated firearms are popular with the military.

gat

Short for "Gatling gun," an early machine gun invented by Richard Gatling in 1861 and first used in the American Civil War. During Prohibition, a gat became synonymous with the Thompson submachine gun; that is, the **Tommy Gun**. It is now a generic term for any **handgun**.

gateshot

First drug fix of the day, specifically heroin (US drug slang).

gateway drug

Drug, usually a **controlled substance**, that when used may lead to the use of more **addictive** substances.

gauge

Term used to denote the **caliber** of a **shotgun**. It is taken as a measure of the number of identical solid spheres, of the same diameter as the bore of the smooth **barrel**, that can be made from a pound of lead (so the 12 identical solid spheres that can be made from a pound of lead fit the internal diameter of a 12-bore shotgun).

gay for the stay, straight for the gate

Refers to the phenomenon of "straight" individuals carrying out homosexual or lesbian relationships while incarcerated, then returning to heterosexual relations once they are out of prison.

GCA

See **Gun Control Act.**

Gein, Ed

Ed Gein was an American **serial killer** and the inspiration for both *Psycho* (1960) and *The Silence of the Lambs* (1991) as well as Leatherface in *The Texas Chain Saw Massacre* (1974). Born in 1906 in Wisconsin, Gein was dominated by his deeply religious mother Augusta, who ruled their repressive household and constantly warned Ed and his brother Henry about the sins of lust and carnal desire. Ed rarely left the farm, especially after his **alcoholic** father died and his brother Henry perished in mysterious circumstances in a fire. Subsequently, Ed became more and more devoted to his mother, never dating or leaving the farm, and after she too died in 1945, he kept her room absolutely pristine while the rest of the house fell into squalor. Although several people in the neighborhood disappeared over the years, it was only when the local hardware store owner also disappeared, leaving a trail of blood that led out the back of her shop, that her son, the deputy sheriff who was already suspicious of the reclusive Gein, apprehended him. When officers went to his farmhouse they were greeted by the sight of the headless, gutted body of Beatrice Worden hanging from the ceiling. During their subsequent search they discovered skulls of other victims fashioned into soup bowls and body organs in jars. Under questioning, Gein admitted to the murder of Worden and another local woman, Mary Hogan, three years earlier, as well as digging up bodies to cut off body parts, wearing suits and masks he had made out of human skin, and necrophilia, among other gruesome practices. The mild-mannered Gein was found to be insane and unfit to stand trial and was committed. Nine years later, he was found fit to stand trial but was judged insane at the time of Worden and Hogan's murders and recommitted to the

Central State Hospital, where he died of cancer in 1984 at the age of 77.

get down
Fight (US contemporary gang slang).

GG
See **ghost gun**.

GHB
GHB (*gamma*-Hydroxybutyric acid) is a popular **date-rape drug** that starts to act within 15 minutes of administration, and has until recently been notoriously difficult to detect thanks to its rapid metabolization by the body. New techniques that involve Nuclear Magnetic Resonance (NMR) Spectroscopy now mean that GHB **metabolites** can be detected up to 24 hours later in the body, with techniques still being perfected that allow its detection up to a month or more after ingestion in the victim's hair. Street names include: blowout; Bruno Mars; cherry meth; easy lay; everclear; fantasy; G; gamma oh; GEEB; Georgia home boy; goop; great hormones at bedtime; grievous bodily harm; G-riffic; Gina; jib; liquid E; liquid X; monkey juice; organic Quaalude; salty water; scoop; soap; water.

ghost detainee
A person whose identity is purposefully unregistered and kept anonymous, and typically held in secret prisons such as a CIA **Black Site**. The US practice of holding ghost detainees rose in the wake of 9/11 terror attacks in 2001, and the practice has been vociferously condemned by various human rights watch organizations.

ghost gun (GG)
A ghost gun is a homemade firearm that, as a result of being DIY (do it yourself), does not have serial numbers and, as a result, is untraceable. Ghost guns appeal to

hobbyists, anarchists, and people who are generally averse to laws and government regulation of any kind, including felons.

A **3-D printed gun** is an example of a ghost gun, but GGs are more often assembled from gun kits that include unfinished parts or leave out one part that must be purchased separately, thereby bypassing federal firearm regulations. Such kits are legal to sell, do not require a **background check**, are easily purchased on the internet, and do not require specialized gunsmithing training or tools to assemble. *See also* **Gun Control Act (GCA)**.

ghost lawyer

A form of ghostwriting, a ghost lawyer will write **briefs** and other legal documents without putting their name on the document. The practice is not necessarily nefarious and can be understood as a form of **pro bono** work if the lawyer does not charge their usual (or any) fees. However, the ethics are debatable.

giallo

Twentieth-century genre of Italian literature and film that encompasses crime fiction, **thrillers** (often **psychological**), mystery and horror. *Giallo* means yellow, reflecting the color of cheap paperback mystery novels in postwar Italy.

Glasgow smile

Popular among Scottish gangs in the 1920s and 1930s, a Glasgow smile describes two characteristic slashes or cuts from the corners of the mouth to the ears, which result in scars giving the victim the appearance of a perpetual smile or grin. It is also known as a Chelsea smile, due to its popularity with a gang known as the Chelsea Headhunters, or a Glasgow, Chelsea, Cheshire, or Birkenhead grin. In Los Angeles, California, Elizabeth Short, the murder victim known posthumously as the

Black Dahlia, was subjected to mutilation including a Glasgow smile.

Glavnoye Razvedyvatel'noye Upravlenie (GU)
Commonly known by its previous abbreviation GRU, this is the Main Directorate of the General Staff of the Armed Forces of the Russian Federation aka Russian military **intelligence**. It is believed to have a far larger **spy** network abroad than Russia's **foreign intelligence** service.

Glock
Austrian manufacturer of **handguns**. ▶ Glock 17 9 mm **pistol** that is the most popular handgun for the military and **law enforcement** agencies in the world. It is popular due to its rugged polymer build, accuracy, and safety features, which mean it is unlikely to accidentally **discharge**. ▶ Glock 19 9mm pistol issued to West Midlands police officers in the UK as an alternative to the Glock 17. It is a compact version of the Glock 17 and was developed by the manufacturer specifically for the military and law enforcement. ▶ Glock 22 The Glock 17's cousin, modified to take 15 **rounds** of .40 **caliber ammunition** while still being light enough to comfortably carry all day. The G22 is used by several law enforcement agencies, including US Marshals, the **Drug Enforcement Administration,** and the **Federal Bureau of Investigation**, and is the most popular police service pistol in the US. ▶ Glock 26 Subcompact 9 mm pistol designed for **concealed carry** and is issued to plainclothes officers in London's **Metropolitan Police**. Like all Glock pistols, it is made from a polymer, which means it is both light and durable.

going postal
Refers to running amok and shooting colleagues in the workplace, named after shootings by US Postal Service workers.

gong
Gun (US/Jamaican contemporary gang slang).

good fellow
"Honest" **thief** who is generous and settles bills on time (US historical slang).

grand jury
A grand jury is a legal instrument that emerged from the **Fifth Amendment**, which stated that "No person shall be held to answer for a capital, or otherwise infamous crime, unless on a presentment or indictment of a grand jury." A regular trial jury has no more than 12 members; by contrast, a grand jury consists of 16 to 26 citizens. It deliberates behind closed doors. Typically, a grand jury is convened to investigate a named individual of felony wrongdoing. Twelve affirmative votes must be returned in order to proceed to an **indictment**.

grandma's house
Gang headquarters or meeting place in a prison or the **cell** of the gang leader (US contemporary prison slang).

Grand Theft Auto (GTA) video game series
Widely considered the most controversial video game series of all time, GTA is an action-adventure style video game that gamifies extreme urban violence. Routinely played by children and teens, players might shoot police, hire or murder prostitutes, engage in gang warfare, torture rivals, and also steal cars. One version was discovered to have a hidden minigame program that allowed

players to have graphic sex with virtual prostitutes. Another minigame allowed players to deal drugs. It remains one of the most popular and profitable video games on the market and continues to break sales records.

Gray List
List of the identities and locations of people of interest whose attitudes or political inclinations toward the US and its policies are unclear or unknown. Those people may possess information or particular skills required by US forces and whose political motivations or attitudes require further **investigation** before the US can attempt to make use of that information and/or skills. (*See also* **Black List** and **White List**.)

green-goods man
Someone who deals in forged currency or bonds (US historical slang).

grey rhino event
Coined by Michele Wucker in 2016, a Grey Rhino event is a "highly probable, high impact yet neglected threat," making it the opposite of a Black Swan event. An example of a Grey Rhino is the Covid-19 pandemic.

G-ride
Gangster ride or stolen car (US contemporary gang slang).

Griess Test
Chemical test that detects nitrites and is used to develop patterns of **gunpowder** residues, which are nitrites, around **bullet** holes.

grifter
Con artist or trickster who **swindles** money out of people through what is usually small-scale, petty **fraud**. Also

known as a scammers, gougers, chisellers, and flim-flam men. The term originated in around 1906 in circuses and carnivals where grifters operated sideshows, often with a gambling element dishonestly fixed in their favor. Its use has been extended to all nonviolent criminals (US slang).

grip
Handle of a **handgun** and portion of the **stock** to the rear of the **trigger** on a long gun.

groove
Spiral or helicoidal cut in a gun **barrel**, which creates the **rifling** that is important in **forensic ballistics**. These grooves impart spin to the **bullet** or projectile on firing. A spinning bullet is more stable in its trajectory and therefore more accurate than one fired from a **smooth-bored** weapon.

grow house
A grow house or **cannabis** farm is an often innocuous-looking house where thousands of cannabis plants might be grown in every room, sometimes tended by marginalized workers. The **drug** gangs who run these farms will hack into the electricity supply to avoid having to pay the enormous bills that result from running the lights, heaters, and hydroponic systems necessary to cultivate their crop.

GRU
See Glavnoye Razvedyvatel'noye Upravlenie.

GSR
See **gunshot** residue.

GU
See Glavnoye Razvedyvatel'noye Upravlenie.

Guantánamo Bay detention camp (2002–)

Also known as Gitmo, this detention camp came into being during the George W. Bush administration as part of the **War on Terror.** Located inside the Guantánamo Bay US Naval Base in Cuba, it was meant to hold high-value or extremely dangerous individuals suspected of involvement with terrorism. Focusing on Muslim militants, some of whom were **ghost detainees**, it became the focus of sustained international criticism regarding its violations of the Geneva Convention, breaches of human rights, credible reports of torture (called "enhanced interrogation") by the US military, and the death of detainees. Attempts by Barack Obama to close the facility failed due to lack of political support. In 2018, Donald Trump extended its charter indefinitely.

gump

Gay male prisoner (US contemporary prison slang).

gun

Synonymous with **firearm** but usually understood to refer to a **handgun (pistol or revolver)**, or, less commonly, to a **rifle (long gun)**. In 2020, there are more guns than people in the US, with 400,000 million in circulation compared to a population of 330 million. Nearly 17 million guns were sold in 2020 alone, and 40 percent of that group were first-time buyers.

Gun Control Act (GCA)

Passed in 1968, in the wake of the assassinations of US Senator Robert F. Kennedy and Dr. Martin Luther King, Jr., the Gun Control Act regulated gun commerce, restricted mail order sales, created a category of persons **prohibited** from possessing a firearm, restricted importation of **Saturday night specials** and similar "junk" guns, and restricted sales of automatic and semiautomatic weapons.

In addition, it required that serial numbers be added to the frames or receivers of firearms so that law enforcement agencies could trace them. Crucially, the law didn't require the rest of the firearm's parts to be marked as well, creating a loophole that set the conditions for the creation of **ghost guns**.

gun moll
Female companion of a male criminal, more specifically a of the mob or the **Mafia** (US historical slang).

gunpowder
Generic term for **cartridge** and **muzzle**-loading **propellant**.

gun rights
The heated debate over the rights of the American citizenry to carry, use, and purchase firearms centers around differing interpretations of the **Second Amendment**, which states: "A well regulated Militia, being necessary to the security of a free State, the right of the people to keep and bear Arms, shall not be infringed." Liberals tend to focus on "well regulated," while conservatives tend to stress "shall not be infringed." There is little middle ground on the issue, with the failure of **Sandy Hook** to increase restrictions of assault-style firearms suggesting there is little political will to change the status quo.

gunshot residue (GSR)
Residues from the powder, **primer,** and **projectile**, as well as from the metallic components of the **cartridge case** and **firearm's barrel**, which are partly expelled from the firearm during firing and partly remain in the firearm, mainly in the bore. Can be important to **forensic evidence** and **investigation**.

gun show loophole

The "gun show loophole" refers to the belief that gun shows are capitalist free-for-alls where vendors will sell guns to anyone, including **prohibited persons**, without a **background check**. However, most event organizers prefer not to run afoul of the law and require their vendors to be **Federal Firearm Licensees (FFLs)**, with all the attendant checks and rules applying.

But at such events, there is nothing to prevent unlicensed dealers and interested parties from showing up and conducting person-to-person transactions in the parking lot. In 2021, it is legal for private individuals (defined as people who do not make their primary income from gun sales) to sell a firearm without running a background check, partly because private citizens have no access to **NICS**. In short, the "gun show loophole" is actually the "private sale loophole" (also known as the **Brady Bill loophole**).

guns in popular culture

Before firearms became defining components of **first-person shooter video games**, they were synonymous with American action films and Westerns. Think Bruce Willis as John McClane running around Nakatomi Towers with a Beretta 92FS, or John Wayne's Winchester Model 1892, which became so closely identified with the Duke that a commemorative model is named after him. Even inside a crowded field of contenders, however, certain makes and models have become stand-alone cultural references. Some examples are: The Colt Python revolver (Rick Grimes/*Walking Dead* gun); the double-action Smith & Wesson Model 29 .44-cal Magnum revolver (the *Dirty Harry* gun); M60 machine gun (*Rambo* gun); the Walther PPK (James Bond gun); and, most recently, the customized Heckler & Koch P30L (*John Wick* gun).

The Internet Movie Firearms Database (imfdb.org) keeps track of all the firearms used in American films, functioning as a kind of pop culture analog of the **National Tracing Center (NTC).**

gun, slang words for

The abbreviated names of certain firearms have, over time, become generic slang for any firearm. Examples include **9** (for 9mm handgun); **gat** (for Gatling gun); and **tommy** (for Thompson submachine gun). The sheer number of slang words for "gun" are too numerous to list, but some examples are: bam bam; banger; **biscuit**; Chicago typewriter; pea shooter; persuader; pew pew pew; **Saturday night special**; side piece; smokepole; and smokewagon.

gun violence

In the US, gun violence and gun crime are not synonymous, largely due to the fact that so many suicides are by firearm. (In the US, suicide is a tragedy, but it is not a crime.) In the twenty-first century, over half of all suicides and 67 percent of all **homicides** in the US involve the use of a firearm. In sheer number of **mass shootings**, the US is an extreme outlier compared to all other countries.

H

hacking

Hacking is the act of gaining access to a computer system by exploiting vulnerabilities in that system. ▶**hacker** Person who gains unwarranted access to a computer system. Hackers contend that they are problem solvers who reveal bugs and flaws in a system and alert companies to vulnerabilities so that they can be fixed. They consider themselves highly skilled and capable of thinking outside the box, looking down on **crackers** who break into computer systems for illegal purposes or personal gain.

hair trigger; heavy trigger

See Trigger pull weight.

half cock

Safety notch on a gun meant to prevent shocks or decocking; the intermediary position of the **hammer** between the notch of the armed and decocking positions intended to prevent release of the hammer without pressing on the **trigger**. This is the safety or loading position of many guns.

halfway house

Halfway house is an umbrella term that applies to non-carceral as well as carceral supervised housing for adults. For example, they can act as "restitution centers," where an offender might be sent in lieu of prison, or be solely involved in drug addiction rehabilitation efforts where no prison time is involved. However, a halfway house is most commonly understood as a residential facility where people released from **jail** (typically non-violent or low-risk offenders) must live before being released back into the community, often as a condition of parole or as part of a supervised program of release. They can be run by state corrections departments, probation/parole offices, and the **Federal Bureau of Prisons (BOP)**. BOPs often contract nonprofits and private companies to run these facilities, which the BOP calls **Residential Reentry Centers (RRCs)**.

hallucinogen

Substance, especially a psychoactive **drug** such as **lysergic acid diethylamide** (LSD), phencyclidine (**PCP**) or **ketamine**, that causes hallucinations, altering perception, experience, and feeling. Hallucinogens are also known as dissociatives and are usually **controlled substances** in the UK and the US. While not highly **addictive**, they can be fatally dangerous and are often misused.

hammer

Part of the firing mechanism on a gun that strikes the **firing pin**, **primer** or percussion cap. In some cases the firing pin is an integral part of the hammer.

handgun

Firearm designed to be held and fired in one hand rather than being shouldered.

handler

Intelligence officer directly responsible for the operational activities of an **agent**. Also known as an agent handler or **case officer**.

handloading

Manually assembling a gun **cartridge case** with a **primer**, **propellant** and **bullet** or **wadding** and **shot**.

happy bag

Bag armed robbers use that contains the weapons, bala-clavas, gloves and other equipment required to carry out robberies.

hardboiled crime fiction

The lone-wolf PI skulking behind a frosted office door is the stuff of hard-boiled fiction. Usually American, tough-talking and tough-acting, he (it is always a "he" in hardboiled crime fiction) is a pro, an unsentimental gunslinger for hire. And the person who hires him is often a woman in distress. These flawed heroes march alone against a corrupt society, taking on the system while adhering to their skewed personal code of honor. Always moral, they won't be cowed or beaten and they never give up on a client or a **case**. Classic exponents of the art include Dashiell Hammett and Raymond Chandler. Their contemporary successors include James Ellroy, Michael Connelly and Dennis Lehane. These authors may not always write about a PI but their prose echoes the classic tropes and their heroes remain slang-slinging modern-day men of myth who take on the world and shoot from the lip.

hardware

One or more (loaded) firearms being carried at the same time.

hate crime

In the US, at the federal level, a hate crime is defined as a criminal act "committed on the basis of the victim's perceived or actual race, color, religion, national origin, sexual orientation, gender, gender identity, or disability." Because it is not illegal to hold bigoted views, hate crimes are distinct from hate *incidents*, which refer to hateful or bigoted acts that are not crimes in of themselves, and "do not involve violence, threats, or property damage." The Hate Crimes Reporting Gap refers to the disparity between hate crimes that actually occur, and those that are reported to law enforcement.

headtopped

Shot in the head (London contemporary gang slang associated with drill music).

heave

Rob. ▶ **heave the booth** Rob someone's house (UK thieves' **cant**, historical slang).

heavy weapon

Weapon intended to be used by more than one member of armed or security forces, as a team, and whose **caliber** is bigger or equal to 100 mm. According to NATO definitions, the term "heavy weapons" means all tanks and armored vehicles, all artillery 75 mm caliber and above, all mortars 81 mm caliber and above, and all antiaircraft weapons 20 mm caliber and above.

hebephile

Someone who is primarily attracted to adolescents or post-pubertal teenagers who are still in the early stages of sexual maturation; that is, usually between 11 and 14 years of age (those attracted to older teenagers are called ephebophiles). Hebephiles are usually solely sexually attracted to these adolescents and do not pursue sexual relationships with adults. As such, they often put themselves in professional and other roles where they have easy access to their vulnerable targets.

Heckler & Koch MP5

The Heckler & Koch MP5 is a range of lightweight, delayed blowback **submachine guns**, with the MP5SF model used by various UK police forces including the **Metropolitan Police**. The MP5SD silenced version of the gun was specifically developed by its German manufacturers for use by special forces.

heel

Rear portion of a **bullet**.

Helicopter Emergency Medical Service (HEMS)

Helicopter Emergency Medical Services, often funded by charities, provide rapid aerial response to a medical emergency.

hemlock

One of the most **poisonous** plants in the world, hemlock (*Conium maculatum*) grows readily in the wild as well as in gardens and, before its tiny white flowers appear, is sometimes mistaken for parsley or carrot leaves. Hemlock poisoning results in total paralysis followed by death due to asphyxiation, although the mind remains unaffected, which means the victim is fully aware of what is happening. It takes only a few drops of liquid hemlock to kill a small animal and a **lethal** dose for a human of prepared hemlock is estimated at around 100 mg. Socrates, the Greek philosopher, was **sentenced** to death by drinking hemlock, sparking the imagination of

Shakespeare and other writers who seized upon this as a murder method in fiction.

henbane

Henbane (*Hyoscyamus niger*) is a plant, the flowers of which are so **poisonous** that smelling them causes giddiness. It contains the tropane alkaloids hyoscine (scopolamine), hyoscyamine, and **atropine**. Among its many symptoms are a dry mouth, blurred vision, photophobia, vomiting, confusion, hallucinations, convulsions, and coma. It was infamously used by Dr. Crippen to murder his wife, although most modern poisonings are the accidental result of overdose after ingesting henbane as a **hallucinogen**.

heroin

Heroin is a highly **addictive** opioid, also known as diamorphine, and is usually sold as a brown or white powder that is smoked, snorted or dissolved in liquid and injected. When smoked it is often heated on a surface such as tinfoil with the resultant smoke inhaled. This is known as "chasing the dragon." It is very easy to overdose on heroin, especially when it is injected, and overdose often results in death from either inhaling vomit or the slowing of breathing to the point where it stops. In the US, where deaths due to **drugs** and especially opiates outnumber deaths due to gun violence, a crime-fiction genre known as Opioid Noir has flourished since Hammett and Chandler highlighted the growing postwar drug crisis, with recent writers such as James Ellroy, James Lee Burke and Don Winslow also shining a light on the opioid epidemic. Heroin's street names include: abajo; A-bomb (heroin mixed with **cannabis**); achivia; adormidera; amarilla; *anestesia de caballo* (heroin mixed with the horse anesthetic xylazine); antifreeze; apodo; arpon; Aunt Hazel; avocado; azucar; bad seed; *baja corte* (diluted heroin);

ballot; basketball; basura; beast; Beyoncé; big bag; big H;
big Harry; bird; birdie powder; *birria*; *birria blanca*; black;
black bitch; black goat; black olives; black paint; black
pearl; black sheep; black shirt; black tar; *blanco*; blue; blow
dope; blue hero; *bombita* (heroin mixed with **cocaine**);
bombs away; *bonita*; boy; bozo; *brea negra*; brick gum;
brown; brown crystal; brown rhine; brown sugar; bubble
gum; burrito; butter; *caballo*; *caballo negro*; *caca*; café;
cajeta; capital H; cardio (white heroin); *carga*; caro;
cement; *certificada* (pure heroin); *chapopote*; charlie;
charlie horse; *chavo*; cheese; *chicle*; *chiclosa*; China; *China
blanca* (white heroin); China cat; China white; Chinese
buffet (white heroin); Chinese food; Chinese red; chip;
chiva; *chiva blanca*; *chiva loca* (heroin mixed with
fentanyl); *chiva negra*; *chivones*; chocolate; chocolate balls;
chocolate shake; choko; chorizo; *churro negro*; *chutazo*;
coco; coffee; *cohete*; *comida*; crown crap; curly hair; dark;
dark girl; dark kind; dead on arrival (DOA); diesel; dirt;
dog food; doggie; doojee; dope; dorado; down; downtown;
dragon; dreck; dynamite; dyno; *el diablo*; engines; *Enrique
Grande*; *esquina*; *esquinilla*; fairy dust; flea powder; food
(white heroin); foolish powder; galloping horse; gamot;
gato; george smack; girl; globo (balloon of heroin); goat;
golden girl; good and plenty; good H; goofball (heroin
mixed with **methamphetamine**); *goma*; *gorda*; *gras*; *grasin*;
gravy; gum; H; H-caps; hairy; hard candy; hard one; Harry;
hats; hazel; heaven dust; heavy; Helen; helicopter; hell
dust; Henry; Hercules; hero; him; *hombre*; horse; hot dope;
huera; hummers; jojee; joy flakes; joy powder; junk;
kabayo; Karachi; karate; king's tickets; *la tierra*; lemonade;
lenta; lifesaver; *manteca*; *marias*; Marrion; mayo; mazpan;
meal; menthol; Mexican brown; Mexican food (black tar
heroin); Mexican horse; Mexican mud; Mexican treat;
modelo negra; mojo; mole; *mongega*; *morena*; *morenita*;
mortal combat; motors; mud; *mujer*; *murcielago*; muzzle;

nanoo; *negra*; *negra tomasa*; *negrita*; nice and easy; night; noise; Obama; old Steve; pants; patty; peg; P-funk; *piezas*; *plata*; poison; *polvo*; *polvo de alegria*; *polvo de estrellas*; *polvo feliz*; poppy; powder; *prostituta negra*; puppy; pure; Rambo; raw (uncut heroin); red chicken; red eagle; reindeer dust; roofing tar; ruby; sack; salt; sand; scag; scat; schmeck; scramble (uncut heroin); sheep; shirts; shoes; skag; skunk; slime; smack; smeck; snickers; soda; speedball (heroin mixed with cocaine); spider blue; sticky kind; *stufa*; sugar; sweet Jesus; tan; tar; *tecata*; thunder; tires; *tomasa*; tootsie roll; tragic magic; trees; turtle; *vidrio*; weights; whiskey; white; white boy; white girl; white junk; white lady; white nurse; white shirt; white stuff; wings; witch; witch hazel; *zapapote*.

H

high roller

Gangster or **drug dealer** making a lot of money (US contemporary gang slang).

highway robber

An archaic British term, a highway robber was a violent criminal who targeted travelers. The phrase, "highway robbery" has since entered common parlance as an expression referring to the overcharging of customers or exorbitantly high yet unavoidable fees. ("Your bank charged you $100 to cash a check? That's highway robbery!")

hitters

A street drug dealer. Typically members of a drug gang, they work for a street boss who runs the entire operation. A street boss's turf is measured in street blocks. Turf wars occur when bosses try to expand their base of operations. A molded gun sleeve traditionally made of leather but now also made of lighter yet durable thermoplastics and tech fabrics. Its purpose is to cradle a firearm so that it may be carried safely on one's person, whether on a belt as an **IWB**, or on shoulder straps. One can buy a generic holster for, say, a .22 pistol, but it is preferred to buy one made to fit a specific make and model, such as a .22 Ruger Single Six LR. Jamming an unholstered gun down one's pants may be **gangsta**, but it's a good way to end up accidentally shooting yourself. (*See also* **unholstering**.)

holding

To have drugs on one's person, either with the intent to use or to sell. Example: "If you're looking for a fix, Alfie's holding."

holding down

Controlling gang turf or an area (US contemporary gang slang).

hollow-point bullet

Bullet with a cavity in the nose to facilitate expansion on impact.

holster

A molded gun sleeve traditionally made of leather but now also made of lighter yet durable thermoplastics and tech fabrics. Its purpose is to cradle a firearm so that it may be carried safely on one's person, whether on a belt as an **IWB**, or on shoulder straps. One can buy a generic holster for, say, a .22 pistol, but it is preferred to buy one made to fit a specific make and model, such as a .22 Ruger Single Six LR. Jamming an unholstered gun down one's pants may be **gangsta**, but it's a good way to end up accidentally shooting yourself. *See also* **unholstering**.

homeboy, homie

Friend from your own area or neighborhood; also fellow gang member (UK/US contemporary slang).

homicide

A homicide, or literally "killing of a man," refers to any instance where a human being kills another, including assisted suicide. A homicide is not necessarily a crime, as there are lawful and justifiable instances, such as killing in **self-defense**. When the killing is unlawful and intentional, it is **murder** (a crime). When the killing is unlawful and unintentional, it is **manslaughter** (a crime).

honey trap

An operation conducted by an **intelligence agent** or **agency**, private detective or other party who intends to gain information by ensnaring an unwary target in a compromising sexual encounter or a relationship, whether real or merely promised. The target may then be vulnerable to blackmail that could lead to them **spying** or conducting other activities for the person or people who set the trap. Private investigators are often asked to set a honey trap or honey pot to catch a spouse who is suspected of cheating. Honey traps are commonly believed to be set by attractive women but in reality can be laid by members of either sex and used to ensnare someone of either gender.

hot pursuit

Hot pursuit is a US **law enforcement** term. If a criminal flees the scene of a crime and a police officer follows them, the officer has the right in "hot pursuit" to enter a property in which the criminal has sought shelter.

howdunnit

In contrast to the **whodunnit**, the howdunnit focuses on how a crime, usually a murder, was committed. These stories generally start with the crime having been committed and with the villain already exposed. They then work backward to expose the truth behind the crime and the **motive** for it.

human intelligence (humint)

Intelligence derived from information collected and provided by human **sources** and often considered the primary or most valuable source of intelligence for agencies such as **MI6**. There are two basic types of humint—overt and **clandestine**. Overt humint involves meeting a target openly, usually as a diplomatic or military representative of a foreign government, and can include methods such as **interrogation** and observation, whereas clandestine humint involves intelligence gathering using secret or clandestine means, also known as **espionage**.

human trafficking

Human trafficking is a form of modern slavery and is the illegal harboring, trade or transport of people through the use of deception and **coercion** for the purposes of exploitation. Victims can be sexually exploited or forced to work, beg or commit criminal acts against their will. They can also have their organs removed and be forced into marriage or domestic servitude. Human trafficking is highly profitable for the organized gangs and criminals who are largely responsible for it. People do not have to be taken across borders in order for trafficking to have occurred; children can be considered trafficked simply if they are taken into an exploitative situation without the need for coercion. Victims of trafficking are often trying to escape extreme poverty, war, violence or lack of opportunity in their country or region. They are often tricked into applying for a job that does not actually exist or where the conditions are completely different to those that were described. They are kept in that situation by violence, force, intimidation, threats against their families, and by the removal of their documents, as well as the imposition of false debts to their traffickers that they can never pay off.

hush money

Money given to keep someone quiet, especially about a crime or **felony** (historical slang and contemporary usage).

hybrid threat

A hybrid threat is the combination of tactics, technologies and capabilities used by adversaries or enemies to gain an asymmetric advantage or edge. These adversaries can include lone attackers, criminals, terrorist organizations and even nation states.

I

IA
See internal affairs.

IAFIS
See Integrated Automated Fingerprint Identification System.

IC
See Intelligence Community.

ICE
See Immigration and Customs Enforcement.

ICP
See initial contact point.

IEPs
See incentives and earned privileges.

IIO
See illegal intelligence officer.

illegal
When used in an **intelligence** context, an illegal is an officer, employee, or **agent** of an intelligence organization who is sent abroad but has no overt relationship with the intelligence service or government for which that person actually works. To all intents and purposes, they are operating as a private person and often under a false identity. This means that they are not afforded diplomatic

protection and can be imprisoned or even executed if caught. They are called illegals because they are operating illegally in the host country. ▶ **illegal intelligence officer (IIO)** Intelligence officer who enters a country with false documents or otherwise circumvents border controls. This means they can stay in that country for an extended period, especially with false documents that allow them to pass **background checks** and to then leave the country similarly undetected. ▶ **illegal support officer** Intelligence officer who has legal residency in a country and whose primary function is to support illegal **agents** by supplying anything they need. They can also gather information and documents that may be useful to future illegal agents.

illegal drug
Drug that is forbidden by law to possess, use, buy, or sell.

imitation firearm
Functional reproduction of an existing **firearm**. The term can also refer to a modern reproduction of an **antique firearm**. Used in crime to fool a victim into believing the weapon is real and to therefore intimidate or terrify them into complying.

Immigration and Customs Enforcement (ICE)
The principal investigative arm of the US Department of Homeland Security (DHS). ICE's primary mission is to promote homeland security and public safety through the criminal and civil enforcement of federal laws governing border control, customs, trade, and immigration.

impact spatter
This type of **bloodstain** occurs when blood hits a surface hard and breaks into smaller droplets. The more forceful the impact, the smaller the droplets, with their density

decreasing as they move further from the source of the blood. Analysis of impact spatter can help to ascertain the relative positions of individuals and objects at a **crime scene** as well as giving insight into what happened.

impersonal communication

In **intelligence** circles, communications between a **handler** and **asset** that do not involve direct contact. Also, secret communication techniques used between a **case officer** and a **human intelligence** asset when physical contact is not possible or desired.

impressed print

Impressed prints are found in soft materials or tissue at **crime scenes** and are formed by fingers, palms, feet, or other body parts pressing into them. They are usually photographed for **evidence** and molds or **casts** can be made of them.

---

incentives and earned privileges (IEPs)

Incentives and earned privileges or IEPs are what prisoners in the UK and the US can earn if they follow the rules and take a constructive part in activities, including their **sentence** plan. These incentives and privileges can include things such as more visits from family and friends, more time outside their **cell**, the right to wear their own clothes instead of a prison uniform, the ability to earn and spend more money, and a TV in their cell. IEPs may be taken away if a prisoner behaves badly or does not comply with the rules. There are three IEP levels.

- Basic level: restricted to a prisoner's legal rights such as some letters and visits. Nothing extra is permitted.

incitement

To incite is to encourage another to commit a crime. In the United States, it falls under 18 US Code § 373, solicitation to commit a crime of violence.

inconclusive

Not conclusive; not resolving doubts or questions; without final results or outcome. Can be used of **evidence** and, in **forensic DNA** analysis, can also mean that there is not enough information to include or exclude a person, or that the sample is not suitable for statistics.

indictable offense

These are the most serious forms of crimes, such as rape and murder. In the United States, they are also known as **felony** crimes.

indictment

Inside the legal system, an indictment is a formal accusation of a crime. An **indicted** person will be given formal notice of the charges against them. For example, a **grand jury** will hand down indictments against a suspected money launderer, who might then attempt to flee the country to avoid having to answer to the charges.

infiltration

Placing an **intelligence officer** or **agent** or other person in a target area in hostile territory. Infiltration methods can be **black** or **clandestine**, gray or through a legal crossing point but under false documentation, and white or legal.

informant

Person who knowingly or unknowingly provides information to an **agent**, a **clandestine** or **intelligence** service, or the police.

informer

Someone who intentionally discloses or provides information about other people or activities to police or a **security service**, usually for a financial reward.

infraction

An infraction (sometimes called a violation) is a petty offense in the US that is punishable only by a small fine. Because infractions cannot result in a jail **sentence** or even **probation**, defendants **charged** with infractions do not have a right to a jury trial.

initial contact point (ICP)

The physical location where an **intelligence officer** or **agent** makes an initial contact or **brush contact** with his **source** or **asset**.

injunction

Court **order** to stop doing or to start doing a specific act.

insanity defense

See **mental disorder defense**.

insect bloodstain

As its name suggests, this is caused by an insect, especially a type of fly that likes to feed on blood and tissue, at the scene. The blood is then regurgitated by the fly as a small, circular stains known as flyspeck. Insects can also move through **bloodstains**, causing further, smaller stains and patterns.

Integrated Automated Fingerprint Identification System (IAFIS)

The **Federal Bureau of Investigation**'s automated **fingerprint** system. It is being replaced by the **Next Generation Identification** system.

Intelink

Intelink is the **classified**, worldwide intranet for the US **Intelligence Community**. The most secure level, Intelink-TS, uses the Joint Worldwide Intelligence Communications System (JWICS) to communicate. JWICS is a 24/7 network that is designed to communicate multimedia **intelligence** worldwide up to the Top Secret/Sensitive Compartmented Information level. Intelink-S is a version accessed through the Secret Internet Protocol Router Network (SIPRNet), and accessed at Secret level and above.

intelligence

Intelligence (intel) is often mistakenly assumed simply to mean information when it is far more complex than that, encompassing both the products of information gathering, processing, evaluation, analysis, and interpretation as well as the process that leads to the gathering of that information and the organizations and agencies involved in that process. To be useful, intelligence must inform policy or decision makers in such a way that it can be acted upon. ▶**intelligence analyst** Professional intelligence officer who is responsible for performing, coordinating or supervising the collection, analysis, and **dissemination** of intelligence. ▶ **Intelligence Community (IC)** All the departments or agencies of a government that are concerned with **intelligence** activity. ▶ **intelligence officer (IO)** Professionally trained member of an **intelligence** service. He or she may be serving in their home country or abroad, either legally or illegally.

internal affairs (IA)

Internal Affairs is the division tasked with investigation accusations of criminal wrongdoing or professional misconduct inside the police force itself. Due to the nature of their work, they typically report directly to the police chief or to a civilian board.

INTERPOL

The International Criminal Police Organization or INTERPOL is the world's largest international police organization, with 194 member countries. Created in 1923, it is headquartered in Lyon, France, and facilitates cross-border police cooperation, supporting, and assisting **law enforcement** worldwide.

interrogation

Systematic process of using techniques to question a captured or detained person to obtain reliable information.

intimate partner violence (IPV)

A more specific term than domestic abuse (which encompasses the entire family, including children, relatives, and household members in general), IPV refers to spousal or partner abuse. This abuse can be psychological, verbal, and financial, as well as physical and sexual, and includes stalking or menacing behavior, both in person as well as over the internet. In 1994, US Congress recognized IPV as criminal behavior in the Violence Against Women Act (VAWA).

IPV

See **intimate partner violence**.

investigation

Detailed, systematic, structured, and objective inquiry to ascertain the truth about an event, situation, or individual, especially after an **allegation** of unlawful or questionable activities. During an investigation, **evidence** is gathered to substantiate or refute the allegation or questionable activity. An investigation is initiated when there are facts or allegations that indicate a possible violation of law or policy.

IO

See **intelligence officer**.

Irish noir

Genre of crime fiction written by Irish writers and largely set in Ireland although the works of John Connolly, one of its exponents, are set in the United States. Irish noir is characteristically bleak, dark, and grim in its realism leavened by moments of gallows humor. It can be further subdivided into genres such as Dublin noir, Ulster noir, and Belfast noir.

IWB

An acronym for Inside the Waistband. It refers to the placement of holsters.

J

jack
Robbery; "doing a jack" is committing a robbery (US contemporary gang slang).

jacket
Prison inmate's rap sheet or information file; also his reputation among other prisoners (US contemporary slang). *See also* **bullet jacket**.

Jack-in-the-Box (JIB or jib)
A collapsible or inflatable dummy that is placed in a car to evade **surveillance** or deceive anyone watching about the number of people in the vehicle. Often the jib is in an empty car while the real occupant(s) are elsewhere carrying out **clandestine** or **covert** activities.

jackrabbit parole
To escape from a prison or correctional facility (US contemporary slang).

Jack the Ripper
Perhaps the most infamous serial killer of all, Jack the Ripper was an unknown murderer who stalked the streets of Whitechapel in the East End of London around 1888, killing and mutilating women, mainly prostitutes. The murders attributed to the person known as Jack the Ripper form only part of what are known as the Whitechapel Murders. The **case file** on these covers 11 cases, 5 of which are almost certainly

attributable to Jack the Ripper, the rest being debatable or definitely not linked to him.

The five believed victims of Jack the Ripper, often referred to as the canonical five victims, are Mary Ann Nichols, Annie Chapman, Elizabeth Stride, Catherine Eddowes, and Mary Kelly, all murdered between August and November 1888, and each of whom had their throat slit and their belly slashed open before being disemboweled. Martha Tabram, also known as Martha Turner, was killed before Mary Ann Nichols and may in fact have been Jack the Ripper's first victim as her throat and abdomen were slashed, although she was not disemboweled. An experienced East End policeman, Inspector Frederick George Abberline, was brought in to head up the **investigation** into the Whitechapel Murders. Wild theories abounded but at least the increased police presence in the area appeared to have scared off the murderer until the night of September 30, 1888, when he killed two more victims, Elizabeth Stride and then Catherine Eddowes, little more than an hour apart.

The killer acquired his name from a letter that was sent to a London news agency, written in red ink and boasting of what the killer had done as well as what he planned to do. The letter was signed Jack the Ripper. Although the police quickly deduced the letter was a hoax and actually written by a journalist, they had already publicized it, subsequently unleashing a deluge of other letters, some of which were clearly hoaxes as well. In November 1888, the body of the woman believed to be the Ripper's final victim, Mary Kelly, was found in her room in Whitechapel, skinned almost to the bone.

There were several more Whitechapel Murders believed to have been the work of different perpetrators, but it is the Ripper murders that have caught and maintained the public's fascination, throwing up a host of possible suspects, some more plausible than others. To this day, the crimes remain unsolved and are likely to remain that way. The Ripper murders not only gave rise to rudimentary criminal **profiling** but were also the first to attract a worldwide media frenzy. They have also inspired hundreds of fiction and nonfiction books, songs, plays, operas, films, and TV series, including a film for Japanese TV featuring your author as Catherine Eddowes.

J jail

Derived from the British word *gaol*, jail is often used interchangeably with prison. However, in the US, jail refers to smaller institutions at the town or county level designed to hold suspects for short stays (but see **Browder, Kalief**). Prisons operate at the state or federal level, and hold inmates who have been sentenced for longer stays. So, when first arrested, suspects go to county jail; after sentencing, they go to state or federal prison.

jail churn

Jail churn refers to people going in and out of the **prison industrial complex**. A marginal individual will be arrested on a minor charge such as vagrancy or public urination, then will either make bail within hours or stay behind bars until processed. If convicted at trial for **misdemeanors**, their sentences are generally short, and they will be released under a year. One in four of this group will be rearrested within that same year. Thus they cycle in and out, with underlying issues such as poverty, mental illness, and addiction, making it nearly impossible for these types of offenders to escape the churn.

Jane/John Doe

Jane Doe and John Doe are standard placeholder names used by **law enforcement** and the courts when a corpse or living person is unidentified, fictitious or must remain anonymous. **Richard Roe** or the surname Roe are also used in court cases when two parties must remain anonymous, most famously in the US Supreme Court case of Roe v. Wade. The surnames Doe and Roe come from an antiquated British legal property process and, interestingly, both reference deer.

jaunt

Derived from joint and can refer to anything from a weapon such as a **shank** to prison currency such as a **magazine** or book of stamps. Used between prisoners so cops and guards won't know what they are talking about (US contemporary prison slang).

Jim Crow laws

Largely concentrated in the American South, Jim Crow legislation consisted of state and local laws that legalized segregation, with the express purpose of creating second-class citizens in the former Confederate States of America. In 1954, school segregation ended with the landmark Supreme Court case Brown v. Board of Education, with the remaining Jim Crow laws (technically) overturned in 1964 by the Civil Rights Act and in 1965 by the Voting Rights Act. Millions of Americans are still alive today who were denied the vote when they turned 21.

jointed

Dismembered or beheaded (US/Jamaican contemporary gang slang).

joint intelligence

Intelligence produced by elements or operatives of more than one intelligence service that belong to the same nation.

joint investigation

Investigation in which more than one investigative **agency** has established investigative authority and the agencies involved agree to pursue the investigation on a joint basis having agreed investigative responsibilities, procedures, and methods.

jolt

"Doing a jolt" means doing time in prison (US historical slang).

judgment (legal)

A judgment is the final decision of the court in a legal proceeding such as a trial,

juke

Hold up, rob, or rip someone off (US/Jamaican contemporary gang slang). Also to hit, beat up, poke, or stab someone (UK/US slang).

just say no

Alert that **undercover** police are in the area (US contemporary gang slang).

juvenile justice system

Inside the criminal justice system, children under the age of 18 are presumed to have different needs from adults. The juvenile justice system strongly mirrors the components of the regular justice system, including arrest, arraignment, detainment, hearings, appeals, incarceration, probation, and parole, and a child has all the same rights as an adult. However, it places overall greater emphasis on habilitation and rehabilitation. Once that person reaches legal adulthood, they can request to have their **juvenile records** sealed or expunged.

juvenile record

Today, it is understood that the brains of children and teens tend to lack impulse control and good judgment. As a result, young people may impulsively commit criminal acts that do not necessarily reflect their character. By having their juvenile records sealed, they have the possibility of starting over, with a clean slate, once they reach age 18. Contrary to how it is depicted in pop culture, the process of sealing is not automatic, and it can be expensive and arduous. Most states require a proactive effort to have juvenile records sealed or expunged (i.e., deleted entirely); and most do not allow those records to be sealed if the juvenile committed a felony offense such as murder.

juvie

An abbreviation of juvenile detention center. Ex: "Jack's in juvie but hopes to come home soon."

K

keister

To hide something such as **drugs** in the anal cavity (US contemporary prison slang).

ketamine

Ketamine (ketamine hydrochloride) is a dissociative anesthetic and analgesic that is frequently used as a **date-rape drug** because it paralyzes its victim for at least a brief period of time. Its dissociative effects are so powerful they can cause auditory and visual hallucinations. When mixed with other depressant drugs and **alcohol**, ketamine's depressant effect on the airways can be deadly. There is also a risk that the temporary paralysis it induces can cause a victim to be unable to clear their airways, thereby choking to death. Ketamine can be detected in urine up to three to five days after ingestion. Street names include: Barry Farrell; blind squid; cat food; cat Valium; donkey; green; green K; honey oil; jet; jet K; K; keller; Kelly's day; K-hold; kit kat; kitty flip; K-ways; purple; Special K; special la coke; super acid; super C; vitamin K; wobble; wonky.

keylogger

Nondestructive program that is designed to log every keystroke made on a computer. The information that is collected can then be saved as a file and/or sent to another computer on the network or over the internet, making it possible for someone else to see every keystroke that was made on a particular system. Using this information, a **cracker** can recreate your usernames and passwords, putting all kinds of data and information at risk. Some companies install keyloggers on employee computers to track usage and ensure that systems are not being used for unintended purposes. Keyloggers are, for obvious reasons, often considered to be **spyware**.

kick up

US **Mafia** term for passing the proceeds of criminal activity up the chain of command.

kidnapper

Historically, a kidnapper is someone who abducts children; also a decoy for street robberies (UK thieves' **cant**, historical slang). The word "kidd" for a child was also thieves' **cant** or historical slang. The contemporary word kidnapper is a direct contraction of the original usage and now means someone who abducts a person of any age.

kill

To cause the death of or end of the life of a person, animal, or plant. In crime fiction, especially **hard-boiled**, detective, and gangster fiction, there are numerous terms for "to kill" including: annihilate; assassinate; blip off; blow; bop; bump; bump off; burn; chill off; croak; cut down; decimate; do for; do away with; do in; eradicate; erase; euthanize; execute; finish; finish off; get; ice; knock off; liquidate; massacre; murder; **neutralize**; obliterate; off; put away; pop; poop; rub out; scrag; snuff; take out; total; waste; whack; wipe; zap; zotz.

As a noun, a kill can be anything that has been slaughtered, including an animal or a person.

Killing, The

Successful Danish **police procedural** TV series (*Forbrydelsen* [The Crime] in Danish) created by Søren Sveistrup and first broadcast on national TV station DR1 on January 7, 2007. Since then, it has been transmitted worldwide with the US remake first airing in 2011. The original version is set in Copenhagen, and revolves around Detective Inspector Sarah Lund, played by Sofie Gråbøl. It is notable in boosting the popularity of the hugely successful genre known as **Scandi noir**.

kite

Originally a worthless check, this now refers to any check. To say you were going to "fly a kite" meant you were going to pass a bad check. Also US prison slang for an illicit letter that is passed from **cell** to cell, sometimes shaped like a kite and used for purposes such as placing orders for **drugs**. ▶**kiter** Someone who writes bad checks (UK/US slang in popular use in 1980s–1990s and still in use today).

kom ind

Danish for "come in," often seen in **Scandi noir**.

L

larceny

Larceny is defined in the US as the unlawful taking, carrying, leading, or riding away of property from the possession or constructive possession of another or **attempting** to commit these acts. Larceny includes **shoplifting**, **pickpocketing**, purse-snatching, bicycle **theft,** and similar acts in which no use of force, violence, or **fraud** occurs.

latent print

One of three categories of **fingerprints** that can be found at a **crime scene**, the others being **impressed** and **patent prints**. A latent print is an impression that is not visible to the naked eye. They are composed of the sweat, skin salts and oils and tiny particles of dirt that we all carry and transfer from our hands even when they appear clean. Latent prints are made visible using magnesium powder, which is dusted over surfaces to illuminate them so they can then be **lifted**. They can also be revealed through the use of chemicals including cyanoacrylate (found in superglue) and silver nitrate.

law enforcement

Generic term for the activities of agencies responsible for maintaining public order and enforcing the law. These include the prevention, detection, and **investigation** of crime, and the apprehension of criminals to protect people, places and things from criminal activity.

lawful search

Examination, authorized by law, of a specific person, property, or area to locate specified property **evidence**, or of a specific person for the purpose of seizing such property or evidence.

L

laws, strange or weird

Many countries have strange or obscure laws that are often left over from archaic legislation, although some are surprisingly modern. In the UK, some examples include:

- All beached whales and sturgeons must be offered to the reigning monarch.
- It is illegal to be drunk in a pub.
- MPs are not allowed to wear armor in parliament.
- It is an offense to be drunk and in charge of cattle in England and Wales.
- It is illegal to handle a salmon in suspicious circumstances.

In the US, some state laws are equally bizarre:

- In Idaho, cannibalism is strictly prohibited and punishable by up to 14 years in prison, except under "life-threatening conditions as the only apparent means of survival."
- In Kentucky, every legislator, public officer, and lawyer must take an oath stating that they have not fought a duel with **deadly weapons**.
- In Maryland, anyone "pretending to forecast or foretell the future of another by cards, palm-reading, or any other scheme, practice, or device" can be found guilty of a **misdemeanor** and fined up to $500, or even serve time in jail.
- In Tennessee, it is a Class A misdemeanor to deliberately hunt, trap, or harm an albino deer.

Strange laws are not confined to the UK and US. In Mexico you may not lift your feet from the pedals if you are riding a bicycle; in Switzerland it is forbidden to hike while naked; and you are not permitted to urinate in the sea in Portugal, although how they police that last one is anyone's guess.

lay

Job. **Hard-boiled** fiction term, as used by Phillip Marlowe in *The Big Sleep* (1939) when he's describing a private detective on a confidential job: "Private—on a confidential lay." Also used to describe a situation: "I gave him the lay"; that is, "I told him where things stood" (as in "lie of the land").

L

lead

Source or potential source of information that may provide a clue or **evidence** in the **investigation** of a crime. Also, in **intelligence** usage, a person with potential for exploitation or any source of information that, if exploited, may reveal information of value in the conduct of an intelligence operation or investigation.

lead bullet

Compact **bullet** formed by a lead alloy.

leave (legal)

A request for permission from the court to do something that is not routine. Typically, in order to obtain a leave from the court, an applicant must fill out paperwork, serve them to the other party, and appear in court to explain why leave should be granted. It's most commonly used to ask to file papers beyond some deadline.

legal thriller
See **courtroom drama**.

legend
See **cover legend**.

leng
Weapon or gun (UK/US contemporary slang).

lethal
Certain to or intended to cause death. Can be used of force, weapons, intent, or quantity, especially where **drugs** are concerned.

lift
A lift is the adhesive tape or another medium used when **fingerprints** need to be lifted, or recovered, and preserved from a **crime scene** or from **evidence**. Electrostatic, gelatin, and adhesive lifts are all common methods.

light weapon
Light weapons, according to NATO definitions, are collective **firearms** designed to be used by two or three persons, though some of them can be used single-handedly.

listening post
Secure site at which signals from an audio operation are received and/or monitored.

Little, Samuel
Samuel Little (b. 1940) has been confirmed by the **Federal Bureau of Investigation** as the most prolific **serial killer** in American history. He has confessed to 93 murders with at least 50 of those having been confirmed so far by **law enforcement**. Little claims to have strangled his victims between 1970 and 2005, although many of those deaths

were initially attributed to overdoses or natural causes. The FBI's **Violent Criminal Apprehension Program** (ViCAP) began to link Little, who was already serving three life **sentences** without **parole**, to these crimes in 2014. He had initially been **arrested** in 2012 on **drugs charges** in California and **DNA** then taken while he was in **custody** linked him to three unsolved homicides in the 1980s. A Texas Ranger went to interview the septuagenarian in 2017 and Little confessed to killing his victims—who were mostly prostitutes or otherwise living on the fringes of society—on camera from behind bars. He drew portraits of 30 of them, many of them African American like himself, and described others as well as how he had killed each one. He has already pleaded guilty to murdering four women in Ohio, and the FBI has provided information about five more homicides in Florida, Arkansas, Kentucky, Nevada, and Louisiana, asking the public for help in identifying the victims. Authorities in Knoxville, Tennessee, have said that a woman named Martha Cunningham, whose body was found in 1975, is also likely to be a victim of Little. Little thought he would never be caught for his crimes because no one was accounting for his victims, but the FBI is now determined to identify each one to bring closure to their families and loved ones.

lividity

Lividity, also known as livor mortis or postmortem hypostatis, is the process by which blood stops flowing around the body when the heart stops pumping after death. The blood normally responds to gravity, which means that someone found lying on their back will have all the blood from their front draining toward the ground. Lividity results in dark purple discoloration of the body, and any part of the body that has been in prolonged contact with a hard surface such as the floor will display signs of it. Lividity starts to work through the body within half an hour of the heart stopping and can continue for up to 12 hours. For the first six hours after it has begun, it can be disturbed by any movement of the body but after that point the blood vessels begin to break down and it cannot be altered. This means that lividity is also used as a reliable indicator of time of death.

load

Combination of components used to assemble a gun **cartridge**. Load also refers to the act of putting **ammunition** into the **chamber** of a firearm.

local nick

Term for local police station used by the police and criminals (UK contemporary slang).

locked-room mystery

The locked-room mystery, a subgenre of detective fiction, involves a **crime scene** from which it is apparently impossible for a perpetrator to get into and out of undetected (i.e., a "locked room"). Typically, the crime is a murder and the perpetrator appears to have vanished into thin air. As with classic detective fiction, the reader is presented with the mystery to be solved along with the clues so they can attempt to deduce what has happened along with the detective or investigator.

loss of life

Prison slang for loss of privileges due to minor infractions. Example: "You're not going to see Pam in the yard today, she's on loss of life."

Locard's Exchange Principle

Dr. Edmond Locard (1877–1966), "the Sherlock Holmes of France," was a French criminologist and pioneer of **forensic** science who came up with a theory that can be summarized as "every contact leaves a trace." He believed that a perpetrator takes something into a **crime scene** and also takes something from it whether that be hair, clothing fibers, blood traces, or **fingerprints**. Both can be used as **forensic evidence**. This became known as Locard's Exchange Principle and is the foundation of all forensic science today.

lock-down

Locking **cells** either at set times or as a response to a particular situation (UK and US contemporary prison slang).

L

logic bomb

Malicious program designed to execute when a certain criterion is met. A logic bomb can be designed to execute when a particular file is accessed, or when a certain key combination is pressed, or through the actioning of any other event or task that is possible to be tracked on a computer. The logic bomb remains dormant until the trigger event occurs.

LSD

See Lysergic Acid Diethylamide.

luminol

Luminol is a powder compound composed of carbon, hydrogen, oxygen, and nitrogen. It is mixed with hydrogen peroxide and an alkali such as sodium hydroxide to create the liquid that is sprayed at **crime scenes** to detect traces of blood. It does so by luminescing in the presence of blood, emitting its characteristic blue glow that is bright enough to see in a dark room. This is caused by a reaction between the hydrogen peroxide and luminol accelerated by the iron contained in hemoglobin. The same reaction can occur in the presence of other substances including feces and bleach.

lysergic acid diethylamide (LSD)

LSD, also known as "acid," is a powerful **hallucinogenic drug** that is sold as blotters; or in liquid form; or as micro dots known as pellets. The liquid form has no taste, but the paper form tastes of paper. LSD **trips** can last for hours and cause disturbing hallucinations as well as euphoria, excitement, paranoia, or aggression, depending on the person's state of mind when they take the drug. LSD is not **addictive**, although prolonged use requires increased dosage. As a **Schedule I** drug, possession of LSD is a felony. Criminal penalties for possession, use, manufacture, or distribution vary widely from state to state. Punishment ranges from a fine to federal prison time. Ironically, the most famous American advocate of LSD, Timothy Leary, was sentenced to 20 years in federal prison for possession of marijuana, not LSD, which was legal in the US during the years of his early advocacy.

LSD's street names include: aceite; acelide; acid; acido; Alice; angels in the sky; animal; Avandaro; backbreaker (LSD mixed with **strychnine**); barrel; Bart Simpson; battery acid; beast; big D; black acid (LSD mixed with **PCP**); black star; black sunshine; black tabs; *blanco de España*; blotter acid; blotter cube; blue acid; blue barrel; blue chair; blue cheer; blue heaven; blue microdots; blue mist; blue moon; blue sky; blue star; blue tabs; *bomba*; brown bomber; brown dots;

California sunshine; cherry dome; chief; Chinese dragons; *Cid*; coffee; *colorines*; conductor; contact lens; crackers; crystal tea; cubo; cupcakes; dental floss; dinosaurs; *divina*; domes; dots; double dome; *El Cid*; electric Kool-Aid; *elefante blanco*; Ellis Day; fields; flash; flat blues; ghost; golden dragon; golf balls; goofy; gota; grape parfait; green wedge; gray shields; hats; Hawaiian sunshine; hawk; haze; headlights; heavenly blue; hits; instant zen; Jesus Christ acid; kaleidoscope; Leary; lens; *lentejuela*; lime acid; live, spit and die; *lluvia de estrellas*; Looney Tunes; Lucy; *maje*; mellow yellow; mica; microdot; *micropunto azul* (white tablet with drop of blue LSD); *micropunto morado* (white tablet with drop of purple LSD); Mighty Quinn; mind detergent; Mother of God; *mureler*; nave; newspapers; orange barrels; orange cubes; orange haze; orange micros; orange wedges; owsley; paper acid; pearly gates; pellets; phoenix; pink blotters; Pink Panther; pink robots; pink wedges; pink witches; pizza; pop; potato; pure love; purple barrels; purple haze; purple hearts; purple flats; recycle; royal blues; Russian sickles; sacrament; *sandoz*; smears; square dancing tickets; sugar cubes; sugar lumps; sunshine; superman; tabs; *tacatosa*; tail lights; teddy bears; ticket; Uncle Sid; valley dolls; vodka acid; wedding bells; wedge; white dust; white fluff; white lightening; white owsley; window glass; window pane; yellow dimples; yellow sunshine; zen.

M

MacDonald Triad
This is the name given to the three classic behaviors
that, if exhibited in childhood, were claimed to be a
predictor of violent tendencies in later life. These
behaviors are: 1) excessive bedwetting beyond the age
of five, 2) cruelty to animals, 3) and fire starting. The
phrase was coined in a 1963 paper entitled "The
Threat to Kill" published in *The American Manual of
Psychiatry* by J. M. MacDonald. MacDonald's research
group was small and unrepresentative, as were subsequent, badly designed groups that bore out his results.
When tested in larger groups with better controls, his
results could not be replicated. The MacDonald Triad
cannot therefore be considered a reliable predictor of
future murderers or serial killers despite the reliance
on it by some authors and even criminologists.

machine
Machine gun (US/Jamaican contemporary gang slang).

machine gun
Also known as a fully **automatic firearm**. A weapon that
fires rapidly and repeatedly without requiring separate
pressure on the **trigger** each time. The gun will continue
to fire until the trigger is released or the supply of **ammunition** is exhausted. ▶ **machine pistol** Fully **automatic
handgun** such as the **Glock 18**. The term machine pistol
can also be used to refer to a **submachine gun**.

made man

Someone who has been inducted into the US **Mafia**.

Mafia

The term Mafia originated with the Sicilian **organized crime** families who formed a loose syndicate although they do not use the word, preferring to refer to themselves as **Cosa Nostra**, meaning "our thing." Through generations of emigration, the Sicilian Mafia spread to the US and Canada, carrying out their traditional activities of protection racketeering or the provision of security services to businesses in exchange for payment and under threat of violence. Smuggling, loan sharking, vote rigging, and murder are other traditional Sicilian Mafia activities, which have been adopted by other organized crime syndicates who emulate the original gangsters. There are now international organizations referred to as Mafias in the media, although they prefer to use their own names such as *Bratva* (Russian), *Yakuza* (Japanese), *La Eme* (Mexican) and *Mutra* (Bulgarian). **Drug trafficking** and prostitution rackets are now major activities for most Mafia organizations.

magazine

Spring-loaded box or tube that holds **cartridges** ready for **loading** into the **chamber** of a repeating or self-loading gun. It may be removable or an integral/fixed part of the **firearm**.

Magnum

Term commonly used to describe a gun **cartridge** that is longer than a standard cartridge or shell of a given **caliber** with an increase over standard performance.

M

mainlining

Act of injecting an **illegal drug**, especially **heroin** or **cocaine**, into a large vein.

malice aforethought

The prior intention to kill or cause harm to a victim. Malice aforethought helps establish the mindset that distinguishes between the charge of **manslaughter**, or **murder**. It is different from premeditation in that it does not refer to a coherent plan of action.

malware

Malicious program that causes damage to a computer or computer system. It includes **viruses**, **Trojans**, **worms**, **time bombs**, **logic bombs** or anything else intended to cause damage upon the execution of the **payload**.

M

Manson, Charles (1934–2017)

Perhaps the most famous conman and cult leader in American history, Manson achieved lasting notoriety for his role in the 1969 death of Sharon Tate, the pregnant wife of director Roman Polanski. Four other innocent people also died in the Tate–Polanski home that night. Manson then instructed his followers, known as his "Family," to murder a random couple, the LaBiancas, and frame the Black Panthers for the deaths. As a lifelong white supremacist and member of the neo-Nazi group, the **Aryan Brotherhood**, Manson was hoping to start a race war, which he called "Helter Skelter." This became the title of a book (1974) subsequently written by Vincent Bugliosi, the lawyer who successfully prosecuted the Manson Family. In 1975, four years after Manson was convicted of first-degree murder and sent to prison, one of his loyal followers, Lynette "Squeaky" Fromme, attempted to assassinate President Gerald Ford.

manslaughter

Manslaughter is a form of **homicide** where one person kills another but without **malice aforethought**. It is a lesser crime than murder but is still a crime; this distinguishes it from **accidental killing**, or from killing in **self-defense**, both of which are not. Manslaughter can be either voluntary (such as **crimes of passion**) or involuntary (such as vehicular homicide where speeding but no drugs or drinking was involved).

marking

Types of marking on a gun include letters, **serial numbers**, words or symbols that are stamped, rolled, cast, or engraved on the **firearm** to designate the manufacturer, model, origin, **caliber** or **gauge**, choke (tapered constriction of a gun barrel), material, or proof that the gun is safe to be used with its designated ammunition. Important in the identification of a gun, markings are often filed off or otherwise removed by criminals who want a weapon to be untraceable.

M

martial arts weapon

Martial arts weapons include the nunchaku, kama, kasari-fundo, octagon sai, tonfa, and Chinese star.

Martin, Trayvon

In 2012, George Zimmerman fatally shot a 17-year-old Black teen named Trayvon Martin, who was walking back to his father's fiancée's townhouse in Sanford, Florida. Police initially refused to detain or charge Zimmerman, who claimed **self-defense** despite the fact that he'd been following an unarmed teenage boy at night. The police claimed that, under Florida's **stand your ground laws**, they had no grounds to arrest him.

Following a massive public outcry, including national media and grassroots campaigns demanding "Justice for

Trayvon," police reluctantly arrested Zimmerman, charging him with **second degree murder** and **manslaughter**. The **stand your ground** defense was not used by his lawyers, but the judge instructed the jury that Zimmerman had no **duty to retreat**, and had every right to invoke stand your ground in self-defense. Following a jury trial, he was acquitted of all charges. Subsequently, the Department of Justice declined to prosecute him on the civil rights (**hate crime**) aspects of the case. In 2016, Zimmerman sold the gun used to kill Martin for $250,000 on an online gun auction site.

At the time of his death, Martin had been wearing a hoodie and holding a packet of Skittles candy, which he had just purchased at a nearby convenience store. The hoodie remains an enduring symbol of Justice for Trayvon.

M

mask of sanity

The name given to the ability of some psychopaths to blend in thanks to their adoption of a mask of apparently normal behavior. Despite this apparently normal, intelligent, and even charming behavior, these psychopaths are unable to experience genuine emotions, and this leads to destructive or self-destructive behavior. It was coined by the psychiatrist Hervey M. Cleckley in his book *The Mask of Sanity: An Attempt to Clarify Some Issues About the So-Called Psychopathic Personality*, first published in 1941 and based on his interviews with patients in a locked institution. Famous criminal examples include **Ted Bundy**, **Charles Manson**, and **John Wayne Gacy**.

mass incarceration

"Mass incarceration" refers to the sheer number of people physically incarcerated in the US, which has the highest number of incarcerated people in the world. Currently, 2.3 million people are being held in a carceral institution, such as a state prison, county jail, mental hospital, or military jail. In other words, 4 million more people are in jail than the combined total populations of Wyoming, Vermont, and Alaska. However, this figure does not tell the whole story: in 2018, 10.6 million people were also going to/getting out of **jail**, with an average stay of 25 days in 2016 (Bureau of Justice Statistics). Many millions more were out with a **bench warrant**, on probation or parole, or otherwise engaged directly with the prison system without necessarily **being inside.**

mass murder

Also known as multicide, a mass murder is the intentional homicidal killing of four or more people at the same time (within 24 hours), in the same geographical location, and often by the same person. When carried out by dictators or authoritarian states, mass murder is called genocide, which is mass killing of entire groups targeted due to ethnicity, race, or religion.

mass murderer

Cousin to the **serial killer**, the mass murderer is notably lacking in definitive warning traits. Typically male and interested in weapons, the mass murderer could be anyone. Though he might have some form of **antisocial personality disorder (APD)**, he is not typified by it. In the US, he is perhaps most closely identified with the figure of the **cult** leader and the school shooter. According to a 2001 Department of Justice white paper on mass murder, other types of mass murderer include "the **pseudocommando**, the disciple (such as the cult disciples of Charles

Manson), the **family annihilator,** the religious/ideological killer, the disgruntled citizen, the disgruntled employee, the hit and run killer (i.e., vehicular homicide with mass casualties), and the psychotic."

master program

In **cybercrime**, a master program is the program a **cracker** uses remotely to transmit commands to infected **zombie drones**, normally to carry out denial of service (DoS) attacks or **spam** attacks.

max out

In reference to prisons, it's slang for the maximum number of years the law stipulates that you can be held on a charge. Prisoners who are "maxed out" can be dangerous, as they have no incentive to maintain good behavior.

MDMA

MDMA (3,4-methylenedioxy-methamphetamine) was originally developed in 1912 by Merck and used in **psychological warfare** experiments by the US Army in 1953. MDMA in its original form was used to lower inhibitions. It did not become known as a party **drug** until the 1970s and was only made illegal in 1985 due to safety concerns. MDMA is particularly dangerous because the pills now being sold on the street may contain a variety of substances including rat **poison, heroin, cocaine,** and **methamphetamine**, while being composed of little or no actual MDMA. A number of deaths, half of them of teenagers, have resulted from taking adulterated MDMA pills. MDMA is also known as: Adam; baby slits; beans; blue kisses; blue Superman; bomb; booty juice (dissolved in liquid); candy; chocolate chips; clarity; dancing shoes; decadence; disco biscuit; doctor; domex (ecstasy mixed with **PCP**); drop; E; E-bomb; essence; Eve; go; goog; green apple; happy pill; hug; hug drug; Kleenex; love doctor; love drug; love flip (taken with mescaline); Love Potion #9; love trip (ecstasy mixed with mescaline); lover's speed; Malcolm X; moon rock; peace; pingaz; pinger; roll; rolling; running; scooby snacks; skittle; smack; slit; smartie; speed for lovers; sweet; tacha; thizz; vitamin E; vowel; white Mercedes; X; XTC; yoke.

medical examiner (ME)

The medical examiner is a medically trained professional who officially investigates suspicious deaths or those that occur in unusual circumstances. The ME carries out post-mortems and can initiate inquests. In the UK, a medical examiner must have undergone formal medical training and will usually also be trained in pathology. In the US, most jurisdictions require formal medical training and further training in pathology, but some have less stringent requirements. A medical examiner has wide-ranging duties and must be able to rely on extensive **forensic** knowledge.

mental disorder and crime

It is a truism oft repeated that people suffering from mental disorder are more likely to be victims of a crime than a perpetrator. It is also true that most individuals with mental disorders are not violent, and most violent individuals do not have a mental disorder.

More to the point, however, poor public policy and the decades-long defunding of social services at federal, state, and local levels has led to a severe lack of support treatments for the mentally unwell, leading to a mental health crisis in the US and criminalizing mental illness. As a result of mental institutions being defunded or shut down across the country, the three largest de facto mental institutions in America are the Los Angeles County Jail, **Riker's Island**, and Cook County Jail in Chicago.

mental disorder defense

Popularly known as the "insanity defense," the mental disorder defense grounds itself in the claim that the defendant was temporarily insane at the time they committed the crime in question. Typically associated with **crimes of passion**, it has also been increasingly used in the US to defend individuals accused of **hate crimes**. In the US, the mental disorder defense was first used in 1859 by New York Congressman Daniel Sickles after he shot his wife's lover in broad daylight in front of the White House. Sickles was not only acquitted, he held and was reelected to his seat in Congress. The notoriety of the case, plus the high profile of everyone involved (the wife's lover was a US attorney and son of Francis Scott Key, lyricist of the "Star Spangled Banner") led to the insanity defense's association with crimes of passion.

M

metabolite

Substance produced by metabolism or that is necessary for the metabolic process. It is what is left after the body breaks down a substance or changes it into another chemical. Most **drugs** metabolize in the body and the metabolites they produce are identified through **forensic toxicology**.

metallic cartridge

Ammunition that has a metallic **cartridge case**.

methamphetamine

Methamphetamine is a stronger form of **amphetamine**. It is highly **addictive** and is the second most popular **illegal drug** globally after **cannabis**. It can be injected, snorted, or swallowed and is a powerful **stimulant** but can cause brain damage and psychosis, among other health risks. Smoking the purer crystalline form known as crystal meth results in an intense high similar to that produced by **crack cocaine**, although it lasts longer. Methamphetamine is a Class B drug in the UK unless prepared for injection, when it becomes Class A. It is also commonly called: accordion; amp; aqua; *arroz*; assembled (crystal meth); *batu*; *begok*; biker's coffee; blue; blue bell ice cream; beers; bottles; *bucio*; Bud Light; bump; *cajitas*; chalk; chandelier; *chavalone*; chicken; chicken feed; chicken powder; Chris; Christine; Christy; clear; clothing cleaner; cold; cold one; Colorado rockies; crank; cream; cri-cri; crink; crisco; Crissy; crypto; crystal; *cuadro*; day; diamond; dunk; *El Gata Diablo*; evil sister; eye glasses; fire; fizz; flowers; *foco*; food; *frio*; fruit; *gak*; garbage; G-funk; gifts; girls; glass; go-fast; go-go; goofball (methamphetamine mixed with **heroin**); groceries; hard ones; hare; Hawaiian salt; hielo; hiropon; hot ice; hubbers; ice; ice cream; ice water; icehead; jale; jug of water; LA glass; LA ice; lemons; lemon drop; light; light beige; *livianas*; *madera*; mamph; meth; methlies quick; Mexican crack; Mexican crank; Miss Girl; *montura*; motor; *muchacha*; nails; one pot; no-doze; paint; *pantalones*; *patudas*; peanut butter crank; *piñata*; pointy ones; *pollito*; popsicle; purple; *raspado*; rims; rocket fuel; salt; *shabu*; shards; shatter; shaved ice; shiny girl; small girl; soap dope; soft ones; speed; speed dog; spicy kind; spin; stove top; stuff; super ice; table; tina; tires; trash; truck; Tupperware; tweak; unassembled (powder meth); uppers; *Ventanas*; *vidrio*; walking zombie; water; wazz; white; whizz; windows; witches teeth; yaba; yellow barn; yellow cake; yellow kind; zip.

M

Mine-Resistant Ambush Protected vehicle (MRAP)

The Mine-Resistant Ambush Protected vehicle (MRAP) was invented by the Department of Defense as a counter-insurgency strategy to be able to fight IED attacks in Iraq and Afghanistan. In 2014, the Los Angeles School Department acquired MRAPS.

Miranda rights

In 1966, Ernesto Miranda's **confession** was tossed following a landmark Supreme Court legal case, Miranda v. Arizona, which ruled that he was unaware of his Constitutional rights upon his arrest, hence what he'd told law enforcement was inadmissible on the grounds of self-incrimination. Since then, law enforcement must convey the necessary information in the famous phrase: "You have the right to remain silent. Anything you say can and will be used against you in a court of law. You have the right to an attorney. If you cannot afford an attorney, one will be provided for you. Do you understand the rights I have just read to you? With these rights in mind, do you wish to speak to me?" Despite what is depicted in television shows, a suspect is generally not Mirandized at the time of arrest but while in custodial interrogation.

misdemeanor

A misdemeanor offense is a low-level crime such as jaywalking, loitering, public lewdness, or intoxication. Annually, 13 million Americans enter the criminal justice system for a misdemeanor arrest, which can have devastating collateral effects and begin the cycle of **jail churn**. Critics point out that misdemeanor arrests disproportionately target low-income or disenfranchised people, who cannot afford court costs or a private lawyer to properly defend them, and will plead guilty even if innocent to avoid jail time.

MI5

MI5 (Military Intelligence, Section 5) is officially known as the **Security Service** and is the UK's domestic and **counterintelligence** security **agency**. It deals with threats to national security including terrorism, cyber threats and **espionage** while protecting the UK's parliamentary and economic interests. It is also concerned with counter-proliferation against regimes that have developed **weapons of mass destruction** (WMDs) and act in contravention of United Nations resolutions, develop **clandestine** weapons, or refuse to sign up to the Non-Proliferation Treaty. MI5 gathers **intelligence**, works in partnership with other national and international agencies, and carries out clandestine and **covert** operations both in the UK and abroad. It is based at Thames House in London and has featured in books, films and TV series, including *Spooks* (2002–2011), which was renamed *MI-5* in the US.

MI6

MI6 (Military Intelligence, Section 6) is officially known as the Secret Intelligence Service (SIS) and is the UK government's **foreign intelligence** service. Its role is the **covert** gathering and analysis of **human intelligence** overseas in order to protect the United Kingdom. Since 1995, MI6 has been headquartered at 85 Vauxhall Cross on the Albert Embankment in London, a building famously featured in the James Bond film *The World Is Not Enough* (1999). Bond is, of course, a fictional MI6 operative and the agency has also been featured in numerous books, films, and TV series, notably those works of John le Carré, a former SIS **agent**, whose real name is David Cornwell.

missing children

Minor children going missing is cause for serious alarm. Once it is reported, it will immediately trigger an **Amber**

Alert. The reasons for a child's disappearance can vary widely, from parental kidnapping to running away from home. These cases are coordinated by the National Center for **Missing and Exploited Children (NCMEC)**.

missing person

A missing person is an individual who has disappeared from their expected location and whose whereabouts cannot be readily confirmed. There are many reasons why adults go missing, including dementia or simply getting lost. A missing person should be reported immediately, though police may not take action until 24 or 48 hours have passed. It is not illegal to disappear from your own life unless it is for purposes of evading the law. When this is the case, a missing person is called a **fugitive**.

MO

See modus operandi.

Mob

Single **Mafia** family or a term referring to all **organized crime** families, or Mafia. ▶**mobbed up** Connected to the Mob. ▶**mobster** Someone who is part of the Mafia or belongs to the Mob.

modus operandi (MO)

The modus operandi (Latin for "way of operating") or MO is the particular way or method in which someone does something. In the context of criminal **investigations** it is the particular method or pattern used by a criminal that indicates their involvement in more than one crime.

mole

Member of an organization such as the police or **intelligence** service who is **spying** and reporting on their own organization. The mole may already be working for the intelligence service or other highly **sensitive** organization when they begin divulging information, or they may be inserted into it for that purpose. Quite often a mole is a potential defector who agrees to spy in return for help defecting. In John le Carré's novel *Tinker, Tailor, Soldier, Spy* (1974), his protagonist Smiley has to hunt down a mole in **MI6**/Secret Intelligence Service. ▶ **mole hunt** Term popularized by John le Carré for an **investigation** conducted into a suspected mole or hostile penetration.

moll buzzer

Someone who only steals from women (US historical slang).

money laundering

Process used to disguise the origin of what are usually large amounts of money obtained from criminal or illicit activity, and to make it seem as if it has come from a legitimate source. The process can include property purchases, shell companies that appear legitimate but do not have any assets or perform any business activities, and investment schemes. Money laundering helps to finance **organized crime** and terrorist activity, threatening national and international security.

Moors Murders

The Moors Murders was a series of murders that took place in and around Manchester in the United Kingdom between July 1963 and October 1965. The murders were carried out by Ian Brady and Myra Hindley and all the victims were children. Of the five victims, who were aged between 10 and 17 years old, at least four had been sexually **assaulted**. Brady and Hindley were **charged** with the murders of three of the victims. Although they both pleaded not guilty, photographs of the moors where the murders took place were discovered in a suitcase belonging to the couple and displayed in court along with pornographic photographs of one of their victims, Lesley Ann Downey, with a scarf tied across her mouth. A tape recording was also played in court of the torture of Lesley Ann Downey who could be heard begging and screaming for help. Brady and Hindley both received life **sentences**. In 1985, Brady reportedly confessed to two more of the murders and later he and Hindley were taken separately to Saddleworth Moor where two of their other victims had been discovered. After a subsequent visit to the moor by Hindley in 1987, the body of Pauline Reade, their first victim, was discovered a hundred yards from where that of Lesley Ann Downey had been found. Myra Hindley was depicted by the press as the most evil woman in Britain and, despite making several **appeals** against her life sentence, was never released. She died in 2002, aged 60. Ian Brady was diagnosed as a psychopath in 1985 and stated that he never wished to be released, repeatedly asking to be allowed to die. He died in 2017, aged 79, and took the whereabouts of the remains of one of his victims, Keith Bennett, to his grave.

Moscow Rules

Ultimate **tradecraft** methods for use in the most hostile operational environments. During the Cold War, Moscow was considered the most difficult operating environment for a **spy** or **intelligence agent** or operative.

motive

Reason someone commits an offense or crime. Intent is a factor in deciding guilt or innocence and therefore establishing motive can be vital along with the other important factors of means and opportunity.

MRAP

See **Mine-Resistant Ambush Protected vehicle.**

mule

In the illegal drug trade, a mule is a person smuggling contraband on their person across the border. Mules might tape contraband tightly to their torso, or, even more dangerously, they might swallow tiny balloons filled with drugs. In money-laundering schemes, a money mule is also known as a smurfer.

Munchausen syndrome by proxy

Mental illness that manifests in a carer or caregiver of a child. In seeking attention for themselves, the carer or caregiver will create symptoms and illnesses in a child, even to the point of harming the child in the process. If the child is harmed, this is child abuse and a criminal offense. Sometimes the child is killed, as in the **cases** of Marybeth Tinning of New York, who is suspected of murdering eight of her nine children although she was only convicted of the death of the youngest, for which she was **charged** with second-degree murder; and the British nurse Beverley Allitt (see **angel of death**), who killed 4 of her patients and was charged with harming 11 others.

M

muppet

Muppet stands for "Most Useless Police Person Ever Trained" and is considered a term of endearment between officers when engaged in banter. Also a general term for a foolish person.

murder

See **first-degree murder; homicide; mass murder; serial killer.**

murderabilia

A portmanteau linking "murder" and "memorabilia," murderabilia is any collectible directly connected to a famous murder or murderer. Virtually anything linked to a sensational crime can be murderabilia, such as the gun that George Zimmerman used to shoot and kill **Trayvon Martin**.

musket

Antiquated military matchlock, flintlock, or wheel-lock shoulder **firearm** with long **smooth-bore barrel**.

muzzle

Forward end of a gun **barrel** from which the **bullet** or **shot** emerges.

M

N

narcissistic personality disorder (NPD)
Traits of a person with NPD include an exaggerated sense of self-importance, preoccupation with dreams of unlimited power, a need for excessive admiration, and an outsize sense of entitlement. Narcissists will resort to lying and criminality to obtain the power and status they believe the world owes them, and are incapable of admitting wrongdoing.

narcissistic sociopathy
When **narcissistic personality disorder (NPD)** combines with **antisocial personality disorder (APD)**, the result is narcissistic sociopathy. The sociopathy will intensify NPD to worsen outcomes. Narcissistic sociopaths will exploit others to obtain their goals and are unable to feel guilt about using others as pawns. They tend to commit crimes because they do not believe laws apply to them.

narcoterrorism
Terrorism that is linked to illicit **drug trafficking**.

National Center for Missing and Exploited Children (NCMEC)
A private, not-for-profit organization established by US Congress to handle cases of missing or exploited children from infancy to age 20.

National Crime Information Center (NCIC)
Launched in 1967 and run by the FBI, the NCIC currently hosts over 17 million records divided into 21 categories of

files: article files (stolen articles); homeland security files; critical infrastructure identification files; boat files (stolen boats); foreign fugitive files; gang files; gun files; identity theft files; immigration violator files; license plate files; missing persons files; protection order files; protective interest files (records on individuals who might pose a threat to the physical safety of protectees or their imme-diate families); securities files (embezzlement, ransoms, counterfeit securities); supervised release files; unidenti-fied persons files; vehicle files (stolen vehicles, vehicles involved in the commission of crimes); vehicle and boat parts files (stolen vehicle or boat parts); and records on stolen license plates. Its purpose is to serve as a clearing-house of data available to law enforcement agencies across the US.

National Cyber Investigative Joint Task Force (NCIJTF)

The **Federal Bureau of Investigation** is responsible for developing and supporting the NCIJTF, which is the focal point for all US government agencies to coordinate, inte-grate and share information related to all domestic cyber-threat **investigations**. It includes 19 **intelligence** and **law enforcement** agencies that work together to iden-tify key players and schemes. It aims to predict and prevent **cyberattacks** as well as pursue the perpetrators behind them.

National Fraud Intelligence Bureau (NFIB)

The National Fraud Intelligence Bureau sits alongside Action Fraud, the national fraud and **cybercrime** reporting center, within the **City of London Police**, which acts as the national lead for economic crime. The NFIB receives the millions of Action Fraud reports of **fraud** and cybercrime. These are used by the NFIB to identify serial offenders, organized-crime groups, and to spot emerging crime types. It does this through assessment and analysis, data matching from different parts of the country and disseminating reports for **investigation**. Bank accounts, websites, and phone numbers that are used by fraudsters can be taken down by the NFIB.

National Incident-Based Reporting System (NIBRS)

This is an incident-based reporting system used by **law enforcement** agencies in the United States for collecting and reporting data on crimes. Local, state, and federal agencies generate NIBRS data from their records management systems. Data is collected on every incident and **arrest** in the Group A offense category. These Group A offenses are 46 specific crimes grouped in 22 offense categories. Specific facts about these offenses are gathered and reported in the NIBRS system. In addition to the Group A offenses, 11 Group B offenses are reported with only the arrest information.

National Instant Criminal Background Check System (NICS)

The Federal Bureau of Investigation (FBI) administers the National Instant Criminal Background Check System (NICS), which debuted in 1998. Before completing any gun sale, a **Federal Firearm Licensee (FFL)** will run the potential buyer's name, date of birth, social security number, and other identifying information through the NICS. Within a matter of minutes, after processing **Federal Form 4473**, that system will return with Denial, Delay, or Proceed, depending on complications in the application, such as having a felony record or presenting falsified/inaccurate credentials. Private citizens do not have access to NICS.

National Integrated Ballistic Information Network (NIBIN)

United States national database of digital images of fired **bullets** and **cartridge cases** from **crime scenes**, operated by the Bureau of Alcohol, Tobacco, Firearms, and Explosives (ATF).

National Missing and Unidentified Persons System (NamUs)

In the US, NamUs acts as a clearinghouse for missing, unidentified, and unclaimed persons, running a database as well as operating inhouse **forensic** services, including **forensic odontology** and **fingerprint** examination, as well as **forensic anthropology** and **DNA** analysis. It also offers investigative support from experienced professionals. NamUs is funded by the National Institute of Justice and offers all of its services at no cost.

national security crime

Crime that impacts or is likely to impact on the national security, defense, or foreign relations of the United States, including but not limited to **espionage**, sabotage, treason and sedition.

National Sex Offenders Public Website (NSOPW)

NSOPW is a website supported by the US **Department of Justice** that allows the general public to search for known sex offenders in all 50 states, the District of Columbia, Puerto Rico, Guam, and numerous Indian tribes.

National Sex Offenders Registry (NSOR)

Administered by the Federal Bureau of Investigation's Criminal Justice Information Services (CJIS), NSOR is a national database of sex offenders that provides information only available to law enforcement. Unlike the **National Sex Offenders Public Website (NSOPW)**, the information in this database is not shared with the public.

National Tracing Center (NTC):

Administered by the **Bureau of Alcohol, Tobacco, and Firearms (ATF)**, the National Tracing Center (NTC) provides data to federal, state, local, and foreign law enforcement agencies regarding domestic and foreign firearms. Its work focuses on tracing the firearms themselves from manufacture, to distribution chain (sellers both wholesale and retail), to buyers. Every legal purchaser of a firearm in the US undergoes a **NICS** check. This information can help link a suspect to a firearm in a criminal investigation and identify potential traffickers. Firearms tracing can detect in-state, interstate, and international patterns in the sources and types of guns used in crimes.

NCIC

See **National Crime Information Center**.

NCIJTF

See **National Cyber Investigative Joint Task Force**.

NCMEC

See **National Center for Missing and Exploited Children**.

need-to-know

In a military or national security situation, need-to-know is a designation regarding the restriction of classified, clandestine, or highly sensitive information. The designation adds another layer of security while discouraging unnecessary sharing.

negligent homicide

It is possible to accidentally kill someone due to reckless or negligent behavior. In the US, this form of criminal homicide often falls under the category of involuntary **manslaughter**. In 2021, for example, a grandfather pled

guilty to negligent homicide after he held his grand-
daughter up to the window of a cruise ship, tragically
causing her to fall to her death.

nerve agent
Potentially **lethal chemical agent** that interferes with the
transmission of nerve impulses.

neutralize
To render ineffective or unusable, or particularly when
used of people, incapable of interfering with a particular
operation. Also to make safe mines, bombs, missiles, and
booby traps and to render harmless anything contaminated with a **chemical agent**.

new number
New York state prison slang for a release inmate
returning to prison based on new charges. If you are
released early on parole, violate it, and are returned to
prison as a result, you keep the original **DIN**. If you serve
your time, get released, and return to prison based on a
new charge, you are assigned a new DIN number (i.e.,
"She's back in with a new number").

Next Generation Identification (NGI)
The **Federal Bureau of Investigation**'s Next Generation
Identification biometric database is gradually replacing
the current **Integrated Automated Fingerprint
Identification System**'s technical capabilities. It is considered the largest biometric database in the world, storing
individual **fingerprint** records and other biometric data
for criminal and civil matters. Its advanced identification
technology provides for fast, efficient, and accurate
fingerprint processing.

NFA

Acronym for "No further action," used when someone is released without **charge** or when there will be no further proceedings in a **case**.

NFIB

See **National Fraud Intelligence Bureau**.

NGI

See **Next Generation Identification**.

NIBIN

See **National Integrated Ballistic Information Network**.

NIBRS

See **National Incident-Based Reporting System**.

nickel

Five-year jail **sentence** (US gang slang).

N

nicotine

Cigarette packets these days often display the warning that "Smoking Kills." But nicotine can kill far faster and more directly when used as a **poison**. One particularly famous murder involving the plant alkaloid nicotine took place in Belgium in 1850. The victim was the Belgian aristocrat Gustave Fougnies, who was fed the poison during a family dinner held for him by his sister and brother-in-law, the deeply in debt Comte and Comtesse de Bocarmé. At the time, there were no tests available that could detect poison in a corpse aside from the procedure developed by British chemist James Marsh that detected arsenic but unfortunately destroyed more fragile plant alkaloids such as nicotine.

Bruising, burns and cuts on Gustave Fougnies's face and attempts by the Comte and Comtesse to clean the body and area with vinegar had already cast suspicion on his death. Pure nicotine is corrosive, which accounted for the burns on Fougnies's face, and police subsequently found vats of pure nicotine and **evidence** of experiments with it on animals in the Comte de Bocarmé's barn. This evidence was, however, only circumstantial—so the magistrate consulted the country's leading chemist, Jean Servais Stas. Stas experimented for three months on organ tissue taken from Fougnies's body and finally managed to extract the liquid nicotine from those tissues using a method involving ethanol, acetic acid and ether. This Stas–Otto method, although since updated, laid the foundations for **forensic** chemistry and remains a fundamental part of **forensic toxicology** to this day.

The Comte de Bocarmé was sent to the guillotine, but this did not deter future nicotine murderers. In 2010, Paul Curry of Kansas was finally **charged** with the murder of his wife Linda by nicotine poisoning 16 years after she died and was later **sentenced** to life in jail. Also in 2010, Morgan Mengel of Pennsylvania tried to kill her husband with Snapple™ laced with nicotine but ended up goading her lover to bludgeon him to death with a shovel. The problem with nicotine as a poison is that, although fast acting, it is difficult to administer in the right **lethal** dose and is difficult to hide in food. This did not deter trained chemist Agatha Christie from using it in her 1934 novel *Three Act Tragedy* (published in the US as *Murder in Three Acts*), or P. D. James in her 1971 novel, *Shroud for a Nightingale*.

NICS

See **National Instant Criminal Background Check System**.

night-vision device

Any electro-optical device used to detect visible and infrared energy and provide a visible image. ▶**night-vision goggles** Electro-optical device that detects visible and near-infrared energy, intensifies the energy, and thereby provides a visible image for night viewing.

9

9 mm **handgun** (UK/US contemporary slang). ▶**9 Mike Mike** 9 mm **handgun** (US contemporary gang slang).

911 or 9-1-1:

US emergency services number for events requiring the immediate services of police or firemen. In the US, 911 is now Enhanced 911 or E911, meaning that nearly all (96 percent of calls to 911 now automatically link to the physical address associated with that phone number. It is a crime to call 911 under false premises, such as a prank.

ninja

Drug cop in the area (US contemporary gang slang).

Ninja Turtles

Prison guards dressed in full riot gear, also known as "hats and bats" (US contemporary slang).

no body case

A "no body" case refers to a suspected homicide where there is no dead body. Contrary to popular belief, such cases can be tried in a court of law, because **circumstantial evidence** (which, in the absence of a body, is all there is) may in fact be used to demonstrate homicide. In the

1990 "woodchipper murder" case in Connecticut, for example, a jury convicted a husband of murdering his wife despite the fact that he'd passed her body through a woodchipper, effectively making her body disappear.

NOC
See **nonofficial cover**.

nonce
Prison term for **pedophile** sex-crime offenders who are usually kept segregated from other prisoners for their own safety as they are considered at risk of attack. The term is of unknown origin but one theory is that it is derived from the acronym NONCE, which stands for "Not On Normal Communal Exercise" and was marked on the door of sex offenders' **cells** so that prison staff would not inadvertently open them while other prisoners' cell doors were also unlocked. Another theory is that it is derived from a Lincolnshire dialectical word "nonse," meaning good-for-nothing. A 1984 entry in the *Oxford English Dictionary* extracted from the *Police Review* states that it is derived from "nancy-boy" (UK contemporary slang for a homosexual).

nonlethal weapon
Weapon or device that is explicitly designed and primarily used to incapacitate immediately while minimizing fatalities, permanent injury to people, and undesired damage to property in the target area or environment.

nonofficial cover (NOC)
Term used by the **Central Intelligence Agency** to describe **case officers** who operate overseas outside the usual diplomatic **cover**.

nonproliferation

Actions taken to prevent the acquisition of **weapons of mass destruction** by preventing or impeding access to **sensitive** technologies, material, and expertise as well as their distribution.

Nordic noir

See **Scandi noir**.

Novichok

Novichok is a group of **nerve agents** that were developed by Soviet Russia in 1971–1993 as part of a program code-named "Foliant." The Russian scientists who developed them claim they are the deadliest ever made. Novichok has never been employed for military purposes but was famously used in the **poisoning** of former Russian military officer and **double agent** Sergei Skripal and his daughter Yulia in Salisbury, UK, in March 2018. Skripal and his daughter survived, but Dawn Sturgess, a woman who came into contact with the discarded perfume bottle that was used to contain the Novichok, later died.

NPD

See **narcissistic personality disorder**.

NSOPW

See **National Sex Offenders Public Website**.

NSOR

See **National Sex Offender Registry**.

NTC

See **National Tracing Center**.

O

OD
To overdose (OD) on a drug. Accidental ODs are common.

officer involved shooting (OIS)
An OIS refers to an instance where a law enforcement officer shoots at a person while they are on duty. It does not mean that a suspect was hit, and also is not used when another person is shooting at the police officer. Depending on police **precinct**, it can also refer to any incident when a police firearm was discharged, including accidental.

OG
Original gang member (US contemporary gang slang).

OIS
See **officer involved shooting**.

omertà
Old rule or law of silence in the **Mafia**, which is mostly no longer upheld by the younger generation of gangsters.

187
California code for murder. A 187 LEO is "murder of a police officer."

one time
Police officer, cop (US contemporary gang slang).

on-scene commander

In the US, the federal officer designated to direct federal crisis and consequence management efforts at the scene of a terrorist or **weapons of mass destruction** incident.

open carry

A person who has a firearm that is plainly visible to the casual observer is practicing open carry. Open carry should not be confused with brandishing a weapon—an act that, depending on the circumstances, may be a crime. In underpopulated states such as Alaska and Wyoming, open carry is seen as being a pragmatic response to the fact that the nearest law enforcement can be hours away. In densely populated and heavily policed cities, however, open carry is generally perceived as a display of hostility. Carrying laws vary by state.

open investigation

An open investigation is an ongoing case being pursued by law enforcement. There is no time limit on how long a case can be open. Law enforcement will not discuss details of an open case with the public but might release information if it may help advance the investigation. For example, the 2020 nonfiction podcast *Down the Hill: The Delphi Murders*, discussed the 2017 murders of Abigail Williams and Liberty German. Because it is still an open investigation, the police will not release details regarding how the girls were murdered. However, because they were seeking the public's help, they released a digital image of a **person of interest** photographed by one of the murdered girls. When the police have identified a suspect they are reasonably certain is guilty, the investigation is considered closed.

O

operations officer (OO)

An operations officer within the **Central Intelligence Agency** may be involved in **clandestine** activities, and spotting, assessing, developing, recruiting, and handling **assets** or individuals with access to vital **foreign intelligence** across issues of national security. An OO's career can include assignments in the **Directorate of Operations'** key areas of activity. These are **human intelligence** collection, **counterintelligence** and **covert** action related to international terrorism, weapons proliferation, international crime, and **drugs trafficking** as well as the capabilities and intentions of rogue nations. Operations officers work mostly overseas on assignments that typically last from two to three years.

opioids

Derived from the opium plant or a synthetic, opioids are highly addictive narcotic drugs that include **heroin**, **fentanyl**, oxycodone, hydrocodone (Vicodin), codeine, and morphine. Due to their high susceptibility to being abused, opioids are **Schedule II** drugs.

order

Written direction of a court or judge to do or refrain from doing certain acts

organized crime

Organized crime describes the activities of a group of people involved in serious criminal activities for what are often substantial profits. Violence can be a feature of organized crime but the main motive is usually financial gain, although some groups, such as terrorist groups, are politically or ideologically motivated. Organized crime activities can include **drug trafficking**, **human trafficking**, **cybercrime**, armed **robbery**, **money laundering**,

O

counterfeit goods, counterfeit currency, tax **fraud**, immigration fraud, and environmental crime.

Organized Crime Drug Enforcement Task Force
Network of regional task forces in the US that coordinates federal **law enforcement** efforts to combat the national and international organizations that cultivate, process, and distribute illicit **drugs**.

original lethal-purpose firearm
Firearm originally manufactured with **lethal** purpose in contrast to weapons **converted** to be capable of live firing with lethal effect.

outfit
Family or clan within the **Mafia**.

over-and-under
Firearm with two **barrels** placed one above the other.

O

overcriminalization
When law enforcement is called to respond to issues that are better addressed through social services, this results in overcriminalization, which creates a burdensome criminal record for otherwise law-abiding citizens, effectively **criminalizing** poverty and despair. Overcriminalization is best understood as a symptom of systematic economic policy failure

P

PACE
See Police and Criminal Evidence Act.

packing heat
To be carrying a firearm (i.e., "His boys pack heat").
(Archaic US slang.)

Patriot Act
In the wake of the terrorist acts of 9/11 and anthrax
attacks of 2001, George W. Bush signed into law the USA
Patriot Act (2001–). Commonly known simply as the
"Patriot Act," its purpose was to strengthen national security and increase the surveillance powers of law
enforcement. It also expanded the definition of terrorism
crimes, and increased the attendant punishments and
penalties. Critics have charged that a number of features
of the Patriot Act are unconstitutional. In 2015, certain
provisions of the Patriot Act expired, but were restored by
and continued under the USA Freedom Act (2015–).

paper
Money. Originating in the US and popularized by gangsta
rappers, this is now in wider use (UK/US contemporary
slang). Also for US police, a report.

paper, on
"On paper" means on **probation** or on **parole** (UK/US
contemporary slang).

paraquat

Paraquat is an organic compound and herbicide that is **toxic** to humans and animals. In humans, paraquat-**poisoning** symptoms include vomiting, blistering, difficulty breathing, kidney and liver damage, and death from multiple organ failure. It is frequently used as a suicide agent in developing countries because it is cheap and readily available, although it is banned in the European Union and tightly regulated in the US. The Paraquat or Vending Machine Murders in Japan in 1985 remain a popular unsolved true-crime mystery with the suspected serial killer, or killers, still at large.

parental child abduction

Also known as parental kidnapping, this distressing form of child abduction happens when a separated or divorced parent takes their child out of the custody of the other parent in defiance of the terms set out by the court. It is the most common form of child kidnapping in the US. The 1993 International Parental Kidnapping Crime Act (IPKCA) made it a federal international kidnapping offense for a parent to take their child out of the country without permission of the other parent.

P

parole

Parole is the early release of a prisoner before they have completed their sentence, and is usually subject to supervision and contingent on good behavior. The word originates from the French *parole*, one meaning of which is promise and began to be used during the Middle Ages for prisoners who kept their word to abide by certain conditions. Prisoners who are given parole are released on **probation**, also known as on license, under certain conditions, including supervision. Parole is granted, or not, after a review of a prisoner by the Parole Board. In the US, prisoners are typically eligible for parole after having served one-third of their original sentence. A "parole eligibility date" is the earliest time an offender might be paroled.

patent print

Patent prints are finger, palm, or other prints that are clearly visible to the naked eye and do not require the use of powders, chemicals or UV light to spot them at **crime scenes**. They are often composed of blood, ink, or other dark substances, and found on hard surfaces such as walls, door and window frames, and paper.

payload

In **cybercrime**, the payload is the part of the **malware** program that actually executes its designated task.

PCP

Phencyclidine, or PCP (the initialism comes from phenyl-cyclohexylpiperidine), also known as angel dust, hog, or peace pills, is an anesthetic that has hallucinogenic properties. It comes in oil, liquid, powder, crystal, or pill form. The oil is yellow whereas the crystals and powder can range in color from white to light brown. PCP can be sniffed, swallowed, injected, or smoked and can lead to users feeling dreamy and euphoric or, conversely, aggressive, panicky, paranoid, and violent. It is addictive and use can result in a severe psychotic state, self-harm, convulsions, and suicide. PCP is a Class A drug in the UK and illegal to use, give away, or sell.

pedophile

Someone who is sexually attracted to prepubescent children. According to the *Diagnostic and Statistical Manual of Psychiatric Disorders* or DSM, this is defined as children under the age of 13, and a person must be a minimum of 16 years of age and at least five years older than the child for their attraction to be considered pedophilia. Most sexual offenders against children are male with an estimated ratio of 10:1 male to female child molesters, although this may be inaccurate as crimes are often underreported. It is not a crime to be a pedophile but it can lead to criminal activity that includes child sexual abuse, rape, grooming, stalking, child pornography, and indecent exposure. Pedophilia is one of the most stigmatized and feared mental disorders, which is considered very difficult, if not impossible, to cure.

peds
Bicycle, often used by **drug** couriers and street gangs for a swift getaway.

peels
Orange jumpsuit worn by prisoners in some prisons and correctional facilities (US contemporary slang).

pellet
Common name for a small spherical **projectile loaded** in **shot** shells. It also refers to a nonspherical projectile used in some **air guns**.

pen
An abbreviation for **penitentiary** (US contemporary prison slang).

penitentiary
In the US, state or federal prison for serious offenders.

pepper spray
Pepper spray is an incapacitating aerosol spray used in policing, especially for riot or crowd control. In the UK, it

is also popular with civilians for self-defense although it is only legal for the police to carry and use it. In the US, it is legal for civilians to carry it for purposes of self-defense, and is regulated by individual states.

persistent agent

Chemical agent that remains able to cause casualties for more than 24 hours and up to several days or weeks after it is released.

person of interest

When an individual is wanted for questioning by law enforcement, they are named as a person of interest. Importantly, a person of interest is not identical to a suspect. For example, a person of interest can be an individual whom the police suspect has information pertinent to the case, or even a person the police suspect is a victim or potential target.

petechial hemorrhage

A petechial hemorrhage is a tiny red dot or mark that appears as a result of asphyxia by external pressure. It can be caused by strangulation, hanging, or smothering. The tell-tale red marks range in size from almost invisible to around 2 mm (.079 inches) and often occur in the whites or conjunctiva of the eyes as well as on the skin of the face and head, the mucous membranes inside the mouth, and behind the ears. For the marks to appear, the victim needs to have been alive when the pressure was applied, which means petechial hemorrhages are particularly useful to determine if a hanging was staged or otherwise. Petechial hemorrhages can occur on the face as a result of a cardiac arrest, and on the lungs and heart in cases of heatstroke or sudden infant death syndrome (SIDS). They can also occur postmortem, although the patterns tend to differ from those that occur before death. A pathologist therefore needs to take all the circumstances into account when examining the **evidence**.

phishing

The fraudulent practice of sending emails that appear to be come from a legitimate source, such as a social networking site, a well-known entity such as eBay, or even a bank. They contain a link that, if clicked, directs the victim to a site that looks very convincing and asks them to verify their account information. This login allows cybercriminals to gather **sensitive** information, which enables them to carry out **cybercrime** such as emptying the account of the person concerned.

phreaking

Phreaking or phone phreaking is the **hacking** of a tele-communications system in order to exploit it by, for example, making international calls or accessing voice-mail for malicious purposes. A phreak or phone phreak is someone who hacks into a telecommunications system in this manner. Phreakers often band together to link hacked systems and create their own networks that bring in billions in revenue for them.

P

PIC

See **prison industrial complex**.

Picasso

To slice up someone's face in prison is "to do a Picasso" (US contemporary prison slang).

pickpocket

Someone who steals money or other valuables from another person's pocket, often through sleight of hand so the victim is not immediately aware.

pinch

To steal money under the pretense of getting change. Also used in a contemporary sense meaning "to steal."

pinched

To get caught by the police or federal **agents** (UK/US slang term).

PIO

See **police information officer**.

PIR

See **priority intelligence requirement**.

pistol

Handgun in which the **chamber** is a part of the **barrel**.

plainclothes

Some police officers, specifically detectives, are expected to wear regular civilian clothing while on duty. While conducting an investigation, these detectives will carry police badges and police-related equipment that clearly indicate they are officers of the law. While undercover officers are technically also plainclothes, they do not carry anything that will link them to their true identity, or to the fact that they are working for the police.

plant

To hide stolen goods or secrete something away (UK thieves' **cant**, historical slang). Also used in a contemporary sense to mean to place or hide an incriminating item such as **drugs** on someone to make them appear guilty of a crime.

plug

To stab or to shoot. Also a **drug** contact or drug supply.

poison

Substance capable of causing the illness or death of a
person or other living organism when ingested or
absorbed. Also, as a verb, to administer poison to a person
or animal.

Poison, so often the murder weapon of choice in the
golden age of Agatha Christie and Dorothy L. Sayers, is
enjoying a resurgence in crime fiction, especially in **cozy
mysteries**. This is in part due to true-crime **cases** such as
that of Alexander Litvinenko with **polonium** but also to
modern toxicology constraints. **Forensic toxicology** tests
are only carried out postmortem if there is **evidence** that
suggests foul play. Even then, tests are only carried out for
the most common **toxic** substances.

police

Law enforcement officers empowered by the state to
enforce law and order, to protect people and property, and
to investigate crime. There are many contemporary slang
terms for the police including: feds; 5-0; rozzers; po-po;
plod; boys in blue; pigs; jakes; **bobbies**; **the Bill** or Old Bill;
peelers (historic slang also derived from Sir Robert Peel).

P

police force ranks

The police force is one branch of the institutional appa-
ratus of law enforcement in the US. It is broken down into
two major divisions: state and federal.

At the *federal* level, the police force consists of the US
Border Control (Homeland Security); US Parks services;
US Marshals; the Washington DC police force, the
Metropolitan Police Department, (unique due to the fact
that DC is not a state); the US Secret Service (which
protects the president of the US), and the **FBI**. The
Attorney General of the US is sometimes referred to as
the country's "top cop"; however, the **Department of
Justice** is not a police department.

At the *state* level, a police force is further broken down into city and municipalities. The organization of a police department follows a hierarchical structure borrowed from the military, and large police departments, such as the Los Angeles and New York Police Departments, will have sub-ranks inside this system. From highest to lowest, the ranks are:

- **Police technician:** entry-level position that involves assisting in follow-up investigations of assigned cases, issuing citations and enforcing parking laws, directing traffic at accident and crime scenes, preparing paperwork for incident reports, keeping records, providing general assistance to the public, and many other support tasks.

- **Police officer/police detective/patrol officer:** law enforcement officers that are generally most familiar to civilians. Most attend a training academy and, after graduation, carry out police work including patrols, **arresting** suspects, and responding to emergency calls. In some departments, such as the New York Police Department (NYPD) and Los Angeles Police Department (LAPD), detectives rank above officers and are additionally ranked third to first.

- **Police corporal:** next rank up from police officer or detective and is a supervisory role, although the title can also belong to nonsupervisory members of a specialist unit.

- **Police sergeant:** duties are usually one step up from those of a police corporal as they actively investigate internal complaints and manage their department as well as supervising their officers, training them, and participating in disciplinary matters.

- **Police lieutenant:** akin to middle managers, liaising between their superiors and the ranks below them to action plans as well as conducting performance reviews and developing their departments. They also work with other law enforcement agencies in the area and act as an ambassador for the police department within their local community.

- **Police captain:** report directly to the chiefs of police or a deputy police chief. They train staff, prepare budgets, handle hiring and promotions, and are even more visible within their community than police lieutenants, running community-policing programs as well as possibly preparing reports on policing in the community.
- **Deputy police chief:** usually found in larger municipal law enforcement agencies, a deputy police chief is responsible for the administration of a police bureau or division. They have the same responsibilities as a police captain but also step in as acting chief of police if required. They also design and implement crime-prevention programs, oversee budgets, and oversee compliance and resources.
- **Chief of police:** the top job, these officers oversee all aspects of a police department, develop programs and procedures, and are responsible for the **deployment** of officers to special investigations. They are usually appointed by elected officials and work closely with mayors and local government officials. As the spokesperson for the police, they address the public and media in crisis situations and are ultimately responsible for any issues or incidents that arise under their watch.

Many towns do not have their own police department and instead rely on **sheriffs** or state troopers.

police information officer (PIO)

A police information officer handles the flow of information to the public. They are particularly important in the event of an emergency, and work with the media to ensure that accurate information and instructions are disseminated in a timely fashion.

police procedural

Subgenre of crime fiction that focuses on the investigative process from the point of view of the police officers involved. Unlike the detective novel, this is usually an ensemble piece based on teamwork that reflects real-life police methodology.

police slang

Like all close-knit subcultures, police forces use slang, which can vary widely among city departments but also inside precincts. Some examples of police slang that have entered into common parlance include: beer run (shoplifting beer); dix (i.e., dicks, meaning detective); drive by (shots fired from a moving vehicle); four fingers (Code 4, no further assistance needed); getting busted (getting arrested); got/give the eye (in view or line of sight); filling out paper (writing required reports); jumper (suicidal person); one roll (getting fingerprints); riding the lightning (tasing someone or getting tased); rollover (vehicle that has rolled over); slim jim (device used to open a locked vehicle); smash and grab (burglary involving a smashed window); and tapping the till (stealing from the cash register). For more examples of police slang, see **10 codes**.

police superintendent

See **police force ranks**.

police tape

The tape, also known as law enforcement tape, used to cordon off a **crime scene** or other hazard where **law enforcement** is involved. This comes in a variety of colors, with yellow, yellow-white, yellow-black, red, and blue-white all being used.

polonium

Highly radioactive, polonium hit the headlines in 2006 when it was used to murder the Russian defector and former Federal Service Security (FSB) officer, Alexander Litvinenko, who drank a cup of green tea laced with polonium-210. It took him three weeks to die and, on his deathbed, he named Russian President Vladimir Putin as the man behind his murder. A UK public enquiry in 2016 found that two former KGB officers, Andrey Lugovoy and Dmitry Kovtun, who had met with Litvinenko the day he fell ill, were responsible for his death. Both deny involvement. Litvinenko's case was the first recorded **poisoning** using polonium-210. Polonium does not kill immediately, although it is **lethal** in very small doses. Victims suffer the effects of radiation poisoning including hair loss, headaches, and diarrhea before they succumb to heart failure.

polygraph test

Popularly known as a lie detector test, polygraphs are used in both criminal **investigation** and the private sector to determine whether a subject is telling the truth. The test measures specific physiological responses to arousal, including respiration, heart rate, and blood pressure, while the subject is asked a series of questions. The problem is that there are no specific physiological indicators of lying and the **Comparison Question Test** used with polygraphs has been shown to be biased against the innocent who cannot think of a lie in response to the control question. The American Polygraph Association claims the test is accurate more than 90 percent of the time while critics claim it is no more than 70 percent accurate; some in the legal and scientific professions regard it as little better than flipping a coin. Most courts do not

P

polymorphic virus

Computer **virus** that will change its digital footprint every time it replicates. Antivirus software relies on a constantly updated and evolving database of virus signatures to detect any virus that may have infected a system. By changing its signature upon replication, a polymorphic virus may elude antivirus software, making it very hard to eradicate.

pool bloodstain

Sustained bleeding from a wound or arterial blood loss causes blood to accumulate or pool at a **crime scene**. If there is no victim or body present, the amount of blood present can indicate the seriousness or even the nature of the injury, and whether that is likely to be fatal.

pop a cap

Shoot at someone (US contemporary gang slang).

posse

Jamaican gang, derived from Spaghetti Westerns, a subgenre of Western film that became popular in the 1960s, called "spaghetti" due to the fact that they were made in Italy. (UK/US/Jamaican contemporary gang slang.)

precinct

The specific geographical area patrolled by a police force is known as its precinct. Large urban police forces will have multiple precincts, each of which will typically have their own specific character, strengths, and weaknesses. For example, the documentary film *The Seven Five* (2014) examined corruption in the 75th precinct of the New York City Police Department (NYPD) in the 1980s.

preliminary inquiry

Review of the facts and circumstances of an incident or **allegation** to determine if the preliminary information or circumstances are sufficient to warrant the initiation of an **investigation** or referral to an investigative entity.

primer

Component in **ammunition** that explodes when struck by the **firing pin**, or under an electric excitement, igniting the **propellant** and discharging the **projectile**. The primer is composed of a primer cup containing priming mixture, the composition of which varies according to the firearm and ammunition used. Primers are also used in flares, mortars, hand grenades, rocket-propelled grenades, and other larger ammunition components. ▶**primer cup** Brass or copper cup designed to contain priming mixture.

printing

In gun culture, "printing" refers to the discernable contours of your gun through your outerwear. To "print" while **concealed carrying** is highly undesirable.

priority intelligence requirement (PIR)

Intelligence requirement that the commander of an operation and staff need to understand the threat and other aspects of the operational environment.

priors

Short for "prior convictions" or criminal record, priors will show up on a **background check**. The simple fact of having them is not indicative of the kinds of crimes committed. Depending on their nature (nonviolent, juvenile offense, violent), they will disqualify applicants from certain jobs as well as from owning a firearm.

P

prison

A prison is a building or set of buildings in which people are held while they are awaiting trial for a crime or are being punished for one. In England and Wales, prisoners are categorized based on the likelihood of the risk of escape, the potential harm to the public if they were to escape, and their potential to cause a threat to the control and stability of a prison. The rules are different for men, women, and young adult offenders. Male prisoners are sent to prisons in one of the following four categories:

- Category A: **high-security prisons** that house prisoners who, if they were to escape, pose the greatest threat to the public, the police, or national security.
- Category B: local or training prisons. Local prisons house prisoners who are brought directly from a local court if they have been **sentenced** or are on remand. Training prisons hold long-term and high-security prisoners.
- Category C: training and resettlement prisons. The majority of prisoners are placed in a Category C prison. They provide prisoners with educational and other opportunities so they can find a job and reintegrate into the community on release.
- Category D: open prisons. These are minimal security prisons that allow eligible prisoners to spend most of their day away from the prison on license to work, attend education or for other resettlement purposes. Open prisons only house prisoners that have been risk-assessed and deemed suitable for open conditions.

Women and young adults are assessed and categorized according to their needs and potential risks before being held in closed or open prisons. If they are categorized as high risk they are given restricted status and can only be held in a closed prison. In exceptional circumstances, women and young adults can be held in a Category A prison. Prison staff regularly assess prisoners throughout their sentence to ensure they are still in the correct category prison.

In the US, prisoners are similarly assessed based on risk factors and also on needs, including medical needs. It is the responsibility of the **Federal Bureau of Prisons** to decide where a prisoner will be designated to serve their sentence. Prisons are categorized as Minimum (also known as Federal Prison Camps), Low (Federational Correctional Institutions or FCIs), Medium (can be FCIs or USPs), High (also known as United States Penitentiaries or USPs) or Federational Correctional Complexes (FCCs) where different category institutions are located close to one another. There are also administrative facilities, which are institutions with specialist missions such as the detention of pretrial prisoners, the treatment of inmates with serious or chronic medical problems, or the containment of extremely dangerous, violent, or escape-prone inmates. Administrative facilities include Metropolitan Correctional Centers (MCCs), Metropolitan Detention Centers (MDCs), Federal Detention Centers (FDCs), Federal Medical Centers (FMCs), the Federal Transfer Center (FTC), the Medical Center for Federal Prisoners (MCFP) and the **Administrative Maximum Security Facility (ADX)**. Administrative facilities, except the ADX, are capable of holding inmates in all security categories.

P

prison abolition movement

As its name implies, the prison abolition movement seeks to abolish prisons altogether. Taking its cues from W. E. B. DuBois, it argues that the carceral logic of the American prison industrial complex emerges from the same predatory capitalist platform that supported American slavery and continues to oppress Black people today. In place of prisons, it proposes decarceration and decriminalization, as well as an expanded system of social welfare to address systemic poverty, structural racism, and mental illness as being among some of the root causes of contemporary criminality.

Critics counter that prison abolition does not solve the real dangers to society posed by habitual and violent predators and organized crime, even as it sends a message that criminals, once caught, will not be held accountable for the actions. The prison abolition movement is distinct from the **prison reform movement**.

prison industrial complex (PIC)

A riff on "military industrial complex," the prison industrial complex is a concept used by prison reformers and abolitionists to summarize the close ties between the prison, the government, exploitative capitalism, and the rise of the surveillance state. It is especially attentive to the corporate exploitation of **prison labor**, and highly critical of **private or for-profit prisons** that rely on imprisoning as many bodies as possible as their business model.

prison labor

The use of prison labor is legal in the US thanks to a provision in the Thirteenth Amendment. The practice ranges from rehabilitative to exploitative. *See also* **chain gang**; **UNICOR**.

prison reform movement

Movements to reform American prisons are older than the United States itself but became prominent in the 1950s and 1960s, when prison populations rose precipitously. They do not seek to abolish prisons but to improve conditions inside. For example, they propose to eliminate cruel and unusual punishment, to obtain legitimate health services for inmates, to improve the quality of food, and to expedite family visits. They also seek to expand GED, literacy, and work training programs that will confer employable skills on the inmate upon their release.

prison slang

Prison slang is unusually variable, institutionally specific, and fast-changing; this is because it hides meaning from guards, but also helps define in-groups and out-groups. Some prison slang that has migrated into common parlance includes: boneyard (conjugal visit); Cadillac job (desirable work); cowboy (someone new on the job); fiend (drug addict); grapes (gossip, i.e., through the grapevine); in the hole (**solitary confinement**); house or crib (your cell); Big House (prison); mando (mandatory); O.G. (original gangster, i.e., a prisoner who has been inside for a very long time); race traitor (someone who socializes outside their race); Ratchet (a nurse); and vic (a victim).

P

prison wolf

Inmate who is straight on the outside but has sexual relationships with other men while in prison (US contemporary slang).

private prison or for-profit prison

See contract prison.

probation

Probation allows a convicted defendant to be released with a shortened or **suspended sentence** for a specified duration dependent on good behavior. Probationers are placed under the supervision of a probation officer and must fulfil certain conditions. If the probationer violates a condition of probation, the court may place additional restrictions on the probationer or **order** the probationer to serve a term of imprisonment.

pro bono

Taken from the Latin phrase "pro bono public" (for the public good), pro bono work is legal work provided without any expectation of monetary compensation. The American Bar Association (ABA) encourages lawyers to donate 50 hours of pro bono work per year to assist low-income individuals or charitable institutions.

profiling

P

Profiling, known as criminal or offender profiling, is a combination of **law enforcement** and **forensic** psychology with few boundaries, no agreed methodology, and little in the way of agreed definitions or terminology. It is the art and science of **crime scene** analysis, forensic psychology, and behavioral science to develop a description of an unknown offender, often a serial offender, and its first use is often cited to be the **case** of **Jack the Ripper**. As well as its application in real-life criminal cases, profiling is a staple of crime fiction, TV series, and films including the popular Netflix series *Mindhunter* (2017–) .

prohibited person

An individual deemed by the US government to be unfit to possess a firearm. Under 18 USC § 922 (g) there are nine categories of prohibited persons. Generally, they include: 1) felons; 2) fugitives; 3) unlawful users of controlled substances; 4) persons who have been adjudicated as mentally "defective" or who have been involuntarily committed to a mental institution; 5) illegal aliens and nonimmigrant aliens; 6) persons dishonorably discharged from the armed forces; 7) persons who have renounced their US citizenship; 8) persons who are the subject of a qualifying domestic protection order; and 9) persons convicted of a misdemeanor crime of domestic violence.

Minors under 18 are not prohibited from handling firearms but cannot personally own a handgun except with the permission of a parent or guardian. If they have a state-issued license, minors can own other kinds of firearms for the purposes of, for example, competing in biathlon competitions; skeet shooting; target shooting; and youth hunting.

projectile

Object (**bullet**, **shot**, **slug**, or **pellet**) that is **discharged** by the force of rapidly burning gases or by other means when a gun is fired.

projection bloodstain

A projection or projected **bloodstain** or spatter is caused by arterial spurting, **expirated** spatter or blood mixing with air from an internal injury, and blood spatter cast off by an object such as a bullet passing through a blood source. Arterial spurting occurs when a major artery is severed and blood is pushed out by the pumping heart, often forming an arcing pattern consisting of individual stains, one for each pump of the heart. Expirated spatter tends to form a fine mist. Projected blood spatter is the result of a blood source being subjected to an action or force greater than the force of gravity.

propellant

Chemical compound inside a gun **cartridge** that burns rapidly when ignited to produce large amounts of hot gas. This gas drives the **projectile(s)** out of the **barrel**.

prosecution (legal)

Inside an adversarial court system, the lawyer for the prosecution is tasked with proving the guilt of the defendant beyond a reasonable doubt.

pro se representation

Pro Se, which is Latin for "on one's own behalf," refers to a defendant acting as their own lawyer. (Pro Per is the same thing, only in state court.) In a quote attributed to Abraham Lincoln: "A man who represents himself has a fool for a client." Nonetheless, important cases have been won by people representing themselves. From 1978 to 1990, for example, inventor Robert Kearns fought and ultimately won an epic patent infringement case against Ford Motor Company and Chrysler. His struggle is the subject of the film, *Flash of Genius* (2018).

pseudocommando

A subtype of **mass murderer**, the pseudocommando typically entertains revenge fantasies starring themselves as military-style commandos. They will stockpile weapons and ammo with the goal of committing a premeditated murder-suicide mass killing. This can also turn into **suicide by cop**, as the pseudocommando type not infrequently hopes to die in a literal "blaze of glory." Its speculated that Stephen Paddock, who committed the Las Vegas Massacre of 2017, could fit this typology: he shot and killed 61 people and injured 867 more, then committed suicide. However, his precise motives remain unknown.

psychological thriller

Thriller that focuses on the often unstable and unreliable psychological and emotional states of both victim and protagonist. Moral ambiguity, complex relationships, and shifting realities are all hallmarks of the genre.

psychological warfare

Use of threats, propaganda, and other psychological techniques to mislead, intimidate, demoralize, or otherwise influence the thinking or behavior of an opponent.

psychopathy

Just as not all psychopaths are **serial killers**, not all serial killers are psychopaths. Psychopaths make up about 1 percent of the population, and they can be highly functional and objectively successful. Those diagnosed with this **antisocial personality disorder (APD)** lack empathy, a sense of shame, and guilt. They also typically possess superior manipulative skills, and understand the difference between right and wrong; they just do not care. Being able to manage psychopathic traits, learning how to appear "normal," and maintaining the **mask of sanity** has helped psychopaths succeed in high-risk professions such as stock brokering, business entrepreneurship, and political office. Famous serial killers diagnosed with psychopathy include Jeffrey **Dahmer** and **Charles Manson**.

P

Public Enemy Era

In the history of the FBI, the 1930s became known as the "Public Enemy Era" due to the sheer number of notorious gangsters who were wanted criminals. They include Bonnie and Clyde, Pretty Boy Floyd, and Ma Barker.

Public Enemy No. 1

Entering popular parlance in the 1930s, "Public Enemy No. 1" quickly became synonymous for gangster bosses. In the 1930s, the FBI named famous gangsters such as Al Capone, John Dillinger, and Baby Face Nelson as Public Enemy No. 1. In 2013, with the escalation of the war on drugs, the Chicago Crime Commission named Sinaloa cartel leader Joaquin "El Chapo" Guzman to the top of its list. (He's currently being held in **Administrative Maximum Security Facility [ADX]** Florence). Inside the FBI, the designation of "Public Enemy No. 1" has morphed into the **Ten Most Wanted Fugitives List**.

pulled

To "get pulled" is to be stopped by the police. Can also mean taken to one side by a senior officer for a minor **misdemeanor** (US contemporary police and UK general slang).

pump

Shotgun (US contemporary gang slang).

pump action

Manual repeating **action** of a **firearm** where all the mechanisms are moved by the back and forward action of the sliding fore-end (the pump), which ejects the spent shell, cocks the hammer and loads a new shell in the **chamber**. By then pushing the slide forward, the shooter pushes the block and **firing pin** into the firing position. This action is repeated every time the gun is fired.

puppy, dog

Gun (US/Jamaican contemporary gang slang).

push, pusha, pushy

Bicycle, often used by **drug** couriers and street gangs for a swift getaway.

Q

quantitative recidivism assessment software (QRAS)
Based on computer algorithms, QRAS are used to predict
the likelihood that a suspect will reoffend. Ostensibly
scientific, these risk assessment reports are better understood as machine-driven versions of the fictional future
crime predictions made by psychic aliens in the sci-fi
short story and film *Minority Report*. As technology ethi-
cists have repeatedly stressed, computers do not emerge
via parthenogenesis as gods fully formed: humans make
them. Because their algorithms replicate the (often
unconscious) biases of their programmers, their predictions do the same.

Q

R

rabbit

Prison inmate who has a history of escape attempts or is planning to escape (US contemporary slang). Also the target in an **intelligence surveillance** operation.

Rader, Dennis

Dennis Rader (b. 1945) was the seemingly devoted family man and churchgoer who was also known as **BTK**, or the BTK killer, because he would bind, torture, and kill his victims. He carried out 10 murders in Wichita, Kansas, between 1974 and 1991, taunting the authorities with correspondence and clues. Rader liked to strangle his victims before taking souvenirs from the scenes of his crimes, although he also shot and stabbed them. He derived sexual pleasure from killing, leaving his semen at the scene of his first crime where he killed four members of the Otero family. He later placed a letter in a book in the local library where he admitted to their killings and wrote, "It's hard to control myself. You probably call me 'psychotic with sexual perversion hang-up.'" He added that he would strike again, stating, "The code words for me will be bind them, torture them, kill them, B.T.K." From then on he was known as the BTK killer and carried on terrorizing Wichita, sending poems and letters to local newspapers and TV stations, and even calling the police to report a homicide he carried out in 1977. After his final murder in 1991, BTK seemed to disappear as Rader focused on his work, family, and roles as president of his church council and Boy Scout leader. Then, in 2004, with the thirtieth anniversary of the Otero killings and attendant publicity, Rader could not resist once more taunting the authorities, sending word puzzles, letters, and even an outline for a BTK story to them as well as to local media. He also dropped off packages containing clues, one of which included a computer disc that led the authorities to Rader's church. They noticed his white van on **CCTV** covering the places where he had dropped off packages and matched him to **crime scenes** through **DNA** taken from his daughter. Rader was **arrested** in 2005 and admitted to all his crimes, and is serving 10 life **sentences** for his murders. His story inspired Stephen King's novella *A Good Marriage* (2010), an episode of Netflix's *Mindhunter* (2017–) and the movie *BTK* (2008).

Rambo

Large knife. Also, "doing a Rambo" is carrying out an armed **assault** or attack (US contemporary gang slang).

rampage killer

A rampage killer and spree killer are very similar; however, the rampage killer is generally understood to kill (or attempt to kill) at least two and generally more victims in a public space. They are thus also **mass murderers**. The psychology of the rampage killer is generally associated with mass school shootings, such as the **Sandy Hook** shootings.

Ramsay

Large knife, named after well-known UK chef Gordon Ramsay.

rankin

High-ranking member of a gang (US/Jamaican contemporary gang slang).

ransom/ransom note

In cases of kidnapping or imprisonment, a sum of money, or ransom, is typically demanded in return for getting the person back. It is a form of **extortion**. The ransom note is the written document that conventionally spells out the kidnapper's demands. In films, the ransom note is often stereotypically crafted using cut-out words and letters from magazines, with the explanation being that the handwriting cannot thus be recognized or analyzed for psychological clues. The ransom note can be the focus of intense analysis for trace evidence, linguistic clues, and other kinds of details that might help identify the kidnapper.

ransomware

A tool of cybercrime, ransomware is malware that encrypts computer data and renders it unusable. Malicious actors will then demand a ransom (usually in bitcoin) in exchange for the decryption key. In 2020 alone, at least eight American cities were crippled by ransomware, including major hubs such as Atlanta, Georgia.

rape

Rape is defined in the US as "penetration, no matter how slight, of the vagina or anus with any body part or object, or oral penetration by a sex organ of another person, without the consent of the victim." **Assault** by penetration is when a person penetrates another person's vagina or anus with any part of the body other than a penis, or by using an object, without the person's consent. *See also* **sexual assault**.

R

rat

Snitch or **informant**. Used by the US **Mafia** and other gangs. To "rat someone out" means to snitch or inform on an **accomplice**.

rate of fire

Number of **projectiles** that can be **discharged** from the **firearm** in a given timeframe such as a minute.

raven

Male operative engaged in Russian **sexpionage** (see **swallow**).

raw intelligence

Colloquial term meaning collected **intelligence** information that has not yet been converted or processed into finished intelligence.

raze up

Cut with a razor (UK and US contemporary prison slang).

reactivation

Restoration of a previously **deactivated weapon's** capacity to fire. Common in the illicit trade and trafficking of guns to avoid or subvert import and other restrictions.

receiver

Someone who receives stolen goods. Also the basic unit of a **firearm** that houses the firing and breech mechanism and onto which the **barrel** and **stock** are assembled. In **revolvers**, **pistols**, and break-open guns, it is called the frame.

recidivism

Inside the criminal justice system, recidivism refers to the tendency of convicted felons to relapse into criminal behavior. Critics have pointed out that this definition is both vague and broad, and lumps in actual criminal offenses with technical violations such as getting caught drinking alcohol. In addition, "data driven" strategies for reducing recidivism, such as **quantitative recidivism**

assessment software, have been shown to use biased or racist algorithms.

In 2019, a US Sentencing Commission report focused on recidivism among federal prisoners showed that nearly 64 percent of prisoners who had been convicted of violent offenses were rearrested within eight years. Those high rates contribute to the argument, made by prison abolitionists, that the current US system is not successful in deterring and rehabilitating inmates but may in fact be contributing to ongoing crime. By contrast, Norway has the lowest recidivism rates in the world as well as one of the lowest crime rates, and is also famous for a humane (as opposed to punitive) prison system that focuses on caring for the offender within a philosophy of restorative justice.

Reducing recidivism and getting felons "out of the life" is one of the key missions of rehabilitation programs and a strategic focus of **halfway houses**.

recoil

Often referred to as a gun's "kick," recoil is the rearward thrust of the gun as it is being discharged. It's a good example of the Newtonian third law of motion: "To every action there is an equal and opposite reaction." Hence, when a **gun** exerts forward force on a bullet, this law of thermodynamics says that bullet will exert an equal force in the opposite direction. Gunplay in television and film does not provide an accurate depiction of the phenomenon of recoil—which refers to what the gun *does*, not to how the shooter reacts—because prop guns shoot **blanks**.

reconnaissance

Mission undertaken to obtain, by visual observation or other methods, information about the activities and resources of an enemy or adversary, or about the geographic and other characteristics of a particular area or facility.

reloading

Reassembling a fired **cartridge case** with a new **primer**, **propellant** and **bullet** or **wadding** and **shot** (see **hand-loading**); or simply rearming a discharged weapon (e.g., by inserting a new **magazine**).

Remington 870

Pump-action shotgun that is the bestselling shotgun of all time. There are specific variants made for police and **law enforcement** including the Police model, which is fitted with a police-specific walnut or synthetic **stock** and is shortened to fit a vehicle-mounted rack and to allow for quick visual inspection of the **magazine**. Police models have Remington 870 Police Magnum stamped on the **receiver**. Remington also makes a Marine model and the MCS (Modular Combat Shotgun) version of the 870.

replica gun

Functional reproduction of an existing **firearm** (see **imitation firearm**). It is also the term used to refer to a modern reproduction of an **antique firearm**.

Residential Reentry Centers (RRC)

Monitored by **Residential Reentry Management Field Offices (RRMs)**, Residential Reentry Centers (RRCs) are federally contracted halfway houses providing criminal offenders with community-based services to help transition them back into society. In addition to supervising felons nearing release, they typically provide employment counseling and other forms of support, with the larger goal of reducing **recidivism**.

Residential Reentry Management Field Offices (RRMs)

A division of the Federal Bureau of Prisons (BOP), Residential Reentry Management Field Offices (RRMs) liaise with the federal **courts**, the **US Marshals**, state and local corrections, and a variety of community groups within their specific judicial districts. There are 22 RRMs in the US, primarily located in major cities in most regions (such as Baltimore, Chicago, Miami, Phoenix, San Antonio, and St. Louis).

restorative justice

In contrast to **retributive justice**, restorative justice seeks to repair the harm inflicted on others by a perpetrator, with the understanding that the perpetrator may themselves be victims of crimes or dark social circumstances, such as a childhood marked by abuse.

restricted target

Valid target, whether that is a person or a place, that has specific restrictions placed on the actions that are authorized against it due to operational considerations.

retributive justice

The idea of retributive justice is based on the concept that any pain inflicted on a victim should be turned back on the perpetrator. This is the Old Testament logic of "eye for an eye." It should not be confused with revenge, which is emotional and tends to widen, not balance, the damage.

R

revolver

Firearm, usually a **handgun** with a revolving **cylinder** of **chambers**, arranged to allow several successive shots to be **discharged** by the same firing mechanism without **reloading**.

RHD

See **Robbery Homicide Division**.

Richard Roe

The name Richard Roe or the surname Roe are used in court cases when two parties must remain anonymous, most famously in the US Supreme Court case of **Roe v. Wade**. The female version is Jane Roe. *See also* **Jane/John Doe**.

ricin

Ricin has been described as "the perfect **poison**," largely because its key ingredient, castor beans, is so easily obtainable, as are instructions on how to extract the **lethal** poison from the beans under nonlaboratory conditions. Once properly prepared, it only takes a pinhead-sized amount of ricin to kill and there is no known antidote. Ricin acts by shutting down the liver and other organs if ingested, or by causing respiratory failure if inhaled. It was notoriously used in the 1978 murder of Bulgarian journalist Georgi Markov in London, who was injected with a ricin **pellet** fired from an umbrella. In 2002, there was an alleged plot to attack the London Underground with ricin. This was known as the Wood Green ricin plot. The suspected contaminated articles recovered were sent to the Biological Weapon Identification Group at the Defense Science and Technology Laboratory at Porton Down in Wiltshire. There was no trace of ricin on any of them, a fact that was suppressed for over two years. Ricin-tainted letters have been sent to former US President Barack Obama, former New York Mayor Michael Bloomberg, federal judges and the Pentagon. These were laced with a crude form of homemade ricin that was not weapons grade.

ride on

Go to another gang area or turf to attack them, usually in vehicles (US contemporary gang slang).

ride with

A prison inmate doing favors for another inmate, including sexual favors, in return for protection, items from the prison commissary, or contraband (US contemporary slang).

rifle

Firearm with a rifled **barrel**.

rifling

Spiral or helicoidal **grooves** inside the **barrel** of a gun designed to make the **bullet** spin, thereby stabilizing it and improving its accuracy. Rifling leaves unique marks on a bullet that can be an aid to **forensic ballistics**.

rigor mortis

Rigor mortis is the stiffening of the body after death that results from the loss of adenosine triphosphate (ATP) from the muscles. Rigor usually starts around two hours after death and spreads at the same time throughout the body, although the smaller muscles, such as those in the face and neck, are affected first. This initial stiffening of the facial muscles leads to the characteristic grimace often reported by **scenes of crime officers**. The initial stage of rigor, known as the rigid stage, lasts from eight to 12 hours, and once the body is completely stiff it stays that way for up to another 18 hours. The muscles then start to lose their stiffness, working in reverse with the largest muscles relaxing first followed by the smaller ones until the entire body is once more flaccid. Because of these scales, rigor mortis is a good method of predicting time of death, although environmental factors such as temperature have to be taken into account.

R

Riker's Island

New York's most infamous prison, the Riker's Island complex is technically not a prison but a jail. Specifically, it is a cluster of 10 jails holding short-term detainees. Capable of accommodating up to 15,000 individuals, its 10 jails are specific to male adults; male adolescents and adults; female adolescents and adults; contagious inmates; and inmates requiring medical attention (infirmary). Visitors are permitted.

In recent years, calls to close Riker's Island have intensified, as the complex has been plagued by substantiated reports of inmate abuse and an institutional culture of shocking violence. In the wake of damning reports, as well as numerous inmate deaths and associated suicides such as that of **Kalief Browder**, in 2017 the New York City Council voted to close Riker's by 2026.

ring

Bullet (US/Jamaican contemporary gang slang).

robbery

Taking or **attempting** to take something of value from its rightful owner or possessor by force, or threat of force or violence, and/or by putting the victim in fear.

R

Robbery Homicide Division (RHD)

RHD is a specific division of the Los Angeles Police Department (LAPD). According to the LAPD website, it is tasked with investigating "select homicides, bank robberies, serial robberies, extortions, sexual assaults, human trafficking, kidnapping, incidents that result in injury or death to an officer, and threats against officers." It has gained a place in pop culture thanks to six seasons of the gritty drama, *Bosch* (2014–), centered around a troubled RHD detective in the LAPD's Hollywood **precinct**.

Rohypnol

Rohypnol (a brand name for flunitrazepam) suppresses the central nervous system and is a type of benzodiazepine. Like other **drugs** in this family, it is a muscle relaxant that lowers inhibitions and causes amnesia. For this reason, it is frequently used as a **date-rape** drug, especially as it intensifies the effects of **alcohol** and other drugs such as **heroin** and **cocaine**. Rohypnol can be detected in urine up to three days after ingestion. Street names include: circle; roofie; roach; rope; ropie; roopie; rophy; ruffie; Mexican Valium.

rolling-car pickup

In **spy** lingo, a **clandestine** car pickup of a person or object executed so smoothly that the car hardly stops at all and appears to have simply kept moving.

Romeo spy

Man, usually an **intelligence officer**, **agent**, or investigator, whose job it is to seduce women who have access to confidential material, in the hope that through pillow talk the women will reveal secrets. Romeo spies were created out of practicality in the Cold War, representing a cost-effective opportunity to steal West German political, military, and security secrets from targets singled out by Markus Wolf, chief **foreign intelligence** officer for East Germany's Stasi, or secret police.

Wolf was so good at his job that, for 20 years, Western intelligence did not even know what he looked like and he was dubbed the "Man Without a Face." He believed that one woman with the right contacts and motivation could provide more secrets than 10 diplomats, and he was right. Wolf deployed young, clean-cut men who usually pretended to be

R

carrying out some kind of humanitarian work or mission, targeting well-educated, upper middle-class women with access to the information the Stasi required, often working for the West German government. The Romeo spies, who had to pass a rigorous screening process, were schooled on the likes, dislikes, and vulnerabilities of their targets, and engineered supposedly chance encounters to meet them. They then proceeded skillfully to seduce them into relationships with good manners and old-fashioned charm.

Despite advertising campaigns warning of these young men, many women fell for them and began relationships, although most subsequently ended those relationships when the Romeo spies moved on to the next stage of their mission and asked the women to **spy** or pass on secrets to them. Some, however, agreed and their **espionage**, along with their relationships, lasted for decades. The Romeo spies were forbidden to marry their targets because the West German government carried out **background checks** on any potential spouse of someone who had access to state secrets, but many also fell for their Juliets. Those who did were sometimes removed back to East Germany, never to be seen by their target again, or suffered an untimely "accidental" death.

Many of the women also fell in love with their Romeos and some fell in love with espionage itself, carrying on even when their Romeo left or was replaced. The Romeo spies program ended in early 1990 when German reunification became inevitable and the Stasi destroyed all documents relating to it. Markus Wolf escaped to Moscow, where he had grown up and learned his **tradecraft**, but surrendered three years later on the Bavarian border and was **sentenced** to six years in prison for treason. He was later pardoned on the grounds that East Germany was a sovereign state when he worked for it and he was therefore entitled to carry out espionage on behalf of that state. He died at the age of 83 on November 9, 2006, the seventeenth anniversary of the fall of the Berlin Wall.

rootkit

Malware program that is installed on a system through various means, including the same methods that allow **viruses** to be injected into a system such as email, downloading unsafe programs or files, and websites designed to introduce malware. Once a rootkit is introduced, it creates a **back door** that will allow remote, unauthorized entry. A rootkit is installed and functions at such low system levels that it can be designed to erase its own tracks and activity from the now vulnerable system, allowing a **hacker** or **cracker** to navigate through entire networks without being exposed. Rootkits can be directly installed from a CD or USB drive to a system that is not normally remotely accessible, sometimes by means of **social engineering**. Rootkits are especially dangerous as they are so difficult to spot.

round

Generic term for a **bulleted cartridge**.

RRC

See **Residential Reentry Centers**.

RRMs

See **Residential Reentry Management Field Offices**.

rule of law

One of the most important cornerstones of a functional democracy, the rule of law holds that *all* individuals are accountable to human laws that are equally enforced and independently adjudicated. The phrase, "No one is above the law," emerges from this legal principle. It stands in opposition to "rule of men," such as a dictatorship or monarchy, where members of a favored family or class can violate laws with impunity.

rush

Immediate and intense surge in sensation felt when smoking or injecting a **drug**. The rush varies in length depending on the drug. Also, to attack (US contemporary gang slang).

RVP

Rendezvous point.

R

S

SACs
See Special Agent in Charge.

SAD
See Special Activities Division.

safe house
Apparently innocuous or unremarkable house or premises established by an organization in order to facilitate **clandestine** or **covert** activity in relative security. Safe houses may be used as a refuge for **agents**, defectors, couriers, escapees, or evaders, for rendezvous, training, briefing, or questioning, or for storage of supplies and equipment. They also act as a place of safety where police witnesses or victims of crime are taken for their own protection.

safety device
Mechanical device in a **firearm** designed to block the firing mechanism during the movement of the mobile parts to prevent unintentional **discharge** when the weapon is properly engaged.

safing
When applied to weapons and **ammunition**, the changing from a state of readiness for use to a safe condition. Also known as de-arming.

samurai
Large knife or samurai-style sword.

Sandy Hook elementary school shooting

In 2012, a young man entered the Sandy Hook elementary school in Newtown, Connecticut, and shot 26 people to death. Twenty victims were children under the age of seven. The event did not result in any new gun control legislation. Instead, schools were incentivized to militarize school grounds (see **1033 program**) and to "harden" security inside. Critics have argued that this approach **criminalizes** childhood and feeds the **school-to-prison** pipeline.

sanitize

To revise a report or other document in such a way as to prevent identification of **sources**, or of the actual people and places with which it is concerned, or of the way in which it was acquired. Sanitization usually involves deleting or substituting names and other key information.

San Quentin State Prison (SQSP)

Also known as "the Arena," San Quentin is the oldest prison in California. At least a dozen films have been set in or made about San Quentin, including the hit *Lincoln Lawyer* (2011). It is considered one of the most dangerous prisons in the US and has the largest number of inmates on **death row** in the country. The number currently stands at over 700. All executions of male and female prisoners occur at San Quentin, irrespective of where they were serving the bulk of their sentence.

SAR

See **Suspicious Activity Report**.

sarin

Sarin was developed in 1937 by the German chemist Gerhard Schrader as an insecticide but the Nazis quickly realized it was more **lethal** than the chlorine gas they had used up until then in **chemical weapons**. So fearful were they of its effects and the possible retaliatory consequences, they did not use it in the Second World War but the Iraqis did in 1988, killing 5,000 Kurds. Sarin became infamous thanks to the 1995 Tokyo subway attack in which a doomsday cult, Aum Shinrikyo, released it during rush hour, killing 12 people and injuring hundreds more. A thirteenth victim died after 14 years in hospital. Odorless and tasteless, sarin works by turning our own nervous systems against us, resulting in convulsions, paralysis, and death within minutes if the dose is sufficient.

Saturday night special

A slang word for any compact small-caliber handgun that is also poorly made and cheap. It emerged in the 1960s due to its association with casual robberies (as opposed to, say, first-degree **homicide** or **organized crime**) of the type primarily motivated by desperation, boredom, and stupidity.

sawed-off shotgun

As its name implies, a sawed-off shotgun is a shotgun manually altered so that its barrel is shorter than 18 inches. This is generally accomplished by sawing the unwanted length off. In the US, sawed-off shotguns are federally restricted.

S

Scandi noir

The long, dark Scandinavian winters have spawned a swathe of crime fiction, TV series, and films known collectively as Scandi or Nordic noir. The murders are brutal; the outlook bleak. Ice-hard detectives crack in the face of their demons and sacrifice all for what becomes a personal crusade. Their colleagues are their family. Frost forms over lonely hearts. The police hero or heroine aches with a longing that can never be fulfilled. There are monsters to be tracked across snowfields and hunted down in urban wastelands while Scandinavian society turns a blind eye. The morals and motivations are complex, the plotlines international. Relentlessly realistic and pared to the bone, Scandi noir reflects the darkest recesses of our souls.

Schedule I, II, III, IV, and V

In 1971, the US **Controlled Substances Act (CSA)** created "schedules" or categories of drugs grouped according to their susceptibility for abuse, their medical use, and their addictive tendencies. According to the US Drug Enforcement Administration (DEA), the five categories range from Schedule I, which are drugs with the highest potential for abuse and no acceptable medical use, such as LSD, peyote, and heroin; to Schedule V, the lowest potential for abuse, such as cough syrup.

school resource officer (SRO)

A school resource officer is not a security guard but a fully empowered law enforcement officer. They are member of the local police force or **sheriff**'s department and assigned to a school, which pays the law enforcement agency for the manpower. Critics argue that SROs criminalize childhood and keep children flowing into the (for-profit) **school-to-prison** pipeline.

school-to-prison pipeline

A well-documented national trend, the school-to-prison pipeline refers to disturbing numbers of children, who can be as young as five, being arrested in schools and funneled into **juvenile justice systems**. It is part of a larger trend of overpolicing and **criminalization**.

S

SCO19
See **Specialist Firearms Command**.

screw
Prison officer (UK and US contemporary prison slang).

search warrant
Legal authorization or court **order** issued by a judge or magistrate for a police officer or other official to search a property, person, vehicle, or premises, and to seize any **evidence** they find. In most countries, search warrants are only issued to facilitate criminal **investigations** and not for civil cases.

Second Amendment
The Second Amendment of the US Constitution affirms the right of the citizenry to keep and bear arms. The Second Amendment is largely why the United States is the most heavily armed country in the world, and the only country where there are more firearms than people. *See also* **gun rights**.

second-degree murder
See **murder**.

secret writing
The official **Federal Bureau of Investigation** definition for this is invisible writing. This can be any **tradecraft** technique that involves invisible messages hidden in, or on, apparently innocuous materials, including invisible inks, microdots and numerous other variations. It can additionally be defined as the use of special inks, also known within the tradecraft as the "dry system."

securing a crime scene

It is the job of the first officer or responder at a **crime scene** to secure it by setting up a cordon, having first prioritized the preservation of life, taken notes of the names of all people at the scene, and considered and recorded the **contamination** risks to **forensic evidence**. They do so by identifying the extent of the scene and setting cordons; controlling access to the scene; covering it if necessary to protect it from the elements and inclement weather; requesting specialist assistance; and then creating a log of the scene, recording all people, police, vehicles, and other agencies that attend the scene from outside the cordon, along with the date and time of arrival and departure, and reason for visit. The first officer or **first responder** also records any initial actions taken to preserve the integrity of evidence. The subsequent highest-ranking officer who attends the scene assumes the role of supervisor, ensures that the above actions have been carried out, and that any emergency preservation of the scene is performed as necessary. They also establish a rendezvous point at the outer cordon and communicate this point to all staff in order that they can report to the crime scene investigator on arrival at the scene.

S

security service

Organization or department of a government charged with responsibility for **espionage**, **counterespionage**, or internal security functions. **MI5**'s formal title is the Security Service.

self-defense

Because US law recognizes the right to protect yourself from harm, killing in self-defense is a form of justifiable homicide and is not a crime. The defendant must believe that they (or a third party they were acting to protect) were in imminent danger of harm, and that they used a reasonable degree of force to prevent that harm from coming to them. However, some states impose a **duty to retreat**, whereas others apply **Castle doctrine** and **stand your ground**. Correspondingly, claims of killing in self-defense may eventually morph into charges of **manslaughter** or second-degree **murder**.

self-radicalization

Process a person follows to advocate or adopt an extreme belief system for the purpose of facilitating or conducting ideologically based violence, or terrorism, to advance political, religious, or social change. The self-radicalized individual has not been recruited by other violent extremists but may seek out direct or indirect contact with other violent extremists for moral or other support and to boost his or her extremist beliefs.

semi-automatic firearm

Self- or auto-loading **firearm** that fires a single shot when the **trigger** is pulled, the fired **cartridge case** is ejected, and a fresh cartridge **loaded** into the **chamber**. The trigger must be released and pulled again to fire another shot.

S

sensitive

When applied to a document, activity, program, place, person, or some kind of information this means it needs protection from disclosure that could cause embarrassment, compromise, or a threat to security. ▶ **sensitive site** Designated, geographically limited area with particular diplomatic, informational, military, economic, national, or state sensitivity.

sentence

Punishment given to a person convicted of a crime. A sentence is ordered by the judge, based on the verdict of the jury (or the judge's decision if there is no jury), within the possible punishments set by law. A sentence is popularly thought of as the jail or prison time ordered after conviction. Technically, a sentence includes all fines, community service, restitution, or other punishment, or terms of **probation**.

serial killer

The first modern serial killer is generally thought to be **Jack the Ripper**, because his crimes were mediatized through the press and caused a public frenzy.

To be classified as serial killing, there must be at least three murders over time (as opposed to all at once), and they cannot be primarily motivated by money in the manner of **contract killers** (but see **black widow**).

The motives of serial killers have been intensively studied, and they are generally grouped into four categories: 1) visionary, 2) mission-oriented, 3) hedonistic, and 4) power or control.

A visionary killer may suffer from hallucinations or delusions, such as claiming that God or the Devil instructed them to kill.

A mission-oriented killer will have a specific mandate, such as ridding the world of prostitutes, or drug addicts, and will often see himself as a kind of vigilante antihero.

A hedonistic killer simply enjoys killing for its own sake. **Jeffrey Dahmer** falls into this type.

A power/control killer feels the need to exert power and/or control over their victims, usually as an expression of a twisted psychology often attributed to the killer's own childhood trauma.

serial number

In weaponry, a number applied to a **firearm** by the manufacturer in order to identify the individual firearm.

serve

To beat someone up badly (US contemporary gang slang).

sex offender register

When a person is convicted or cautioned in relation to a sexual offense, or has committed a sexual offense but been found not guilty due to insanity or a disability in the UK, they are added to the Violent and Sex Offender Register (ViSOR). In the US, there is also a central Sex Offender Registry (SOR).

sexpionage

Use of sex, seduction, romance, or a relationship, or the promise of any of those, to carry out **espionage**. It has been a time-honored trick up a **spy**'s sleeve, or elsewhere, since the days of Mata Hari—the Dutch exotic dancer and courtesan who was convicted of spying for the Germans during the First World War and executed by firing squad,— and well before that. **Spies** have used sexpionage to blackmail, elicit secrets, and lure valuable **sources** into relationships and even marriage (see **honey trap**, **Romeo spy**, **swallow,** and **raven**).

sextortion

Sextortion is the latest wrinkle in the **extortion** racket. A form of sexual exploitation and online **blackmail** scam, it typically consists of an online abuser threatening to reveal the victim's compromising or embarrassing digital photos unless the victim cooperates, usually by providing more compromising photos or sexual favors of some kind. Though it can involve **child sexual abuse material** if the victim is a minor, sextortion can occur among people of any age.

sexual assault

Sexual or indecent **assault** is a sexual act inflicted on someone without their consent that causes physical, psychological and emotional violation. It can involve forcing or manipulating someone to witness or participate in any sexual acts. Not all cases of sexual assault involve violence, cause physical injury or leave visible marks but are not less serious for that. ▶ **sexual assault kit (SAK)** Envelope, box, or other container that includes items for collecting and preserving materials including fibers, hairs, and bodily fluids that may provide **evidence** from sexual assault victims, the **accused,** or suspects in sexual assault **cases**.

shake down

Unscheduled search of a prison cell.

shank

To stab, to **assault** someone with a knife, dagger, or similar sharp object. It can also refer to a homemade knife or weapon, usually fashioned out of something that is not ordinarily used as a knife (e.g., the end of a toothbrush filed down until it is sharp). When used in prison it means to stab with a homemade knife (contemporary slang).

shellin'

Shooting.

sheriff

In the United States, the sheriff is an elected official providing law enforcement services for a county or other subdivision determined by the state. They work for—and uniquely answer to–the people of that county. (By contrast, a police force services a municipality, town, or city, and its officers are not elected but hired.) Sheriffs have the same law enforcement powers as police officers but they are "constitutional officers," and there are no minimum requirements for the job.

Shipman, Harold

Harold Frederick Shipman (1946–2004) was a general practitioner of medicine (GP) nicknamed Doctor Death as the UK's, and one of the world's, most prolific serial killers. Shipman is believed to have killed at least 218 of his mostly elderly female patients with **lethal** injections of diamorphine between 1975 and 1998 in Hyde, Greater Manchester, where he practiced at a medical center. Detectives believe the total could be closer to 250 although Shipman was only found guilty of 15 murders at Preston Crown Court in 2000. In 1975, Shipman had been caught forging prescriptions of Demerol for his own use and was required to attend a **drug** rehabilitation program. Over the years, people became suspicious of the high mortality rate among his patients, but the police dismissed the concerns of those at Shipman's medical center and a local funeral home who were suspicious about the high number of Shipman's elderly female patients who were being cremated. The posthumous Shipman Inquiry in 2005 blamed the force for assigning inexperienced officers to the **case**. It was only when he was caught forging the will of Kathleen Grundy in 1998 in an attempt to defraud her estate of £360,000 that Shipman was finally apprehended. His attempted **fraud** along with the abnormally high mortality rate at his practice made detectives look closer. The body of Kathleen Grundy was exhumed and found to contain traces of

S

diamorphine. Shipman never confessed to his crimes and insisted Grundy had been an addict, but computer **evidence** showed that he had written up his medical notes about her after her death. Shipman hanged himself in Wakefield prison in 2004, on the eve of his fifty-eighth birthday, apparently to ensure that his wife Primrose would receive his full NHS pension. The Shipman Inquiry revealed some of the extent of his crimes, with his youngest suspected victim having been only four years old. It also led to changes in standard medical and funeral procedures in the UK.

shiv

Knife, razor or other sharp weapon fashioned out of something that is already sharp or lends itself to the purpose, and often homemade in prison. To shiv means to slash, stab or cut someone with the aforementioned sharp object (contemporary slang).

shooty

Shotgun (US/Jamaican contemporary gang slang).

shoplifter

Someone who steals items and goods from shops (historical slang and still in contemporary use).

Short-Range Agent Communication (SRAC)

Device or gadget that allows an **intelligence agent** and their **case officer** to communicate secretly over a short distance.

shot

Small **pellets** of varying sizes and weights that are used as the **projectiles** in **shotgun cartridges**. ▶ shotgun A firearm with a **smooth bore**, normally designed to be fired from the shoulder and which usually **discharges** a **cartridge** containing a number of small **pellets** or **shot** or a single solid **slug,** or any other **load** that can be carried by the cartridge. ▶ **shotgun cartridge** Centerfire or rimfire cartridge **loaded** with small-diameter **shot**. ▶ **shot size** Numerical or alphabetical designation related to the average diameter of a **pellet**. The number system varies from country to country.

show me your back
"Leave or get lost" (US contemporary gang slang).

side-by-side
Firearm with two **barrels** arranged adjacently in the horizontal plane.

signal
In **spy** lingo this means any form of **clandestine tradecraft** that uses a system of marks, signs, or **codes** for signaling between operatives. ▶ **signal site** Prearranged fixed location, usually in a public place, on which an **agent** or **intelligence officer** can place a predetermined mark in order to alert another agent or officer to the commencement or of operational activity. This might be something like a chalk mark on a lamppost or a tiny piece of tape stuck to a particular wall.

sign-of-life signal
Signal emitted periodically to confirm that an **intelligence agent** or officer is safe.

SIG Sauer P226
Full-size **semiautomatic pistol** popular with military and **law enforcement** services across the world including the SAS, US Navy SEALs, the British Army, the **Federal**

Bureau of Investigation, and multiple US police forces such as the NYPD and the Texas Rangers. Made of steel, it comes in 9 mm, .357 SIG, or .40 S&W varieties with a longer-than-average barrel that gives it better ballistic performance and accuracy.

single action

In relation to **firearms**, this means the **hammer** must be pulled back manually or **cocked** prior to utilizing the **trigger** to operate the firing mechanism.

single shot

Firearm without a **magazine**, holding a single **round** of **ammunition**.

skaghead

Heroin addict (contemporary slang).

skinner

Pedophile (US contemporary prison slang).

sleeper

In **intelligence** terms, an **illegal agent** in a foreign country, or placed in particular territory, who does not engage in intelligence activities until activated or told to do so.

S

sleeving

Practice common in gun conversions by criminals to overcome weaknesses in a **barrel** caused by the presence of venting holes or in an attempt to provide a barrel that **chambers** available **ammunition** correctly. It involves replacing an existing gun barrel with a metal tube or to inserting a tube inside a weak barrel.

slide action

Repeating mechanism in a gun where the **loading** is done by moving a part of the **firearm** parallel to the **barrel**. Also called **pump action**.

slug

Unique **projectile** in a **shotgun cartridge**.

small arms

According to NATO's definition, these are individual **firearms** capable of being carried by one person and fired without mechanical support. They, especially but not exclusively, include **handguns**, shoulder weapons, light **machine guns**, **submachine guns**, and **assault rifles**.

SMG

See **Submachine gun**.

"smoking gun"

See **evidence**.

smooth bore

Firearm with a **barrel** with no internal **rifling**, typically a **shotgun**.

sneak

Petty **thief** of small articles. A morning sneak would go down to the servants' quarters just as they were up and busy in the kitchen and steal whatever they could find. They would also do the same in shops as they opened. An evening sneak would so the same at closing up time (historical slang). From this we get the contemporary sneak thief who steals small items after entering through open doors or reaching through open windows.

SO
See **special operations**.

---

social engineering

In relation to **cybercrime**, social engineering means to deceive someone for the purpose of acquiring sensitive and personal information such as credit-card details or usernames and passwords. This can be by means of a telephone call purporting to come from your bank or ISP (Internet Service Provider) informing you, say, of new username and password guidelines being implemented by the company, and asking you to reveal your current ones so they can be changed. Social engineering is very convincing and works on even sophisticated users of systems.

---

sociopathy
Like psychopathy, sociopathy is **antisocial personality disorder (APB)** that can be predictive of criminal behavior. From a medical perspective, sociopathy and psychopathy have clear distinctions. For example, both sociopaths and psychopaths lack empathy. However, a sociopath will let you know they don't care, whereas a psychopath will often successfully convince you that he does. Sociopaths are frequently loners incapable of maintaining relationships; the opposite is true of psychopaths, who maintain friends and family to mask their true nature.

soft-point bullet
Semi-jacketed **bullet** where a portion of the core is exposed at the nose of the bullet.

solitary confinement

Inside the prison system, solitary confinement is the isolation of a prisoner inside a special cell with little to no contact with others, including the guards. It is the norm inside **supermax** prisons. The practice is frequently targeted by prison reform movements, which consider it **cruel and unusual punishment**, and the United Nations deems solitary confinement over 15 sequential days to be torture. In 2016, Albert Woodfox was released from prison after an astonishing 43 years in solitary confinement in Louisiana State Prison. He is the last surviving member of the Angola Three: a group of men accused of murder, who claimed—truthfully—that they were innocent.

sound moderator

Also known as a sound suppressor or a silencer. A device that attaches to, or is permanently fixed to, the **muzzle** of the **barrel** of a **firearm** and reduces the noise or report produced by a discharging **cartridge**.

source

In **intelligence** and policing terms, a person, thing, or activity from whom or from which information or services are obtained.

S

spam

Spam is unsolicited email, otherwise known as junk email. Spammers gather or buy lists of email addresses, which they use to bombard users with this unsolicited mail. Usually these emails are simply advertising a product or service but sometimes they can be used for **phishing** and/ or to direct someone to websites or products that will introduce **malware** into their system. Most mail services have spam filters and these should be employed whenever possible. Spam emails should be deleted immediately and the links they contain should never be clicked.

Special Activities Division (SAD)

The Special Activities Division (SAD) of the **Central Intelligence Agency** carries out **clandestine** activities and operations through two divisions: the Political Action Group (PAG) and the Special Operations Group (SOG).

special agent

Detective or investigator who works for the federal government in the US, most famously for the **Federal Bureau of Investigation**. Operatives who work for the **Central Intelligence Agency** in **clandestine intelligence** are not known as special or secret **agents** but as officers.

Special Agent in Charge (SAC or SAIC)

When used specifically in reference to the FBI, a Special Agent in Charge (SAC or SAIC) is the head of a regional office, such as Seattle, Washington, or Norfolk, Virginia. However, due to their size and complexity, field offices in New York City, Los Angeles, and Washington, DC, are instead headed by Assistant Directors in Charge, who are supported in their duties by a number of SACs with specific areas of responsibility.

special operations (SO)

Operations that demand unique tactical techniques, methods of engagement and employment as well as equipment and training, and are often conducted in hostile, restricted or politically **sensitive** environments. Special operations, often referred to as special ops, are usually at least of the following: time-sensitive, **clandestine**, conducted with and/or through indigenous forces, conducted in low visibility including at night, requiring regional expertise and/or a high degree of risk. They can include **reconnaissance**, **psychological warfare** operations, **counterterrorism**, humanitarian assistance, and hostage search and rescue. Unsurprisingly, it is often special forces that conduct special ops.

spice

Spice is a **synthetic** cannabinoid that some people consider more damaging than **heroin**. Although some people call it "fake weed" because its mixture of shredded herbs and synthetic chemicals is similar to **cannabis**, its effects are very different and much stronger. Spice is often sold as incense or some kind of natural product, but it is dangerous and its use can, in some instances, be fatal. It can act as a relaxant, but it can also cause paranoia, aggression and violent behavior. Spice is highly **addictive** and has spread rapidly through the UK's homeless population, being both cheap and strong, although its strength can vary widely.

Spice's street names include: black mamba; bliss; Bombay blue; fake weed; genie; K2; skunk; Yucatan fire; and zohai.

spoofing

Cybercriminals and **crackers** will often cover their tracks by spoofing or faking an IP address, or masking or changing the sender information on an email so as to deceive the recipient as to its origin. They can make an email appear as it if comes from a safe source, such as a trusted friend or well-known organization so that you are more likely to click on the link it contains, which will then introduce **malware** in some way into your system, either by taking you to a site that injects it into your system or by directly injecting it so that crackers can access your computer and data.

spotter

Also known as an assessor. In **intelligence**, an **agent**, **asset**, or **illegal** whose job it is to find and assess people in positions of value or potential value to an intelligence service.

spray and pray

Originally a military insult referring to the use of an auto, or semiautomatic weapon, and firing it in long bursts in the general direction of the target without attempting to take aim. It has since migrated to **first person shooter games** as a reference to style of play.

spree killer

A spree killer distinguishes himself from the serial killer in that he kills two or more victims in a very short period of time. By contrast, a serial killer may wait months, years, and even decades between kills. The identity of the spree killer is generally immediately known, whereas the serial killer is generally unknown until after they are caught. The **rampage killer** is a subset of both spree killer and **mass murderer**.

spy

A spy can be an **intelligence officer** who works for a government **security service** or an **asset**, **agent**, or foreign **source** who works for that service. Intelligence officers normally recruit and handle agents or assets who do the actual spying work and then send or deliver that information to their **handler** or **case officer**. The handler may have protective diplomatic status, also known as official **cover**, and be based in an embassy, or may have nonofficial cover. Spies can steal or gather military, governmental, economic, and technical secrets, among others, or information that is of value to the nation state or

S

security service that employs them. Spies can also carry out industrial **espionage**, sabotage, or spread disinformation to the benefit of the country that employs them. Most countries spy on their allies as well as their enemies, although they do not officially admit to or comment on these operations. In addition, the security services and police **infiltrate** terrorist and other organizations to obtain information and possibly preempt attacks as well as protect national security. Spying, or espionage, is strictly controlled by law in most countries and there can be severe penalties, including expulsion and execution in some countries, if a spy is caught. ▶ **spy dust** Also known as *metka*, which is the Russian for "mark," spy dust is a chemical marking compound composed of nitrophenyl pentadienal (NPPD) and **luminol**. It was developed and used by the KGB (now the FSB) to track a foreign agent, officer, or individual, who would unwittingly leave a trail once they had walked across or even brushed against it. Spy dust was smeared on door knobs and sprinkled on the floors of apartments occupied by foreign persons of interest in Moscow and beyond. Its existence was only revealed to the West when a defecting agent informed American security services in 1984 and they got hold of a sample of it. ▶ **spy fiction** Spy fiction is a subgenre of the mystery and **thriller** genres. It focuses on **espionage** and usually features an agent or agents working for intelligence agencies. The Bond Series by Ian Fleming is perhaps the most famous example of spy fiction; John le Carré is considered to be one of the best exponents of the art. ▶ **spyware** Software designed to gather information about a user's computer use without their knowledge. Sometimes spyware is simply used to track a user's internet surfing habits for advertising purposes so it can then show you relevant

S

ads. More dangerously, spyware can also scan computer files and keystrokes, create pop-up ads, change your homepage, and/or redirect you to unsafe websites. A common scam is to generate a pop-up ad informing you that your system has been infected with a **virus** or some other form of **malware** and then force you to a webpage that has the solution to fix the problem. Most often, spyware is bundled with free software such as screen savers, emoticons, and social networking programs.

SQSP
See **San Quentin State Prison.**

squeal
To inform on an accomplice, or reveal hidden plans.

SRAC
See **Short-Range Agent Communication**.

SRO
See **school resource officer.**

stainless-steel ride
Prison term for death by **lethal** injection (US contemporary slang).

stalking
There is no strict official legal definition of "stalking" in the UK or the US, but it is an offense that can include acts such as following a person, watching, or spying on them, or forcing contact with them through any means, including social media (see **cyberstalking**). In many cases and when taken in isolation, the behavior might appear innocent, but when carried out repeatedly so as to

amount to a course of conduct, it may then cause significant alarm, harassment, or distress to the victim. The effect on the victim is to curb their freedom and make them feel as if they constantly have to keep a watch out or look over their shoulder, and can be extremely distressing. Stalking has been known to escalate to other crimes of physical violence including murder.

stand-your-ground

In some US jurisdictions, if a person is threatened with violence, they have a legal right to stand their ground, which is to say, to meet force with force, without attempt to defuse or run away. It extends from the same self-defense philosophy underpinning the **Castle Doctrine,** which permits the use of deadly force against trespassers within your home; by contrast, stand-your-ground applies wherever you go. Critics have pointed out that whites using the stand-your-ground defense against Black attackers are significantly more successful than Blacks using the defense against white attackers. This controversial legal reasoning informed law enforcement's initial refusal to charge the man who shot and killed an unarmed Black teen named **Trayvon Martin**. Stand your ground applies on a state-by-state basis.

state's evidence

See **turning state's evidence.**

station

Overseas **Central Intelligence Agency** office or operational hub that is usually located in an official building such as an embassy. The officer in charge of it is known as the chief of station (COS).

statute of limitation
Legal time frame within which criminal **charges** must be filed against an **accused** or the **case** may no longer be prosecuted.

steel-jacketed bullet
Steel metallic envelope surrounding the core of a compound **bullet**.

steel shot
Soft steel **pellets** made specifically for use in **shotgun cartridges**.

steganography
The practice of hiding a digital file inside another, usually an image, so that, for example, a child pornography image can be hidden inside another graphic image file, audio file or other file format.

stimulant
Drug that immediately increases energy and alertness along with increases in blood pressure, heart rate, and breathing.

stock
The part of a shoulder **firearm** that is held for firing and to which the **action** is attached. It is used to steady the firearm against the shoulder when firing.

stone
Bullet or **crack cocaine** (contemporary slang).

stop and search
A police officer can stop and search (S & S) someone in the US or the UK if they have "reasonable grounds" to suspect they are carrying **illegal drugs**, a weapon, stolen property,

or something that could be used to commit a crime. You can only be stopped and searched without reasonable grounds if it has been approved by a senior police officer. This can happen if it is suspected that serious violence could take place, the suspect is carrying a weapon or has used one, or they are in a specific location or area.

straight pull action

A **bolt-action** gun in which the bolt handle does not need to be rotated for locking and unlocking but can be handled by a straight backward and forward motion of the shooter's hand.

strap

Gun (UK and US contemporary slang). ▶**strapped** Armed with a gun, carrying a gun (US contemporary gang slang).

strapped

To be carrying a firearm (i.e., "He came to the hostage negotiations fully strapped"). Probably derives from the straps used to support the carrying of so-called long guns, a generic category of "not handguns" that includes rifles, **AK-47s,** and **Uzis.**

straw purchase

Refers to any sale where a third party purchases an item on your behalf, such as teens giving money to an older sibling to buy alcohol specifically for them. Straw purchases are not always illegal, but it is always illegal to conduct a straw purchase of a firearm. If the straw purchaser knows or has reason to believe that the gun will be used in a crime, then they have committed a federal felony punishable by up to 10 years in prison and a $10,000 fine; the person for whom the firearm was straw-purchased can be charged with conspiracy to

S

violate federal law, with the same punishments and penalties.

strip

Area where **drugs** are sold (contemporary slang).

strychnine

Strychnine is a **poison** that was popular in the Victorian era as it was widely used in cities for pest control. Not the most subtle of poisons, strychnine causes frothing at the mouth followed by muscle spasms that grow so intense they asphyxiate the victim. The 1987 death of waxwork-museum owner Patsy Wright from cold medicine laced with strychnine remains unsolved, and in 1993 the Turkish president Turgut Özal was apparently assassinated by strychnine poisoning. Dame Agatha Christie used strychnine as the murder method in several of her novels and short stories, as did Sir Arthur Conan Doyle and, more recently, Stephen King.

stun gun

Handheld contact weapon that uses a temporary high-voltage, low-current electrical **discharge** and delivers an electric shock that briefly disables, or stuns, the recipient.

S

submachine gun (SMG)

An **automatic firearm** that frequently **discharges pistol caliber ammunition** and is generally used with two hands.

succinylcholine (SUX)

Fast-acting **drug** that paralyzes all the muscles in the body in less than a minute. It has no sedative effect, so the recipient remains fully awake. Succinylcholine has been suggested as an excellent murder weapon by the writer and pharmacist James J. Murray as it metabolizes into two substances already present in the body: succinic acid and choline. The only slightly elevated levels of these found during an **autopsy** could therefore easily be overlooked unless there was other **evidence** indicating criminal activity.

suicide by cop

Suicide by cop is based on the US concept of, and training of officers in, the **use of (deadly) force**. A suicidal individual will deliberately behave in a threatening fashion, such as waving around a weapon, in hopes of forcing police officers to use deadly force against them. The second form is a desperation move, such as a fugitive who decides that life is not worth living once they are caught, and they will goad the officer into killing them. This second form was famously used as a plot device in the dark thriller, *Se7en* (1995).

summary offense

Summary offenses are a lesser form of crime than **misdemeanors**, and typically result in a fine rather than a jail sentence. They include parking tickets, loitering, low-level harassment, petty shoplifting (such as stealing a bag of chips), and contempt of court. They are called "summary offenses" because they do not require a jury trial, hence the judge can hand out the fine in a "summary" (on the spot) fashion.

supermax prison

"Supermax" is the common term used to refer to an **Administrative Maximum Security Facility (ADX)** in the US. They exist to provide long-term housing for prisoners deemed too violent and dangerous to be kept in regular federal institutions. Inmates are kept in **solitary confinement**, which is both punishment and protection from other prisoners. They are also typically kept under round-the-clock surveillance using **CCTV** cameras.

surveillance

The laws around surveillance in the US are evolving slower than the surveillance technologies themselves. In general, surveillance refers to the monitoring of the activities of a given group of individuals. It is also used by governments as part of **intelligence** gathering. The global rise of smart cities, which embed information and communication technology (ICT) in the urban fabric itself to directly coordinate with law enforcement, signals the expanding norms of a surveillance society.

suspended sentence

When a prison term is not imposed if the defendant does not get into further trouble for the period they would have spent in jail or prison.

Suspicious Activity Report (SAR)

A Suspicious Activity Report alerts **law enforcement** in the US and the UK and elsewhere to possible economic crime or terrorist financing. The reports are made by financial institutions and professionals such as accountants, solicitors, and estate agents. They provide information from the private sector to law enforcement that would not otherwise be available and are vital in helping to tackle **money laundering, fraud,** and other economic crimes. They also help to locate sex offenders, trace terrorist suspects, and detect and prevent organized and other serious crimes.

SUX

See **succinylcholine**.

swag

Booty or plunder from a **robbery** or **burglary** (contemporary slang).

swallow

A swallow was a female Russian **agent** or officer who was employed to seduce targets in **honey-trap** operations and effectively act as an **undercover** prostitute. The apartment in which she operated was known as a swallow's nest and was a double apartment where she would carry out her seduction in one room while the KGB recorded everything that happened from an adjoining room or apartment. Her male equivalent was known as a **raven**.

SWAT team

An acronym for Special Weapons and Tactics, SWAT teams have become ubiquitous in US police forces, and the subject of dozens of films and television shows. Created to handle unusual "high risk" incidents of crime, their numbers increased in the wake of the **War on Drugs** and the **War on Terror**. They are the most visible expression of the militarization of the police.

swatting (SWATting)

A form of criminal harassment and a variation of **suicide by cop**, SWATting starts when a malicious actor falsely claims that a high-risk situation is unfolding at a given address, knowing that this will activate the SWAT team. In 2019, a gamer and serial swatter named Tyler Barriss started a chain of events that led to the shooting death of a random man in his home. Barriss was sentenced to 20 years in prison on assorted charges, such as making a false report to the police. Lawmakers are currently proposing new laws to make swatting itself a federal crime.

sweep

In **spy** lingo, to physically and/or electronically examine a room or area in order to detect any **clandestine** devices such as **bugs** or concealed electronic-listening devices.

swindler

A cheat or confidence artist who sets out to target and defraud honest tradesmen (UK thieves' **cant**, historical slang, also in contemporary use). In contemporary use, it is anyone who cheats another out of money or possessions. Elaborate scams are nothing new and even back in the sixteenth century gangs of swindlers were setting up stings, renting respectable houses in the most desirable parts of town, and giving themselves the roles of "masters, servants, porters, clerks, outriders and shopmen." They then obtained credit through this show of opulence and proceeded to order goods, which they then sent to the countryside to be sold or bartered for other commodities. If they bartered for goods, these were then brought to London to be sold in turn.

Everything they bought was paid for with counterfeit money and their profit margins were huge on the goods they sold. Once they had bled a town and its tradesmen dry, they moved on, swapping roles so that whoever had played the master now posed as a servant or outrider and so on. They also ran another scam where they would answer newspaper advertisements from distressed tradesmen looking for credit, promising to find them the money they needed once they had taken a deposit from them. Of course, those tradesmen never saw that deposit again or the

S

promised loan, and were left in an even worse position. Many of them were then faced with ruin and the debtors' prison. These swindlers could be compared to the **grifters** in the United States and **con** artists and tricksters the world over who still practice today, although nowadays most often using the internet.

sword

A long, bladed weapon; also knife.

synthetic drug

Drug created artificially from chemicals, especially one made to resemble a natural product.

T

tak

Danish for "thanks, thank you or please," and a word that often occurs in **Scandi noir**.

take someone out of the box

To kill someone, usually a member of a rival gang (US contemporary gang slang).

taking the fifth, pleading the fifth

See **Fifth Amendment**.

tartan noir

A genre of crime fiction set in Scotland and written by Scottish writers or those based there, tartan noir has its roots in the work of Robert Louis Stevenson and William McIlvanney and was influenced by American **hard-boiled** fiction writers such as Raymond Chandler and James Ellroy. It is claimed that Ellroy coined the term when referring to Ian Rankin as "the king of tartan noir" although Rankin may have coined it himself when he asked Ellroy to sign a book for him stating that he was a big fan and that he wrote tartan noir. Rankin and Val McDermid spearheaded this new wave of Scottish crime writing that now includes multicultural elements but retains its overtones of cynicism and a particularly world-weary point of view.

tax

To steal. Taxed—stolen (contemporary slang).

taxine

Unusual **poison** derived from yew tree seeds, berries, needles and leaves. It was used in Agatha Christie's *A Pocketful of Rye* (1953), where the victim is fed marmalade laced with taxine. Death is so rapid that the tell-tale signs of taxine poisoning–staggering, seizures, respiratory and heart failure–are often missed and it is only postmortem that the cause of death is discovered.

tear up

A fight or to beat up (US/UK contemporary prison slang).

technical surveillance

Use of optical, audio, or electronic monitoring or listening devices or systems, including vehicle trackers, to surreptitiously collect information.

teef

To steal (originally Jamaican slang, now in wider contemporary use).

"10" codes

10 codes (ten codes) are shorthand codes used by law enforcement over police scanners as well as private individuals, such as truckers, who might use Citizens' Band (CB) radio. **10-4**, meaning "affirmative/understood," is probably the most widely recognized of the "10" codes, closely followed by **10-20**, "Where are you? (slang: What's your twenty?)" Among police departments, however, meaning of the 10 codes can vary widely. In California, for example, 10-16 is a request to pick a lunch order, but in Nevada it refers to a domestic violence call. 10-100 means "officer is taking a bathroom break," leading to the joke 10 code, 10-200 (2 x 100), which stands for "officer pooping."

10-8

US police **code** that means an officer or unit is in service and available for calls. An officer will check on the radio or advise that they are ready for another call by "taking a 10-8." Officers may use it in conversation to describe a suspect who fled from them, saying the suspect "got 10-8."

10-4

US police **code** that means "affirmative." It can be used to answer "yes" to a question or to advise that everything is OK.

Ten Most Wanted Fugitives List

In 1950, FBI director Herbert Hoover issued the first "Ten Most Wanted Fugitives List," and it received so much publicity that he implemented it as a feature. The list is not ranked. In order to appear on the list, an individual 1) must have committed serious crimes and/or be considered a dangerous menace to society as a wanted fugitive; and 2) the nationwide publicity resulting from appearing on the list will contribute to the likelihood they will be caught. Today, the list is hosted by the FBI website.

10-13

US police **code** that refers to an officer's status or conditions. A dispatcher may ask an officer for their "10-13" to determine if everything is OK or if they need help; 10-13 can also refer to weather conditions, crowd issues, or the status of a victim or suspect.

1033 program

In 1997, under the Clinton administration, political pressure to support the **"War on Drugs"** resulted in the 1033 program. To bolster local police forces, the **1033 program** transferred the military's extra or outdated gear to state and local authorities, including **school resource officers**

(SROs) and state park officers. The transfer is not automatic; eligible entities must apply for it and pay for the cost of shipping. In addition to tactical clothing and technology, this military gear includes **armored resource vehicles**. The accelerating militarization of the US police and school resource officers has been viewed with alarm by human rights watch groups.

10-20

US police **code** that refers to the location of an officer or call. Some departments require their officers to provide their 10-20 whenever they initiate radio communications. Calls for service always include a 10-20, so the officer knows where to go.

thallium

Agatha Christie used thallium in her 1961 novel *The Pale Horse*, with the narrative resting on the fact that it is a handy **poison** for a murder thanks to it being odorless and tasteless as well as easily blended with food and drink. Thallium is also highly detectable as it remains in body tissue for weeks. Although it was once widely available in rat poison, it is now tightly controlled. It was used in the 1991 murder of Robert Curley by his wife, Joann, in Pennsylvania and of a computer engineer named Xiaoye Wang in New Jersey in 2011, who was poisoned by his estranged wife, Li. Thallium was also the poison of choice for women in Sydney, Australia, in the 1950s. In 1952–3 there were a hundred thallium poisonings with 10 deaths resulting from them. The majority of the perpetrators were female and the victims male. Investigators initially thought that Alexander Litvinenko, murdered in 2006 in London, had been poisoned with thallium as he had the classic flu-like symptoms, failing eyesight, and his hair had fallen out, but the poison was later found to be **polonium**.

The antidote for thallium is Prussian Blue, which, ironically, is derived from **cyanide**.

THC

Tetrahydrocannabinol or THC is the main psychoactive constituent in **cannabis**.

theft

Theft is the act of stealing or of taking another person's property without their permission or consent with the intention of unlawfully depriving them of it. ▶ **thief** A thief is someone who acts by stealth to steal or take another person's property without their permission or consent and with the intention of unlawfully depriving them of it.

third-degree murder

See **manslaughter**.

13th (Thirteenth) Amendment

In the wake of the US Civil War, the Thirteenth Amendment was passed by US Congress on January 31, 1865, and ratified on December 6, 1865. The Thirteenth Amendment abolished slavery and involuntary servitude in the US, but left in an important caveat: ... "except as punishment for a crime." Known as the **penal labor exemption**, that caveat opened up a path to the **prison industrial complex** and the ongoing use of **prison labor** along highly racialized lines.

3-D printed firearm

A plastic firearm that can be reproduced by a 3-D printer with the appropriate blueprints. Under the terms of the **Undetectable Firearms Act** of 1988, they are illegal to make in the US. Currently, 3-D printed firearms mostly serve as weapons in an ideological battle, as there are easier and cheaper ways for criminals to acquire more effective illegal firearms on the **black market** or just make one themselves. Nonetheless, in the not-too-distant future, it's entirely possible that the technology will advance to the point where 3-D printed guns are both inexpensive and sophisticated, making this technology highly relevant in the ongoing battle over **ghost guns.**

thriller

The thriller genre is wide-ranging and can best be characterized by the emotions it evokes including excitement, anticipation, fascination, fear, and tension. Suspense is a crucial element along with action and uncertainty. A good thriller keeps its audience on the edge of their seats, either literally or metaphorically, until the final act or denouement. There are multiple subgenres including action thrillers, **spy fiction**, **psychological thrillers**, romantic thrillers, historical thrillers, political thrillers, and **courtroom dramas**. The thriller genre encompasses books, films, and television.

TIC

Taken Into Consideration (UK police acronym).

time bomb

When related to **cybercrime**, a time bomb is a malicious program designed to execute at a predetermined time and/or date. Time bombs are often set to trigger on special days such as national holidays or on anniversaries of global events to make a political statement. When it executes, a time bomb can do something innocuous such as displaying a particular image, but it can also do something far more damaging such as stealing, deleting, or corrupting system information. The time bomb remains dormant until the pre-set trigger time arrives.

T

Tommy or Tommy Gun:
Slang for "Thompson submachine gun" made famous by the Chicago mobs during Prohibition (Archaic US slang).

tool
Gun; to be "tooled up" is to be equipped with a weapon, especially a gun (contemporary slang).

tooling
Pickpocketing using an implement or tool to open the pocket (historical slang).

toss
In **tradecraft**, placing a drop, or passing on an item, by throwing it while on the move by foot or by vehicle (see **car toss**).

total metal jacket
Projectile in which the **bullet** jacket encloses the whole core, including the base. (See **full metal jacket**.)

touch
To **arrest** (historical slang).

toxic
Harmful, destructive, deadly or **poisonous** to a living organism. ▶**toxicity** Degree or level to which a substance is **poisonous** or can harm somebody or something.

toy
Depending on the context can refer to a gun, car, **drugs,** or item of drug paraphernalia (UK and US contemporary slang).

trace evidence
Trace evidence is created when objects make contact and is often transferred by heat or created by contact friction. Dr. Edmond Locard demonstrated the importance of trace evidence with the formulation of **Locard's Exchange Principle. Forensic** scientists use trace evidence to reconstruct crimes as well as in accident **investigation** to establish what happened. Examples of trace evidence include **gunshot residue**, blood, **fingerprints**, and fibers as well impressions such as **bullet** holes and bitemarks. Trace evidence is vulnerable to **contamination** and the scene must therefore be preserved and the evidence collected following established procedures and guidelines.

tradecraft
Operational and particular methods, techniques, skills, and equipment used in the organization and performance of **intelligence** services and activities, especially techniques and methods for handling communications with **agents** such as **dead drops**.

transcript
Official written record of everything that was said at a court proceeding, a hearing, or a deposition.

transfer bloodstain
This is when a bloodied surface comes into contact with another surface and some of the blood is then transferred to that new surface. Transfer **bloodstains** can be especially useful in establishing the sequence of events and also raise the possibility of **fingerprint** and other **trace evidence** in the bloodstains.

transportation

Transportation was an alternative to hanging as a punishment in seventeenth- to nineteenth-century England, initially being used when death was considered too severe a penalty and later as an alternative for what had previously been capital crimes. It was a cheaper way than prison to remove a criminal from society as the only cost was that of the passage. As well as convicts, transportees included political prisoners, debtors, and prisoners-of-war from Ireland and Scotland. The Transportation Act of 1717 permitted the courts to **sentence** prisoners to seven years' transportation to America. Although seven years was the usual term, sometimes the sentence was for life. If they were freed after seven years, they had to make their own way back home and usually could not afford to do so, staying on in the colonies to work and therefore acting as some of the first settlers in Australia.

Prisoners were sent to the Americas from 1610 until the American Revolution in 1776, when transportation was suspended by the Criminal Law Act. The first transportations to Australia started in 1787 and continued until 1868. Around 162,000 men, women, and children were transported to Australia, some as young as nine years old. Estimates of the numbers transported to America vary between 50,000 and 120,000. Alternative transportation destinations included Bermuda and, unsuccessfully, to Ghana and Senegal. Other countries that practiced transportation include the then Soviet Union and France, most notoriously sending the army officer Alfred Dreyfus, wrongly convicted of treason in 1894, to its penal colony on Devil's Island in a case that became known as the Dreyfus Affair.

trap-and-trace device

Device that captures incoming electronic or other impulses that identify the source of a wire or electronic communication.

trash cover

Federal Bureau of Investigation term for an intentional search of a specific person's rubbish at their home or business in an effort to find information relevant to an ongoing **investigation** when "no reasonable expectation of privacy exists."

tray eight

.38 **caliber handgun** (US contemporary gang slang).

tree jumper

Rapist of women (US contemporary gang slang).

trial by media, tried in the media

The phrase, which originated in the television age, now refers to rushed coverage by a 24-hour streaming news and social media postings less interested in ethical journalism than in "engagement" that drives up ad revenues. One of the most famous cases of trial by media was that of Richard Jewell, a heroic security guard later named a **person of interest** in the 1996 Centennial Olympic Park bombing in Atlanta, Georgia. Though the FBI later cleared him and found the actual bomber, his reputation was shattered. Jewell's story has since been told in the hit nonfiction series, *Manhunt*, as well as the Clint Eastwood film, *Richard Jewell* (2019).

trigger

Part of a **firearm**'s mechanism, which is squeezed or pressed by the finger to cause the firearm to **discharge**.
▶ **trigger guard** Loop that partially surrounds the trigger to reduce the possibility of accidental **discharge**.

trigger pull length

Often conflated with **trigger pull weight**, trigger pull length refers to the length of time it takes to pull the trigger back before it fires. It is generally the case that a "heavy" trigger also has a "long" trigger pull length. Trigger pull length is not to be confused with "length of pull (LOP)," which refers to the distance between the center of the trigger and the back center of the butt plate/ **recoil** pad; that is, the part of the buttstock that touches the shoulder when the firearm is raised and aimed.

trigger pull weight

Trigger pull weight is often described as being "heavy" or "light." A single-action trigger is light: its one job is to release the hammer. A double-action trigger tends toward heavy: its two jobs are to 1) cock the **hammer**, then 2) release it.

Target pistols are designed to have light trigger pull weights (also sometimes called a hair trigger) because lightness of pull means greater accuracy. By contrast, a heavy trigger pull weight (and long **trigger pull length**) is desirable for **concealed carry**, as such triggers must be pulled with conscious intent and will not fire when dropped, and are thus safe to carry when **holstered** on one's person. Serious shooters will practice various hand exercises to build up finger strength.

trip

Common name for the **hallucinogenic** experience produced by taking a **drug** such as **lysergic acid diethyl-amide** (LSD) or **ketamine**. If someone takes enough ketamine that they completely dissociate and are unable to feel or experience the world around them, then this is colloquially known as "falling into a k-hole."

triple agent

Agent who serves three **intelligence** services but who, like a **double agent**, knowingly or unknowingly withholds significant information from two services at the instigation of the third service.

Trojan

In relation to **cybercrime**, a Trojan, or Trojan Horse, is a malicious program disguised to look like a valid program. This makes it difficult to distinguish from programs that are supposed to be on a system. Once introduced, a Trojan can change information, steal passwords, destroy files and carry out any other illicit task for which it was designed. It may also remain dormant until a **cracker** accesses it remotely to take control of the system. A Trojan is very similar to a virus but cannot replicate.

trophy

Many serial killers collect a trophy or souvenir from their victims or **crime scenes**. This can include clothing, jewelry, or an actual body part. **Ed Gein**, on whom both *Psycho* (1960) and *The Silence of the Lambs* (1991) are based, turned body parts from his victims into household items including bowls created from skulls and a wastebasket from human skin as well as masks from human faces. **Ted Bundy** displayed his victims' heads in his apartment while **Jeffrey Dahmer** kept his victims' genitals in a lobster pot. The Ukrainian serial killer Anatoly Onoprienko kept underwear from all his female victims and even gave some of it to his then girlfriend. Killers who keep trophies such as jewelry will often give it to a family member or close friend. Others like to take out a trophy or look at it to enable them to relive the crime and the satisfaction, including sexual satisfaction, they gained from it. Trophies are not confined to

T

serial killers–the "Shoe Rapist" James Lloyd took pairs of shoes from his victims. He was convicted of four **rapes** and two **attempted** rapes, but police believe the figure was much higher, as 126 pairs of shoes were found in his possession after his **arrest**.

turning state's evidence

When a criminal admits guilt, then testifies against their associates (i.e., stands as witness for the state) in exchange for leniency in sentencing or immunity from prosecution, this is called "turning state's evidence." A form of **ratting**, it is not a legal term but slang.

turnover

Official term for the handing of an **intelligence agent** from one **case officer** to a new one; that is, turning them over to another.

twelve

Slang for police. Possibly derived for a **10 code**, specifically 10-12, which can mean "visitors are present."

two

"A two" is a two-year **sentence**. Similarly "a four" is a four-year sentence, "an eight" is an eight-year sentence, and so on (US/UK contemporary prison slang).

201 file

File that contains the personal or "personality" information of a **Central Intelligence Agency** operative. It can also refer to a US military personnel file.

U

UMBRAGE
Central Intelligence Agency's **hacking** group, part of its
Remote Development Branch, that allegedly stores
hacking signatures and techniques stolen from other
nation states, including the Russian Federation. They then
allegedly use these signatures or "fingerprints" during
their own attacks to misdirect and then, according to
Wikileaks, make it appear as if they emanate from
elsewhere.

unauthorized disclosure
Communication, leaking or physical transfer of **classified**,
or unclassified but **sensitive**, information to an unauthorized recipient, including the media.

unconditional discharge
Sentence in a criminal **case** in which the defendant is
released without imprisonment, **probation** supervision or
conditions.

undeclared
Intelligence officer, **asset, agent,** or action whose affiliation to an intelligence service or **agency** is not formally
identified to a **foreign intelligence** or **security service**,
government, organization, or other entity.

undercover
Covert, **clandestine,** or secret work, especially by the
police or for **espionage** purposes, is known as

"undercover" and is normally carried out by officers or **agents** in plain clothes or disguise who try to blend in with the community or organization they are investigating or **infiltrating**.

Undetectable Firearms Act of 1988

Signed into law by Ronald Reagan, the Undetectable Firearms Act of 1988 (18 USC § 922(p)) effectively requires all handguns to incorporate metal components that show up on standard building security metal detectors, as well as imaging technologies used at airports. It is "illegal to manufacture, import, sell, ship, deliver, possess, transfer, or receive any firearm" that is otherwise undetectable by these standard security means. It also prohibits guns being produced in forms other than their conventional shape. Nonetheless, in 2016, a company developed a handgun that looks and **prints** like a smartphone; despite lawmakers' objections, it remains for sale and is likely to remain so, as it must be unfolded into the shape of a regular handgun in order to be fired.

unholstering

The act of removing your firearm from its holster is viewed as preparedness to self-defend and/or provocation to violence. Police protocols place unholstering a firearm under the guidelines of **use of force**. From a disciplinary standpoint, an officer unholstering will prompt a review of the conditions under which that decision occurred. It is reasonable to expect law enforcement officers to unholster their firearm when called to a named high-risk situation; that reasonable expectation has led to at least one fatal **SWATting** incident, where the blame did not lie with the officers but with the false report of a hostage situation.

UNICOR

Officially the Federal Prison Industries (FPI), UNICOR operates under the umbrella of the Department of Justice. Established in 1934 as a wholly owned government corporation, its purpose was to help prisoners acquire labor skills that would allow them to transition back into society as productive members. It is not focused on turning a profit, although it is self-sustaining and receives no tax dollars. Today, it continues to sell goods and services provided by inmates. Hourly pay ranges from 23 cents to $1.15, and all products are, naturally, made in America.

unilateral operation

Clandestine or secret operation or activity conducted without the knowledge or assistance of a **foreign intelligence** or **security service**, host country, foreign organization, or other entity.

United Nations Office on Drugs and Crime

The United Nations Office on Drugs and Crime (UNODC) helps member states fight **illegal drugs**, crime, and terrorism, and operates throughout the world in an extensive network of field offices.

United States Secret Service (USSS)

Federal **law enforcement agency** mandated by US Congress to carry out the dual missions of the protection of national and visiting foreign leaders and criminal **investigations**.

unknown subject (unsub)

The subject of a criminal **investigation** whose identity has not been determined is commonly referred to as an "unsub."

up on it

Successful **drug dealer** or someone who has a lot of knowledge about drugs (US contemporary gang slang).

use of force

In a police context, "use of force" is a general rubric that permits police to use physical force to the extent it is required to restore order or secure compliance from a suspect. Because it exists on a continuum, is situationally dependent, and can result in the death of suspects, "use of force" is often brought up in accusations of police brutality.

US Marshals

Under the aegis of the **US Department of Justice (DOJ)**, US Marshals serve the federal courts. Created in 1789 by the Judiciary Act of the first Congress, they are the oldest continuous law enforcement agency in the US. In 1877, the great abolitionist Frederick Douglass was a US Marshall serving DC. Over the centuries, US Marshalls represented the federal government in the unorganized territories; enforced federal law in Southern states after the Civil War; and helped protect the first Black student attending the University of Mississippi in 1962. Today, they are responsible for "apprehending wanted **fugitives**, providing protection for the federal judiciary, transporting federal prisoners, protecting endangered federal witnesses, and managing assets seizure" (US Department of Justice).

Uzi

Designed in the 1950s by Captain (later Major) Uziel "Uzi" Gal of the Israeli Special Forces, the Uzi is a type of open bolt submachine gun. Its innovation was a telescoping bolt design that allowed the magazine to be housed in a pistol grip, creating its now-iconic shape. Inexpensive to manufacture, reliable in the field, and easy to operate, the Uzi was quickly adopted by the Israeli military. Since then, it has become extremely popular among military outfits, police units, and security companies around the world. There exist micro and mini versions in pistol form.

V

validation

In **intelligence** terms, the process that confirms that the
need to collect or produce a particular piece of intelligence is sufficiently important to justify the dedication of
intelligence resources, does not duplicate an existing
requirement, and has not been previously satisfied.

vehicle-borne improvised explosive device (VBIED)

Formal technical term for a car bomb.

VENONA

The top-secret US codebreaking operation during the
Second World War that deciphered Soviet **intelligence** messages transmitted between Moscow and
other cities concerning US **spy** and other activities
was known as the VENONA project. From the traffic,
the Americans discovered that the Soviets had over
three hundred **assets** of various kinds inside
numerous US government agencies.

Violent Criminal Apprehension Program (ViCAP)

A **Federal Bureau of Investigation** program that maintains a nationwide data information center to collect,
collate, and analyze violent crimes. ViCAP **analysts**
examine crime data and patterns to identify potential
similarities between crimes, and identify homicide and
sexual assault trends and patterns.

virus

A computer virus is a malicious program or **code** that attaches itself to another program file where it can replicate itself and then infect other systems. A computer virus spreads from one system to another when the infected program is used by the other system. It can therefore spread rapidly and easily on networked systems and can also be transmitted via other media such as a CD or memory stick. It can also be emailed with an attachment. A virus is different from other **malware** such as adware and **Trojans** in that it can self-replicate.

visit

To leave prison for some purpose; such as, "I'm going on a visit" (US/UK contemporary prison slang).

volunteer

In **intelligence** terms, someone who initiates contact voluntarily to offer information or services to an intelligence service or government, whether by calling, writing, or walking in to an embassy or other government office, often in return for political asylum, out of greed, or a desire for revenge. Also known as a walk-in.

VX

VX (O-ethyl S-diisopropylaminomethyl methylphosphonothiolate) is a liquid **nerve agent** that is entirely manufactured in the UK. It is tasteless, colorless, odorless, and a hundred times more potent than **sarin**, penetrating the skin and causing paralysis that leads to rapid respiratory failure. VX is classified by the United Nations as a **weapon of mass destruction**. In February 2017, it was used to kill Kim Jong-nam, the half-brother of North Korean leader Kim Jong-un, at Kuala Lumpur airport.

V

W

wadding

Plastic or fiber filler **loaded** in **shotgun cartridges** to isolate propellant from **pellets**.

walk-in

See **volunteer**.

wardriving

Wardriving is the act of driving around in a vehicle to find an open, unsecured Wi-Fi network that will then be added to a map of exploitable zones to be used at a later date or passed on to others. The range of a wireless network will often go beyond the bounds of the building it covers, creating public zones that can be exploited to gain entry to the network and carry out **cybercrime**.

War on Drugs

When Nixon declared drug abuse to be "**public enemy number one**," he started what has since become known as the "War on Drugs." It is not a literal war but a metaphorical one. Its goal is reducing the illegal drug trade, both globally as well as in the US. Its goals are worthy, but critics argue that it has been politicized and racialized to unjustly target people of color, even as it criminalizes addiction to prescribed medicines, such as **opioid** painkillers, instead of targeting the suppliers or developing treatment programs.

W

War on Terror

In the wake of the 9/11 terror attacks in 2001, the Bush administration initiated what has since become known as the "War on Terror," giving rise to the creation of the Department of Homeland Security (founded in 2002) and granting it special powers under the **Patriot Act.** Originally, its target was primarily the Islamic State (ISIS) and extremist Muslim groups believed to be operating under its influence. It has since broadened its reach to cover "domestic terrorism," though what that is remains poorly defined.

weapon of mass destruction (WMD)

Chemical, biological, radiological, or nuclear weapon capable of creating widespread damage or destruction, and of causing mass casualties.

whack

To kill (US/UK contemporary prison slang).

White List

The identities and locations of people who have been identified as being of **intelligence** or **counterintelligence** interest and are expected to be able to provide information or assistance in existing or new intelligence areas of interest. (*See also* **Black List** and **Gray List**.)

whodunnit

Often interchangeable with the detective fiction and **cozy mystery** genres of crime fiction, the whodunnit focuses on deducing who committed a crime, usually a murder, by solving a series of clues. There are traditionally lots of plot twists and red herrings to confuse the reader before the protagonist is exposed in the denouement.

W

window of detection
Time period within which a **drug** can be detected in a biological sample such as urine.

wiseguy
Made man, someone who is a member of the US **Mafia**.

WMD
See **weapon of mass destruction**.

worm
A worm is very similar to a computer **virus** as it is a destructive, self-contained program that can replicate itself and is therefore favored by cybercriminals. Unlike a virus, a worm does not need to be a part of another program or document. A worm can copy and transfer itself to other systems on a network without any kind of user intervention and can prove devastating if not isolated and removed. A worm replicating out of control can consume system resources such as memory and bandwidth until a system becomes unstable, and can cause an enormous amount of damage.

written statement
Permanent, written record of the pretrial testimony of the **accused**, suspects, victims, complainants, and witnesses.

W

Wuornos, Aileen
Aileen Wuornos (1956–2002) was that rare thing: a female serial killer. The survivor of an abusive and horrifyingly chaotic childhood, Wuornos was born in Michigan to a father who killed himself while in prison for child molestation and a mother who

abandoned her young family. Raised by her grandparents, Aileen was sexually abused by her grandfather and had sexual relations with her brother, giving up a baby for adoption in her early teens. She lived as a vagabond in adulthood, hitchhiking and earning money as a sex worker.

Briefly married, Wuornos already had a long criminal history by the time she met Tyria Moore in 1986 in Florida and began a relationship with her. From 1989, when the body of Richard Mallory was found in a junkyard, until 1991, Wuornos murdered at least six men along the Florida highways where she plied her trade as a sex worker, shooting all of them. Moore and Wuornos were traced through palm and **fingerprints** left in the crashed car of another missing man and Moore did a deal with prosecutors, getting Wuornos to confess to all the murders over a taped phone conversation.

Wuornos claimed she had killed Mallory in self-defense as he had **raped** her, and it later turned out that he had served 10 years in prison for **sexual assault**, although this was not revealed in court. Wuornos also claimed the other five killings were in self-defense, although she later retracted this. She was given the death penalty for all six killings, spent 10 years on death row and was executed by **lethal** injection in 2002 when Governor of Florida Jeb Bush lifted a temporary stay of execution and a team of psychiatrists deemed her mentally competent, even though at least one state-appointed attorney expressed severe doubts about her mental state. Wuornos is the subject of several documentaries and was depicted by Charlize Theron in the film *Monster* (2003), for which Theron won an Academy Award.

X

X-Files, The

The X-Files was a long-running science-fiction TV series focusing on the activities of two **Federal Bureau of Investigation special agents**, Fox Mulder and Dana Scully, played by David Duchovny and Gillian Anderson, respectively. The series ran from 1993 to 2018 and focused on **investigations** into paranormal activity, with Mulder a strong believer in the supernatural while Scully remained skeptical until she became a reluctant believer, explaining away the paranormal with science. Some episodes were based on real-life events; both the US and the UK, along with other global powers including Russia, run military and **intelligence** programs that investigate, or have investigated, paranormal events and suspected activity.

XO

Executive officer, the second in command of a military unit in the US.

X-ray

X-rays are used to identify human remains, among other **forensic** uses, usually of the spine, upper leg, or skull. A side X-ray of the skull can be used to identify a body with 97 percent certainty whereas cervical, or neck, vertebrae provide a greater than 98 percent accuracy. An X-ray can also be used to display and locate any foreign objects in a body, such as a **bullet,** and to help detect various traumatic and pathological changes. It can help identify sharp-force injuries and the weapon used, as well as being helpful in motor-vehicle related deaths. X-rays are also helpful for complex injury evaluation in victims where abuse is suspected. ▶ **X-ray fluorescence (XRF) spectroscopy** Nondestructive analytical technique that uses X-rays for elemental analysis and is particularly useful in **forensic** science. Compared to other forensic techniques it is fast, often giving results within minutes, and portable XRF machines can be taken to **crime scenes** to analyze and produce results on the spot. XRF is used to analyze rock, soils, paints, inks, **gunshot residue,** and even counterfeit coins.

X

Y

yardie
Member of a Jamaican gang, or a gang mostly composed of Jamaicans, involved in the **drug** trade and prone to torture and extreme violence. Can also be used by Jamaicans to refer to a fellow Jamaican (UK/Jamaican contemporary slang).

yeng
Gun (US/Jamaican contemporary gang slang).

You all right/you want anything?
Used by **drug dealers** to ask someone if they want any drugs (UK/US contemporary gang slang).

Z

zero day

A zero-day vulnerability is one that is as yet unknown to the creators of the software, and is potentially exploitable thanks to that security hole or vulnerability. It is also as yet unknown to antivirus or anti-malware vendors. A zero-day exploit is the **code** that **hackers** use to exploit this hole. The term "zero day" refers to the number of days the owner of the software has known about the vulnerability. Zero-day exploits and codes are extremely valuable, and a thriving market has grown to trade them, largely fueled by government **intelligence** agencies. Some infamous programs that employed zero-day exploits include Stuxnet, a **virus** that attacked Iran's Natanz uranium enrichment plant, and Operation Aurora, an attack by what are believed to be Chinese hackers who broke into the systems of Google, Adobe, and a dozen other companies. The **Central Intelligence Agency** allegedly uses zero-day exploits in **malware** that can penetrate and infest both the Android phone and iPhone software that runs or has run presidential Twitter accounts. Of course, this means that as long as they conceal this vulnerability from Google and Apple, these phones remain hackable by the CIA.

Z

Zodiac Killer

The Zodiac Killer is the name given to the as yet unidentified **serial killer** who carried out murders in Northern California from the late 1960s or earlier until the early 1970s. The name "Zodiac" came from a series of letters sent by someone, assumed to be male, claiming to be the perpetrator to the Bay Area press. The letters contained four cryptograms, only one of which has been solved to date. There are so far 7 confirmed victims of the Zodiac Killer, 2 of whom survived, with another possible 28, although the killer himself claimed 37. There have been a number of theories and claims as to the true identity of the killer and in 2018 the Vallejo police department submitted the envelopes he used in his correspondence for **DNA** testing but have never released the results to the public.

zombie, zombie drone

A zombie is a **malware** program that can be used by a cybercriminal to remotely take control of a system. It can then be used as a zombie drone for further attacks, such as denial-of-service (DoS) attacks, without a user's knowledge. Zombies can be introduced to a system by simply opening an infected email attachment, but are also often inadvertently downloaded through file-sharing sites, chat groups, adult websites, and online casinos that force you to download their media player to have access to the content on their site and then use the installed player as the delivery mechanism for the zombie.

Z

zoning

Surveillance technique in which the surveillance area is divided into zones, with surveillants assigned to cover a specific zone or area.

Z

ACKNOWLEDGMENTS

This book came about thanks to the launch of another book, serendipity, and a couple of glasses of wine. That other book was Jonathon Green's *The Stories of Slang* and those glasses of wine unleashed a torrent of ideas that I decided to share with his editor, Duncan Proudfoot, one of which was a dictionary of crime. He loved it, told me I should write it and then convinced me I actually could. Two years later, I handed him the completed manuscript. It marked not just a new departure for me but my return to being published after a prolonged period caring for a seriously ill family member. I am forever grateful to Duncan, a gentleman as well as a fine editor, for believing in me and for opening the door once again to a world I love.

I am also grateful to Lisa Moylett, my astounding, indefatigable agent who nurtures her authors while eating LA lawyers for breakfast, and to Jamie Maclean, Zoe Apostolides, and Elena Langtry who make up the rest of the hotbed of creativity that is CMM. You all not only rock but you are some of the most genuinely wonderful people I know.

Of course, I must thank Jonathon Green because without him this book would never have happened, and the other authors at CMM who are so mutually supportive. I'm also grateful for Jonathon's occasional prod on Twitter when I get something wrong and even when I get something right.

Thanks also to the team at Little, Brown who have shaped this book, especially the eagle-eyed Howard Watson, who copyedits with precision and flair, and Rebecca Sheppard, who calmly and efficiently pulls everything together. I am writing this months before the book is launched but I know you will do that brilliantly too.

One of my oldest friends, Sean Lashley, was a serving officer with the Metropolitan Police Service for many years and helped me out with acronyms and police slang, much of which I heard from him as he recounted tales of what had gone on at the nick. Huge thanks too to my other sources whom I cannot name but who were immensely helpful. You know who you are and you all do a fine job.

Finally, my heartfelt gratitude to my friends, family, and fellow writers, often interchangeable, who have been there for me through good times and bad. There are too many of you to name but, again, you know who you are and I love you all equally. Except maybe my daughter. I might love her a little bit more.

ABOUT THE AUTHOR

Amanda Lees was born in Hong Kong. She is the author of the bestselling satirical novels *Selling Out* and *Secret Admirer* (Pan), which have both received critical acclaim and have been translated into several languages. Her major YA thriller trilogy, *Kumari, Goddess of Gotham*, was nominated for the *Guardian* Children's Book Prize and the Doncaster Book Award. It also featured as Redhouse Book of the Month and Lovereading4kids Book of the Month. Amanda appears regularly on BBC radio and LBC and was a contracted writer to the hit series *Weekending* on Radio 4. She has written for, or contributed to, the *Evening Standard*, *The Times*, *New Woman*, *US Cosmopolitan*, and Bulgaria's *Vagabond* magazine. Amanda has conducted a love coaching phone-in from the sofa of *Richard & Judy* and wooed the viewers on Channel 5 Live. She won an award at the Hungarian Györ Film Festival for a short film she produced, a psychological thriller called *Pros and Cons*.